ALASTAIR SAWDAY'S
SPECIAL

D0268682

INDIA

Design: Caroline King

Maps & Mapping: Bartholomew Mapping, a division of HarperCollins, Glasgow

Printing: Canale, Italy

UK Distribution: Portfolio, Greenford, Middlesex

Published in 2003

Alastair Sawday Publishing Co. Ltd
The Home Farm Stables, Barrow Gurney, Bristol BS48 3RW
Tel: +44 (0)1275 464891 Fax: +44 (0)1275 464887
E-mail: info@specialplacestostay.com Web: www.specialplacestostay.com

First edition

Copyright © 2003 Alastair Sawday Publishing Co. Ltd

All rights reserved. No part of this publication may be used other than for the purpose for which it is intended nor may any part be reproduced, or transmitted, in any form or by any means, electronically or mechanically, including photocopying, recording or any information storage or retrieval system without prior written permission from the publisher. Request for permission should be addressed to Alastair Sawday Publishing Co. Ltd, The Home Farm Stables, Barrow Gurney, Bristol BS48 3RW, UK.

A catalogue record for this book is available from the British Library.

This publication is not included under licences issued by the Copyright Agency. No part of this publication may be used in any form of advertising, sales promotion or publicity.

Alastair Sawday has asserted his right to be identified as the author of this work.

ISBN 1-901970-36-1

Printed in Italy

The publishers have made every effort to ensure the accuracy of the information in this book at the time of going to press. However, they cannot accept any responsibility for any loss, injury or inconvenience resulting from the use of information contained therein.

A WORD FROM
ALASTAIR SAWDAY

I was born in Kashmir, my mother seeking the cool of the Himalayas during the long Indian summer. Though I left while still a baby, India has somehow worked its way into my consciousness, assisted by parental tales of the Raj and stories of my great-grandfather, a missionary in Mysore.

Yet, it is hard to 'know' India. The country's mystifying miscellany is legendary and will lure the curious traveller for as long as people travel. There is no limit to the ingenuity of the theatre that Indian life presents. At every turn you will see people behaving in ways that are unexpected and, often, unexpectable. The challenge of daily survival calls up resources that most of us here cannot imagine. Yet there is a richness to the texture of Indian culture that beggars belief.

So India remains hard to resist, whatever the tales of illness and hardship that emerge from travellers' encounters with the country. Yes, it is infuriatingly bureaucratic – but whose fault is that? And it demands a transformation in the traveller's attitude to time. Yes, it is unspeakably litter-strewn, but that is partly to do with poverty and a different attitude to public space. Yes, it adds a new dimension to the word 'heirarchy', but at least there is social order and you usually feel safe. And so on – a mass of confusing impressions will assault you and you may never make sense of it all.

Hence this book. With it you will find relief amid the confusion. If your whole day has been a long series of risks and unknowns, you may appreciate being able to retreat to a place that we have chosen for you. (Note that getting it wrong in India can be traumatic: when an Indian hotel is bad it is very, very bad.) But this book gives you much more than safety and relief: you can dazzle yourself with a night in a Rajah's palace in the grandest of styles, or you can camp out in a wildlife reserve. You can stay with a retired army colonel among the tea plantations in a little bungalow or flop about on the beach with luxury at your elbow in Kerala. The book can provide you with all the fascination you need – just trust us and trust the people to whom we are introducing you. They will make your holiday and give you a measure of real independence that has often been hard for travellers to this vast and extraordinary country.

Let us have your tales, for we will learn from them.

Alastair Sawday

ACKNOWLEDGEMENTS

This is a delicate one to write, for Toby is my son. But he did rescue this book from oblivion. We were about to decide against doing it when he offered to give it a go. So we tossed him into the very deep end. His determination to get it done, whatever the odds, has been admirable. Many would have come home, especially when the heat in Delhi reached 45 degrees. I also greatly admire Miriam Turner for sticking (literally, in that heat) by him and helping to produce this book. They both deserve our immense gratitude – and probably the gratitude of thousands of next season's travellers to India.

So do Martin and Annie Howard – whose generosity and kindness to Toby made the book possible. There were others, whom Toby has mentioned in his own acknowledgements.

Alastair Sawday

Series Editor:	Alastair Sawday
Editor:	Toby Sawday
Assistant to Editor:	Miriam Turner
Editorial Director:	Annie Shillito
Production Manager:	Julia Richardson
Web & IT:	Russell Wilkinson, Matt Kenefick
Copy Editor:	Jo Boissevain
Editorial:	Roanne Finch, Danielle Williams
Production Assistants:	Rachel Coe, Paul Groom, Beth Thomas
Accounts:	Bridget Bishop, Sheila Clifton, Jenny Purdy, Sandra Hassell, Christine Buxton
Sales & Marketing:	Siobhan Flynn, Julia Forster
PR:	Sarah Bolton
Writing:	Toby Sawday, Miriam Turner, Joanne Lane, Sasha Lillie, Caroline Sylge, Jo Boissevain
Inspections:	Toby Sawday, Lucinda Carling, Sasha Lillie, Miriam Turner, Laura Smith, Joanne Lane, Caroline Sylge, Ranjith Henry, Rachel Kellett

Photo of entry 7 © Robin Harris, Photo of entry 6 © Carolyn Sylge, Photos of 138, 145, 149 © Tim Griffith

ACKNOWLEDGEMENTS

This book begun as a mad project in a vast country – we
entered blind and with little encouragement. Yet there have
been certain people without whom we may have had to pull
the plug. I cannot do justice to the immense debt of gratitude
I feel towards Martin and Annie Howard, who gave me a bed,
an office, introductions galore and precious support when
spirits were low. Without these two remarkably generous
Delhi-wallahs, the book may never have come into being.
Two other people of a rare nature cannot go unmentioned –
Patrick Bowring's unquestioning kindness to a stranger gave
a home to 'the Delhi office', and the chilled wine and
calming words of Simon Blazely made hurdles less daunting.
The unflappable Leric Reeches of Banyan Travel pulled rabbits
from hats when I had only dared to hope for hamsters and was
a beaming face amid humourless hoteliers. The youthful charm
and easy nature of the wonderful Anuranjani Nagar (also of
Banyan) made dealings a joy. Mini Chandran of Sundale Tours
gave her time and trade secrets when common sense might
have suggested otherwise, giving the book a much-needed
boost. Thank you, Anjuli, for wielding the maternal iron-fist –
your mooti and meals held off several assaults on my health.
The enthusiasm of the many people who have fallen in love
with India has been invaluable – thank you to Bob Bradnock,
Rachel Kellett, Ruth Pitts-Tucker, Patricia Scott-Bolton,
Ollie Rance and countless others. Special thanks are due to
Western & Oriental Travel, and their Indian partners Banyan
Tours & Travel, whose advice and experience rescued the book
and the mood. Lastly, I would like to thank Miriam Turner,
without whose company, tireless help and love I might well have
given up. This book is as much hers as it is mine.

Toby Sawday

WHAT'S IN THE BOOK?

CONTENTS

INTRODUCTION

These books are founded upon a passion for the unpretentious, the genuine and the unique. Our criteria for deciding whether a place is special may appear obscure – we have no 'star' system and do not include somewhere just because it has all the right 'facilities'. What counts, for us, are people, architecture, history, views and, above all, atmosphere. A faded 17th-century palace run by a generous, spirited family would be chosen in preference over a slick, designer hotel with all the five-star trimmings but surly staff.

India has long been a magnet for all sorts of people, from the British royal family on their imperial wanderings, to the gap-year saunterer on a shoestring. India's entrepreneurs have leapt in to offer beds, creating a hotel landscape with everything from the ghastly to the gorgeous, from the dirt cheap to the stupendously expensive. With so many people jostling for business, there are many places that don't make the mark. Finding out which ones do is the hard part.

Types of properties   Like anywhere in the modern(ising) world, India has suffered from rampant and tasteless construction, aided by easily floutable regulations and cheap labour. The worst offenders have been low-budget chains of business and package tourism hotels, which we have avoided. In short, we have weeded out those places, both modern and old, which we find drab, bad value, ugly, homogenous or unfriendly.

Beware of the terms used to describe hotels

The prefixes 'palace', 'fort', 'haveli' (town mansion), 'resort' and even 'hotel' are used liberally and loosely in India. Use the write-up and price as guidelines for what to expect, as a 'palace' can be little more than a six-room guest house that once housed a maharaja's poodle, whilst a 'resort' might only have a small pond and a plastic elephant slide. We have avoided the downright fraudulent and have, occasionally, asked the owners if we can remove a prefix such as 'palace', in order not to disappoint.

Heritage Hotels

India's royalty has seen better days. Indira Ghandi removed the privy purses from the royal families and limited the land they could own, thus many maharajas found themselves with vast palaces that they could no longer maintain. The savvy among

INTRODUCTION

them made the right moves, while most refused to believe it was happening and went down with the dynastic ship. A few have led the way, using great imagination to turn their stately piles into beautiful Heritage hotels that are architecturally and historically fascinating, if a little rough around the edges, and some truly first-class hotels, with all the trimmings and the price tag. Others, however, watched this success and jumped on the Heritage bandwagon, creaking open their doors to the public but making almost no concession to the traveller.

Be guided first by our descriptions, and then by the price. Use your imagination and expect a little dustiness – these are India's relics – and try to see these buildings for what they are (were, sometimes) – wonderfully ornate, lavishly decorated monuments.

Boutique hotels

Boutique hotels are a relatively recent phenomenon. They tend to be small (often with around 20 rooms), expensive, heavily styled (minimalism is popular) and privately owned.

Hotels

This category includes established hotels that do not come under the 'Heritage' banner.

Homestays

There are some wonderful family houses that have opened as homestays, giving you a chance to glimpse (predominantly middle-class) Indian home life from within. Some are simple, though many are extremely comfortable. Nearly all have been thrown open to you because the owners love having people from foreign lands passing through their lives. Though many of the host families have moved away from a strictly traditional Indian lifestyle, you must be aware that you are staying in someone's home, and respect the customs and practices of the family. The experience can be rich; relaxed, conversational meals can ramble into the night and friendships are easily forged – be prepared to join in. Privacy can be hard to come by, but do not be afraid to ask for a little time out.

Guesthouses

Our guesthouses tend to be more friendly, less anonymous than hotels although perhaps less intimate than homestays. They are often private houses that have been partially converted, and tend not to have the same mod cons as hotels.

INTRODUCTION

Eco-lodges

Chosen for their commitment to reducing their impact on the environment, these places tend to be simple and relaxed and to have more soul than luxury. Run by people who are passionate about India and her environment, and often deeply involved in their local communities, eco-lodges are for those who prefer to know that the money they spend goes towards good causes rather than for those who want a pampered, anonymous stay.

Tented Camps

A far cry from the musty-canvas-and-soggy-sleeping-bag experience you might associate with tents, these have more in common with comfortable hotel rooms – fresh linen, flush toilets and four-poster beds, with the added luxury of being under canvas (some are even air-conditioned!).

Many family-run places will not appreciate guests sunbathing on their lawn. Please be respectful of those people who live and work where you are staying.

Choosing your special place

We try to make your decision as easy as possible, by giving you an honest write-up describing the style and atmosphere of the place. The write-ups will tell you how formal or relaxed a place is, what the hosts are like and how the overall atmosphere feels. You should be able to tell whether you can get the privacy you're after, or if you're likely to be drawn into the heart of a lively family. You can then decide how you want to spend your holiday – and your money.

Though we have tried hard to avoid any misrepresentation, photos can paint a somewhat different picture from reality. If we give a web site address for the place, take a look at it for a fuller picture.

After you have read the write-up and seen the photo, your best indicator of whether the place is for you is the price. There is a massive range in this book. As a general rule, needless to say, the more expensive a hotel, the more luxurious it will be.

The size of the hotel is a great indicator of the atmosphere. A two-room guesthouse will have a far cosier atmosphere than a resort with a hundred cottages.

N.B. Though we have tried hard to avoid plastic furniture, shiny curtains and embossed wallpaper, you will often find small

INTRODUCTION

flurries of kitsch in modern Indian interior design. Plastic chairs are a common sight in India. It's all part of the experience.

How to use
this book

Map

When you've pawed through guidebooks and taken advice to give you an idea of the region you'd like to visit, look at the map at the front of the book to find your area. The numbers on the map correspond to the entry number at the bottom of each property page.

Or, of course, you can peruse the book first using the map page number at the bottom of the entry page to find the entry number on the map.

Our mapping is only approximate, so you absolutely must check the precise whereabouts of the hotel, especially for the more remote places, by getting in touch with the owners or visiting their websites. Almost all of the places in the book can pick you up from nearby airports or railway stations, though you will often have to pay for each journey.

Rooms

We tell you about the range of accommodation in doubles, twins, singles, suites and family rooms as well as apartments and whole houses. The first price shown is for a double room. Indian hotels rarely have such things as 'standard doubles', preferring instead to grade their rooms according to levels of regality – going up from maharani to maharaja to vice-regal for example.

Rooms have their own bathrooms, unless we say otherwise.

A/c suggests air-conditioned rooms, while *air-cooled* has only rudimentary cooling machines.

To those used to the soft comfort of European mattresses, Indian beds and their pillows can seem unyielding. Do not be afraid to ask for another mattress.

Bathrooms

Water is in short supply in India and baths are the first casualty of water restrictions. Though they are available in many of our special places, baths are by no means standard; showers are always available. Be sparing with water – shortages have become a huge, often life-threatening, problem even in areas with apparently high rainfall. Do double-check bathroom details when booking if they are important to you.

INTRODUCTION

Prices

Prices given are for two people sharing a room in peak season, unless we say otherwise. Single rates are nearly always available – expect to pay 15-40% less. Indian hotels tend not to include breakfast in the price; we say where it is included.

Though room prices were correct at the time of going to print, do check for changes on arrival or when making a booking. Most are prices for the 2003-4 season, so if you are reading this book in 2005, be prepared for a possible 10% increase – or check the hotel web site. See inside back cover for our price band table.

Prices in India, especially the south, can almost double during the Christmas and New Year period. We do not mention these prices in the book, so PLEASE check before making a booking for those times of year.

During low season it is often possible to negotiate reduced rates (you may even find half-price rooms). If the hotel appears quite empty, this usually suggests that you'll be able to bargain. City hotels are less likely to offer discounts.

Taxes

The hidden taxes – 'luxury', 'service', 'sales' – in India can add up to 25% to your hotel bill. The more expensive the hotel, the higher the taxes. If you are concerned, make sure that you find out when making your booking what taxes to expect. The Indian government is constantly changing the rules, but the latest budget (2003) promised to encourage tourism through the reduction in related taxes. We say where room taxes apply. However, we have not mentioned the taxes on food, which will very rarely amount to more than 10%.

Where we do not mention tax, it is included in the price.

Every state has its own economies, rules and restrictions that affect how expensive it is to be a tourist. Competition in the Goan tourism market has meant that prices in the lower brackets are at an all-time low. However, Kerala is riding a wave of popularity while the building of hotels has yet to catch up. Therefore, though quality tends to be pretty high, the average room is more expensive than in Goa.

INTRODUCTION

Seasons

We only print the peak season prices, as most foreign travellers do not want to visit India in the climatically extreme off-peak times. However, during monsoon and high summer, and during winter in the lower Himalayas, you can get wonderfully cheap rooms.

Symbols

There is an explanation of these on the inside back cover of the book. Treat them as guidelines rather than as an unequivocal statement of fact and check anything particularly important to you.

Quick reference indices

At the back of the book is a quick reference section to direct you to the places that suit you.

Practical Matters

Visas

Unless you hold an Indian passport you will need to get a visa to enter the country. This is issued after you have stamped your feet in a queue outside the Indian High Commission (www.hcilondon.net) in Holborn, London. It's a cunning trick to print off the application form from the web site before going, to save time and to avoid losing your place in the queue to someone else who has thought ahead (the site also gives stacks of good info on each state, plus maps and links to other useful sites). A typical tourist visa lasts for six months and costs approximately £30. Applications by post take around six weeks.

Phones and Phone Codes

The numbers printed include the country code (91).

Calling India from the UK – dial 00, then the full printed number from the book.

Dialing within the country – omit the first two digits printed (+ 91), replacing them instead with a single 0 before you dial the remaining digits.

Calling another country from India – dial 00, followed by the country code, then the area code (again, omitting the first 0). For example, Alastair Sawday Publishing (01275 464 891) from India: 00 44 1275 464 891

INTRODUCTION

Calling an Indian mobile phone from within India – all numbers begin with 9. However, if you are calling a mobile phone that belongs to someone from outside the state from which you are calling, you must prefix the number with 0.

For more detailed information on using phones in India, see page 248.

Meals

We tell you if our special places offer meals, and the average price per person. In many places there is no option but to eat in, in which case you are offered full-board prices. Hotels tend to be open to non-residents for meals, while homestays are not. It is best to ask your hosts where to go, as certain Indian kitchens should be given a wide berth.

Indian food has both wonderful and terrible reputations. Scores of travellers come home with horrific stories about 'Delhi-belly' and holidays spent almost exclusively in the bathroom (normally thanks to others' careless hand-washing or a brush with an unwashed salad). Yet others fall in love with the magical cuisine – inventive, hugely varied and with ingredients we would be pushed to even spell. (Vegetarians find themselves in the rare and welcome position of being in the majority.) Dishes change as you pass from state to state, reflecting the dizzying array of different regional ingredients – coconut and fish dominate the dishes of the southern coastal areas and in the Himalayan region the influences are Tibetan and Chinese. Not all of it is tongue-searingly spicy either, as restaurants have wised up to the feeble palates and relatively weak constitutions of western travellers.

You can buy a wholesome, tasty meal for less than £1 in many cheap restaurants, but can pay European prices in the more upmarket hotels. Such hotels offer relative safety from the fear of food poisoning, but you are never entirely free from the threat. We have, as far as is possible, weeded out those places that have reputations for poor food hygiene.

Tipping

In a standard hotel, Rs50 per day per main person is about right. Alternatively, 10% of the total bill as a tip to spread between various parties should suffice. Bear in mind that a 2km rickshaw ride should be about Rs15 – so a rail porter getting

INTRODUCTION

Rs10 for carting your luggage is more than enough. You do
not need to tip more than a few rupees to the waiter at a
cheap *dhaba* (road-side café). The lack of obvious gratitude
from those you tip is hard to get used to, but doesn't mean
they are not pleased to receive the offering.

Booking

Try to book well in advance, especially if you plan to travel
during the peak season. Some places in popular areas will be
booked up almost a year in advance for the Christmas and
New Year period. Hotels close to major cities can also be
busy with weekenders, so beware.

Certain smaller hotels and many homestays only accept
pre-booked guests.

Many hotels ask for a percentage of the room price as a non-
refundable deposit and some homestays will even ask for the
entire amount before confirming the booking. With only two or
three rooms, they struggle to cope with last minute cancellations.
Though credit or debit cards can be used for pre-payment in
larger places, international transfers can be arranged when
making bookings for those places without card machines.
Ask your bank for more details.

Cancellations

Please give as much notice as possible when making a
cancellation, and make sure you check the property's policy
when booking – this can often be found on their web sites.

Payment

Cash (Indian rupee) is accepted everywhere, but many places in
this book also take credit cards and foreign currency. The most
commonly accepted cards are Visa and MasterCard, though
others might work in larger hotels. Smaller hotels tend not to
accept card payments because of the high bank charges, though
they may often change small amounts of foreign currency for
you. Although metropolitan areas have plenty of cash machines,
it's best to carry enough cash to last until the next major city.
You can also often pay for your hotel bill with foreign currency
(dollars and euros are most widely accepted). See the symbols.

INTRODUCTION

Electricity

The current in India is 220/240 volts, 50 Hz. Virtually all hotel rooms will have at least one socket that will take a 2-pin plug. For UK travellers, a European adaptor plug (available in airports) will do the trick. Though Indian batteries are cheap they tend to be of poor quality.

Public Transport

India's extensive transport system is at the same time both antiquated and modern – though certainly an experience. For more information see the travel section at the back of the book.

Environment

We try to reduce our impact on the environment by:

* printing on recycled paper. Megamatt is made up of 50% recycled and de-inked fibres from pre- and post-consumer waste. There is no use of chlorine in the de-inking process.

* planting trees. We are officially Carbon Neutral®. The emissions directly related to our office, paper production and printing of this book have been 'neutralised' through the planting of indigenous woodlands with Future Forests.

* re-using paper, recycling stationery, tins, bottles, etc.

* encouraging staff use of bicycles (they're loaned free) and car sharing.

* celebrating the use of organic, home-grown and locally-produced food.

* publishing books that support, in however small a way, the rural economy and small-scale businesses.

* running an Environmental Benefit Trust to stimulate business interest in the environment.

* working to establish an organic standard for B&B's (preliminary meetings have taken place).

* publishing *The Little Earth Book*, a collection of essays on environmental issues and *The Little Food Book*, a hard-hitting analysis of the food industry. *The Little Money Book* is under way, too. See our web site www.fragile-earth.com for more information on any of these titles.

Subscriptions

Owners pay to appear in this guide. Their fee goes towards the high costs of a sophisticated inspection system and producing an

INTRODUCTION

all-colour book. We only include places and owners that we find positively special. It is not possible for anyone to buy his/her way into our guides.

Internet Our web site www.specialplacestostay.com has online pages for all the places featured here and from all our other books – around 3,500 Special Places in total. There's a searchable database, a taster of the write-ups and colour photos.

For more details see the back of the book.

Disclaimer We make no claims to pure objectivity in choosing our Special Places to Stay. They are here because we like them. Our opinions and tastes are ours alone and this book is a statement of them; we hope that you will share them.

We have done our utmost to get our facts right but apologise unreservedly for any mistakes that may have crept in. Feedback from you is invaluable and we always act upon comments. With your help and our own inspections we can maintain our reputation for dependability.

You should know that we do not check such things as fire alarms, swimming pool security or any other regulations with which owners of properties receiving paying guests should comply. This is the responsibility of the owners. On the inside back cover we give the entry numbers of those places that had not been inspected by ASP at the time of going to press.

And finally Though India, for many, is a hugely daunting country and one that is cause for stories of both magic and misery, it is a thrilling place in which to travel. Read, talk, learn about this country – take from it what you want and revel in the unexpected.

Toby Sawday

HOW TO USE THIS BOOK

explanations

❶ rooms

All rooms, in this example, are 'en suite'.

❷ room price

The price shown is for one night for two people sharing a room. A price range incorporates room differences. We say when price is per week.

❸ meals

Prices are per person for a set two-course meal. If breakfast isn't included we give the price.

❹ closed

When given in months, this means for the whole of the named months and the time in between.

❺ directions

Use as a guide; the owner can give more details, as can their web sites.

❻ map & entry numbers

Map page number; entry number.

❼ type of place

❽ price band

Price ranges, see last page of the book.

❾ reservation number

❿ symbols

See the last page of the book for fuller explanation:

 smoking restrictions exist
 credit cards accepted
premises are licensed
 food served
working farm
 air-conditioning
 internet connection available
swimming pool

sample entry

RAJASTHAN

Neemrana Fort-Palace
Neemrana, 301 705, Rajasthan

If the marauding hordes descending on this maze of a palace got as lost I did, the inhabitants might never have been defeated. The warren spreads over 10 layers, the ramparts and colonnaded walkways leading to open courtyards and as confusing as an Escher sketch. A sensitive, modest, yet beautiful restoration of near ruins, this 'non-hotel' is a powerful example of the triumph of good taste and moderation over the evils of standardised luxury. Built over ten years, the rooms have slowly taken shape, reflecting the mindfulness of history that runs throughout this special place. Some have their own jarokha balconies facing out onto plains peppered with plots of bright mustard, while others have bathrooms open to the skies. You can sleep in the old royal court, or in a tent atop the highest turret. All are simply furnished with colonial and Indian antiques in the eclectic style so well executed here. This place embodies holiday calm – there are no TVs or phones in the rooms, just endless corners, courtyards and lush gardens to sit and read – one of the few hotels where one can always have a turret or courtyard to oneself. *The smaller rooms are very cosy. Yoga, meditation.*

rooms	43: 21 doubles, 1 single, 18 suites, 1 family room for 4. Some A/C.
price	Doubles Rs2,200–Rs3,300. Singles Rs1,100. Suites Rs4,400–Rs6,600. Family room Rs12,000. Plus 10% tax. Peak season: September–March.
meals	Breakfast Rs200. Lunch, & dinner Rs400.
closed	Rarely.
directions	2 hours southwest of Delhi along NH8 to Jaipur. Turn right at the signs in Neemrana Village.

	Mr Ramesh Dhabhai
tel	+91 1494 246 006
fax	+91 11 2435 1112
e-mail	sales@neemranahotels.com
web	www.neemranahotels.com
res. no.	+91 11 2435 6145

❼ Heritage Hotel   ❾

❻ entry 37   map 5   E+f ❽   ❿

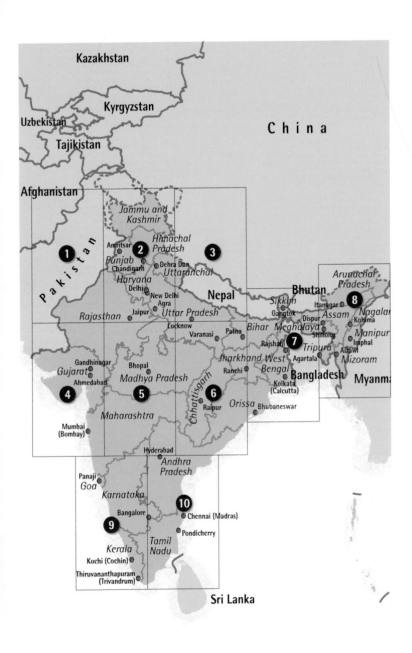

A guide to our map page numbers

© Bartholomew Ltd 2003

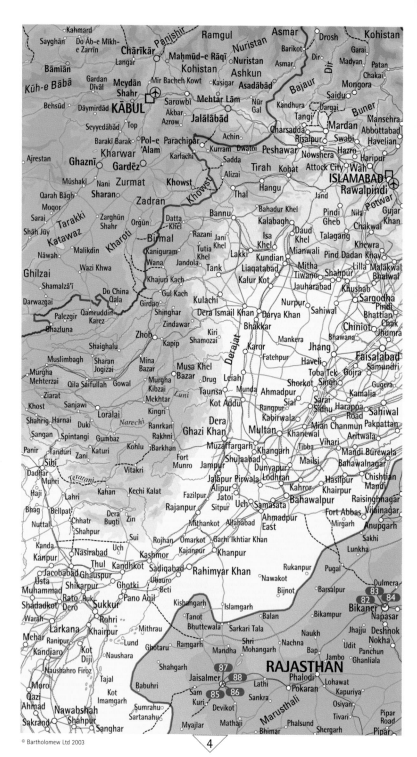

Map 1

© Bartholomew Ltd 2003

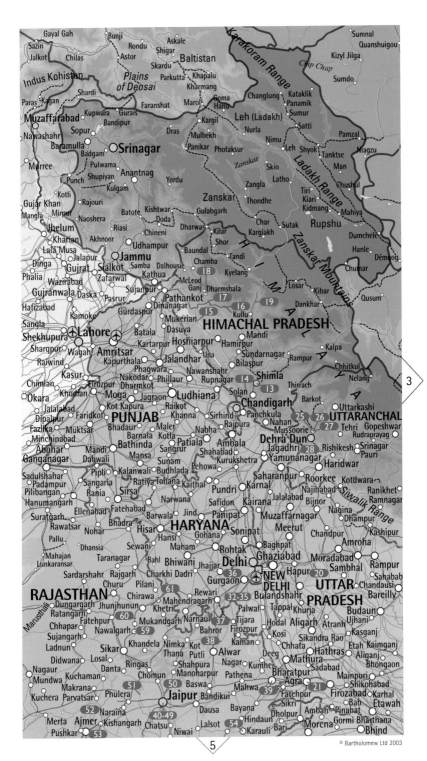

Map 2

© Bartholomew Ltd 2003

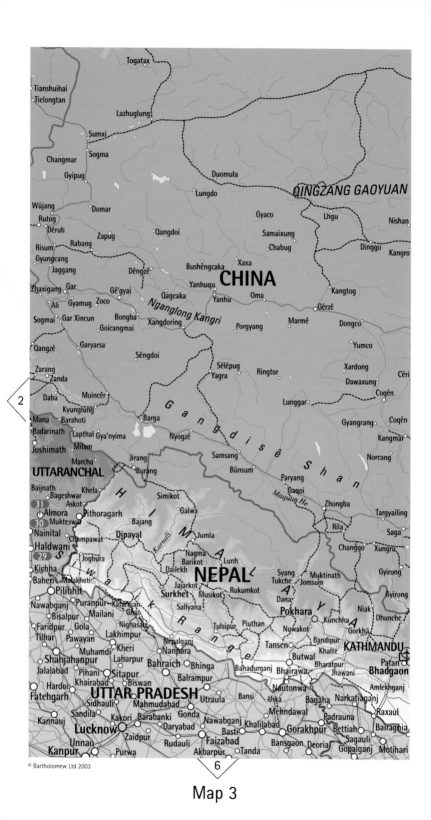

Map 3

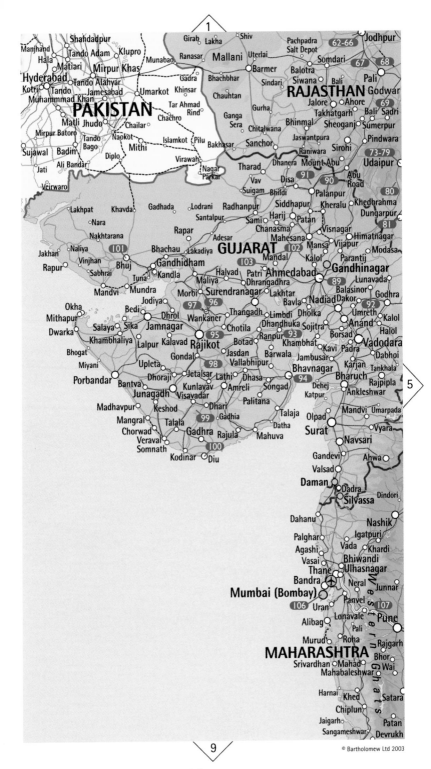

Shahdadpur
Manjhand
Hala
Matiari
Hyderabad
Kotri
Tando
Muhammmad Khan
Mirpur Khas
Tando Adam
Klupro
Munabao
Girab
Lakha
Shiv
Ranasar
Mallani
Uterlai
Pachpadra
Salt Depot
62-66
Jodhpur
Somdari
67
68
Barmer
Balotra
Tando Alahyar
Jamesabad
Umarkot
Khinsar
Gadra
Bhachbhar
Sindari
Siwana
Bali
Pali
PAKISTAN
Tar Ahmad
Rind
Chauhtan
Gurha
Chitalwana
Godwar
RAJASTHAN
Jalore
Ahore
Bali Sadri
69
Sumerpur
Matli
Jhudo
Chailar
Ganga
Sera
Bhinmal
Takhatgarh
Sheoganj
Mirpur Batoro
Tando
Bago
Naokot
Chachro
Islamkot
Pilu
Jaswantpura
Raniwara
Sirohi
Pindwara
73-79
Sujawal
Badin
Ali Bandar
Diplo
Mithi
Virawah
Bakhasar
Sanchor
Dhanera
Mount Abu
Udaipur
Jati
Nagar
Parkar
Tharad
Vav
Suigam
Bhildi
Disa
Abu
Road
91
90
80
Veirwaro
Lakhpat
Khavda
Gadhada
Lodrani
Radhanpur
Siddhapur
Palanpur
Kheralu
Khedbrahma
Nara
Santalpur
Sami
Harij
Patan
Visnagar
Dungarpur
81
Nakhtarana
Rapar
Adesar
Chanasma
Mahesana
Mansa
Vijapur
Himatnagar
Jakhan
Naliya
101
Bhachau
Lakadiya
GUJARAT
102
Mandal
Kalol
Parantij
Modasa
Rapur
Vinjhan
Bhuj
Gandhidham
103
Ahmedabad
Gandhinagar
Lunavada
Sabhrai
Tuna
Kandla
Halvad
Patri
89
Balasinor
Okha
Jodiya
Mundra
Morbi
Surendranagar
Dhrangadhra
Lakhtar
Bavla
Nadiad
Dakor
92
Godhra
Mithapur
Bedi
Dhrol
97
96
Thangadh
Limbdi
Dholka
Umreth
Kalol
Dwarka
Salaya
Sika
Jamnagar
Wankaner
Chotila
Dhandhuka
Sojitra
Borsad
Anand
Halol
Khambhaliya
Lalpur
Kalavad
Rajkot
95
Botad
Ranpur
93
Khambhat
Kavi
Padra
Vadodara
Dabhoi
Bhogat
Gondal
Jasdan
Vallabhipur
Barwala
Jambusar
Karjan
Tankhala
Miyani
Upleta
98
Lathi
Dhasa
Bhavnagar
Bharuch
Porbandar
Bantva
Dhoraji
Jetalsar
Amreli
Songad
94
Dehej
Rajpipla
Junagadh
Kunlavav
Visavadar
Dhari
Palitana
Katpur
Ankleshwar
Madhavpur
Keshod
Dhari
Gadhia
Talaja
Datha
Olpad
Mandvi
Umarpada
Mangral
Chorwad
Talala
99
Rajula
Mahuva
Surat
Vyara
Veraval
Gadhra
Navsari
Somnath
Kodinar
100
Diu
Gandevi
Ahwa
Valsad
Daman
Dadra
Dindori
Silvassa
Dahanu
Nashik
Palghar
Igatpuri
Agashi
Vada
Khardi
Vasai
Bhiwandi
Thane
Ulhasnagar
Bandra
Neral
Junnar
Mumbai (Bombay)
106
Panvel
107
Pune
Uran
Lonavale
Alibag
Pali
Murud
Roha
Rajgarh
MAHARASHTRA
Bhor
Srivardhan
Mahad
Wai
Mahabaleshwar
Harnai
Khed
Satara
Chiplun
Patan
Jaigarh
Sangameshwar
Devrukh

5

© Bartholomew Ltd 2003

Map 4

© Bartholomew Ltd 2003

Map 5

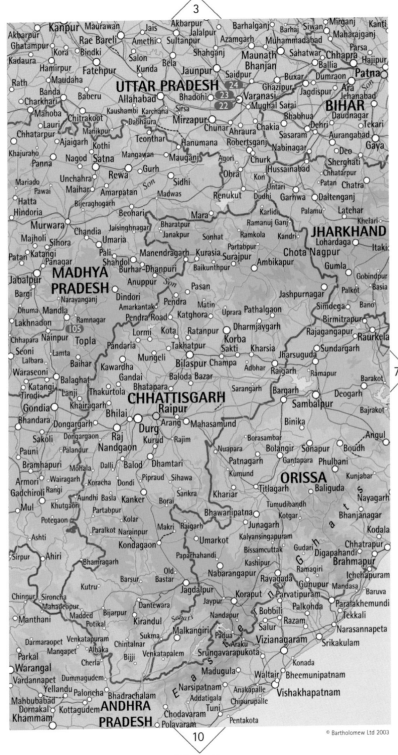

Map 6

© Bartholomew Ltd 2003

Map 7

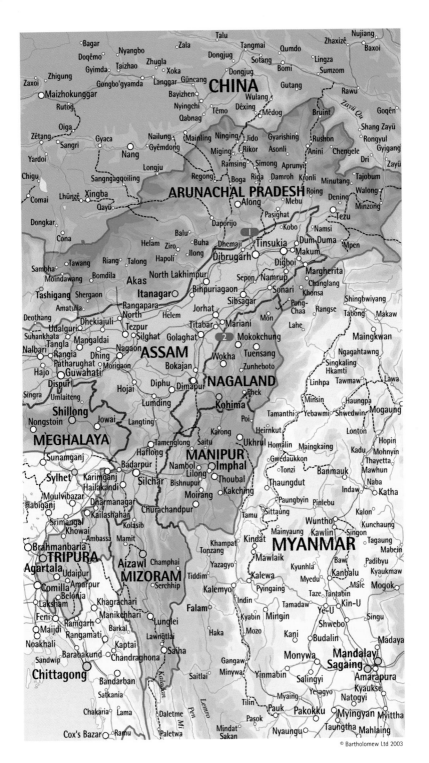

Map 8

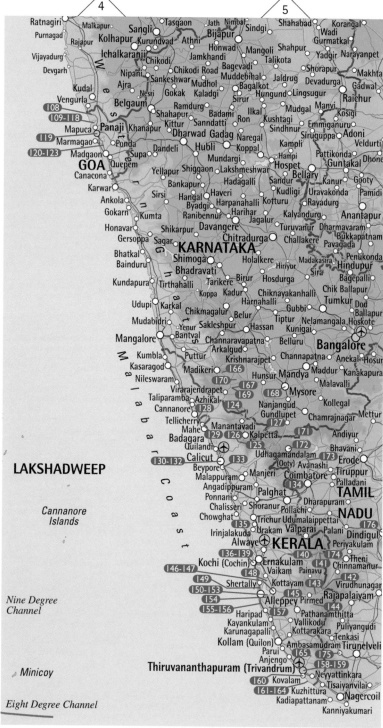

Map 9

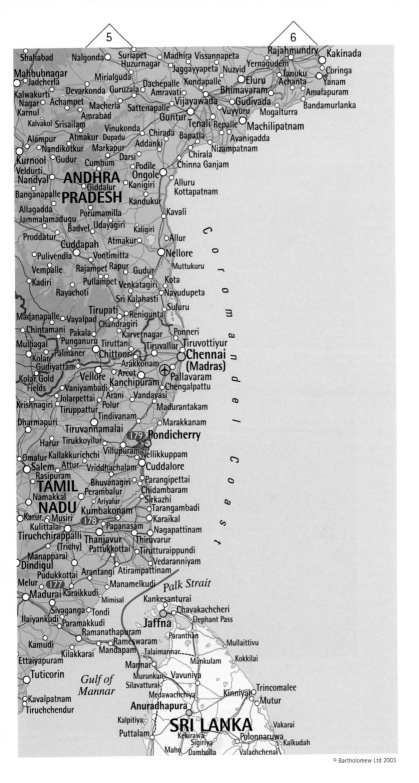

Map 10

Photography by Toby Sawday

assam
sikkim

Mancotta Chang Bungalow

Purvi Discovery (P) Ltd, Jalan Nagar, Dibrugarh, 786 005, Assam

In the middle of a working Assam tea estate, this 157-year-old bungalow was built by British tea planters. Raised on wooden stilts to make it easier for former planters to climb onto their elephants, and to protect them from floods and jungle animals, it's a spacious, airy place with two levels of verandas. Varnished dark wood floors, beds and writing desks give a gentlemanly feel to the rooms, which are elegant and very comfortable. Meals are taken in the dining room or on a veranda, and the food alternates between Indian and continental – Indian wins out every time. There's a place to watch videos and a small library of books. After the rain, take some time to sniff the air, sip some tea and enjoy the rich pea-green of the tea bushes. The Jalan family, who own the bungalow, have been in the area for five generations – Manoj and Vineeta will make you feel at home and arrange local tours, including to Rukmini Island for birdwatching and adventure sports. The guides are exceptional, particularly Hemanta, who is full of stories. If you're in a big party, there's a second, cosier bungalow a short drive away, though it is near a road. *Croquet, boating, tea tasting.*

rooms	6 doubles.
price	Full-board only, Rs5,500. Plus 10% tax. Peak season: November-May.
meals	Included. Full-board.
closed	Rarely.
directions	In the middle of Mancotta Tea Estate, just outside Dibrugarh. 5km from train station; 15km from airport.

Mr Ranjeet Das

tel	+91 373 2301 120
fax	+91 373 2301 944
e-mail	purvi@sancharnet.in
web	www.purvidiscovery.com

Guesthouse

Thengal Manor

Jalukanibari, Na Ali, Jorhat, 785 001, Assam

A slice of another life – and although the architecture is thoroughly colonial the family that owns it is Assamese, and immensely distinguished. It is on a grand scale, almost opulent, though there is gratifyingly little hint of the 'hotel'. The furniture is a handsome mix of antique and reproduction, with original objects from all over the world. Solidly upholstered and deeply comfortable furniture – perhaps a mahogany drum table and a Louis IV-style sideboard, heavy floral curtains, giant-chequered floor, white walls and old-fashioned ceiling fans. The bedrooms are magnificent: maybe a four-poster bed, dark but elegant wooden pieces, red polished floors with attractive rugs and plain walls; all are big enough to have their own sitting areas and dressing rooms. Somehow it is very European, despite the epic space and ceiling fans, but in the middle of a green sea of tea plantation. The colonial style re-emerges in the splendidly colonnaded quadrangular veranda, with polished red floors and white cane chairs. There are a sitting room, dining room and lounge – space galore. *US dollar cash is the only foreign currency they accept.*

rooms	5 doubles. Some a/c.	
price	Rs1,500-Rs1,950. Whole house Rs8,500. Plus 20% tax. Peak season: October-April.	
meals	Breakfast Rs150. Lunch & dinner from Rs250.	
closed	Rarely.	
directions	15km from Jorhat along the Na Ali (new road) towards Titabor. Signed.	

	Mr S M Hussain
tel	+91 376 2339 519
fax	+91 376 2320 242
e-mail	muja_did@yahoo.com
web	www.heritagetourismindia.com
res. no.	+91 376 2320 479

Guesthouse

F   map 8   entry 2

Netuk House

Tibet Road, Gangtok, 737 101, Sikkim

From here you can see the third highest mountain in the world, Mount Kanchanjunga. From nearby you can see Everest. Netuk House has a Buddhist serenity to unwind the most frenzied traveller. Pema and his wife are gifted with a rare kindness and a passionate devotion to Sikkim's culture. Expect no unnecessary luxuries, only the most attractive simplicity. The furniture is made locally, carved and then brightly painted with 'lucky' floral designs. Each room has a veranda with chairs and tables and eye-stretching views to the mountains (though the two rooms in the main house have space rather than views). Bedcovers and blankets are of traditional material and all is plain, but utterly right. Because it is dark inside it is best to be out and about during the day. You usually eat with the family, a delightful experience, and the food is very good — specialities include squash root, nettle soup, ferns with cottage cheese. Pema's cousin, a monk educated in the USA, often shares dinner. The mountain range within Sikkim's borders is one of the most magnificent in the world.

rooms	10 doubles.
price	Full board only, Rs3,600. Plus 10% tax. Peak season: September–November; March–June.
meals	Included. Full-board.
closed	Rarely.
directions	300m from MG Marg (main market). Call guesthouse for directions as there are no signs.

	Mr Pema Namgyala
tel	+91 3592 222 374
fax	+91 3592 224 802
e-mail	slg_netuk@sancharnet.in

Guesthouse

Nor-Khill

Stadium Road, Gangtok, 737 101, Sikkim

The huge and beautifully decorated lobby was originally the King's ballroom when this was the royal guesthouse. The royal charm lives on, in the serenity, the designs and the fabulous food (nettle soup and bamboo shoots, perhaps, or chicken momo, served with the local tipple Chang). As a hotel it is individual and luxurious in the nicest possible way, with fine wooden-floored bedrooms and some original pieces, and much satisying detail: old silver, engraved breakfast pepper and salt pots, hand-woven tray mats and chair covers, wooden floors throughout and a general sense that the house has known good times. The King and his American wife, Hope Cook, had a hand in the decoration and he held his parties here. When Diamond Oberoi bought it he spruced it up but left it largely intact. There is a Sikkimese altar in the main corridor with two circular seating areas at each end covered with hand-woven material in bold colours. There are wall-hangings, intricate painted designs, an old wood-burning stove, a stone floor and lots of red. If it was good enough for the Dalai Lama and Shirley McLean it may do you.

rooms	32: 28 doubles, 4 suites.
price	Full-board only, Rs4,800. Suites Rs6,500. Plus 10%. Peak season: September-December; March-June.
meals	Included. Full-board.
closed	Rarely.
directions	Just above the Palzor Stadium on Stadium Road.

	Mr Basudev Sahoo
tel	+91 3592 220 064
fax	+91 3592 225 639
e-mail	newelgin@cal.vsnl.net.in
web	www.elginhotels.com
res. no.	+91 33 2226 9878

Heritage Hotel

map 7   entry 4

Bamboo Resort
Sajong, Rumtek, 737 101, Sikkim

It's an east-meets-west sort of place, with low double beds, Sikkimese cushions and rugs and all the vibrancy of Sikkimese culture. Although the building is of solid stone there is a big emphasis on bamboo; there is plenty of it about and it is part of the décor. The floors are all of grey marble and the feng shui bedrooms, each a different colour to represent an element, are a main feature. Indeed, the whole building was built according to feng shui principles. Helen is Swiss and Topgay Sikkimese; they met at a meditation centre in San Francisco and have been planning this building for many years. Helen is fired-up, energetic and passionate about ecology; Topgay is calmer – a lovely presence. They make a great team (both are Buddhists) and the house reflects their beliefs. They grow food organically and buy locally, have a large herb garden, a beautiful meditation room and a steam room and will run yoga and meditation courses. They are genuinely committed to ecological principles and the whole place is an inspiration – as is the area and the setting. When we saw the building it wasn't quite finished – so do check. *Language courses.*

rooms	10 doubles.
price	Full-board only, $60-$70. Peak season: March-May; September-November.
meals	Included. Full-board.
closed	Rarely.
directions	From Gangtok 25km along Rumtek Road to Sajong village. Ask for the statue factory, from where the resort is signed.

Helen & Topgay Takapa
tel +91 353 202 049
e-mail info@sikkim.ch
web www.sikkim.ch

Yangsum Farm Homestay

Yangsum Farm, P.O. Rinchenpong, District Gyalsing, 737 111, West Sikkim

Based near the small bazaar village of Richenpong, this is a delightful working farm run by Thendup Tashi and his two sisters Dorji Lhaden and Pema Chuki – unassuming, switched-on hosts who have only just opened their home to guests. Built by their grandfather in 1833, the place has a gentle, calming atmosphere. Come to write, draw or walk, or help out on the 44-acre farm which grows everything from cardamom and tea to avocados, oranges, ginger, mangoes, vegetables. The wooden-floored bedrooms are basic, decorated with Sikkimese fabrics and family photographs; the bathrooms are shared but spotless. Check out the traditional Buddhist altar room, where you can meditate, should the mood take you. There's a communal sitting room indoors and a courtyard where you can enjoy the sunshine. The food is superb – be brave and try the local dishes that incorporate nettles, ferns and bamboo; other Indian food is served, too. Thendup and Pema are likely to accompany you on some great walks, including those to a rhododendron forest, an aristocratic Lepcha house or Buddhist monasteries far quieter and more remote than any on the Sikkimese tourist route.

rooms	3: 1 double, 2 singles.
price	Full-board only, Rs2,400. Singles Rs1,200. Peak season: March–December.
meals	Included. Full-board.
closed	Rarely.
directions	2km down from small bazaar village of Richenpong, in the centre of West Sikkim. 4 hours drive from Bagdogra airport.

	Mr Thendup Tashi Tsechutharpa
tel	+91 3595 245 322
e-mail	yangsumfarm@yahoo.com
web	www.yangsumfarm.com
res. no.	+91 3592 222 633

Homestay

 G **map 7 entry 6**

Photography by Quentin Craven

kolkata & west bengal

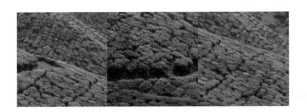

Fairlawn Hotel

13/A Sudder Street, Kolkata, 700 016, Kolkata and West Bengal

Heinz ketchup on the tables, posters advertising Somerset and Assam tea, old furniture (some of which has been painted), heavy brown floral curtains, bric-a-brac everywhere – this is an oasis in the frenzy of Calcutta, utterly devoted to the past and determined to hang on. You can see why it is so popular, though: the rooms are big and airy, you are served banana custard for lunch, the devoted staff who have been there for ever wear white gloves and cummerbunds at dinner, there are several lounges and a large, green and pleasant garden and you are made to feel immensely at home. Avoid, if you can, the three window-less rooms and if you are single (it's a fine place for singles) ask for No 9. There's a rooftop garden on the annexe, chairs and tables on the main roof and space to be yourself. It is all rather wonderful, a place to be calm, to create, to paint or write a novel. The atmosphere is welcoming and 'family' and people come back year after year. The bar is a watering place for expatriates of every hue and for locals intent on a gossip. They probably find it.

rooms	20: 13 doubles, 5 triples, 2 singles.
price	$42. Triples $56. Singles $33. Plus 16% tax. Peak season October–March.
meals	Lunch & dinner from Rs150.
closed	Rarely.
directions	Next to the Indian Museum & opposite the Salvation Army.

	Mrs Violet Smith
tel	+91 33 2252 1510
fax	+91 33 2252 1835
e-mail	fairlawn@cal.vsnl.net.in
web	www.fairlawnhotel.com

Heritage Hotel

The Elgin

18 H.D. Lama Road, Darjeeling, 734 101, Kolkata and West Bengal

Diamond Oberoi is indeed a member of the hotel family but this is his own creation in the old home of a maharajah's daughter. He went to school in town and loves it still; he has the quiet elegance of his own hotel and enjoys chatting to guests during the months when he is here. The walls of the bar are hung with prints by the Anglo-Indian artist, Gordon Douglas, and elsewhere there are lithographs and paintings and old photos of Darjeeling. A piano player plays during dinner – for which you will probably want to dress up – and afterwards you can withdraw to one of the many cosy corners. Built as a home, the hotel still has some of the domesticity of the house. There are open fires and a long garden in which to relax – and take tea whenever you want it. A gazebo has enchanting white wooden tables and chairs. Diamond owns the Nor-Khill and the Silver Oaks too, but not the Windamere – which is somehow more self-consciously British. You are right in the centre of town yet secluded. Almost perfect.

rooms	25: 20 doubles, 5 suites.
price	Full-board only, Rs4,100. Suites Rs6,500. Plus 10% tax. Peak season: March-June; September-December.
meals	Included. Full-board.
closed	Rarely.
directions	5-minute walk from Chowrasta, the main square; 7-minute walk to the Chock Bazaar bus stand; 10-minute walk from Darjeeling Station.

Mr Badal Majumder

tel	+91 354 2254 114
fax	+91 354 2254 267
e-mail	newelgin@cal.vsnl.net.in
web	www.elginhotels.com
res. no.	+91 33 2226 9878

Heritage Hotel

E map 7 entry 8

Windamere Hotel

Observatory Hill, Darjeeling, 734 101, Kolkata and West Bengal

To quote the brochure "The Windamere's… enduring, slightly eccentric charm resists… absolute definition." It is pure, ureconstructed Raj — yet Jan Morris wrote of it as a latter-day paradise. It is a buoyant reminder of a more leisured age, one which treated travellers with ceremony, and it still resists the concept of travel as an 'amusement' industry. No modern brashness, TV, slot machines, kiosks — just irresistibly personal service, such as a hot water bottle for each foot and a fire lit in your bedroom. The brass sparkles, the silver gleams and all is wholesomely clean. The plumbing is old but superb; the bathrooms have enamelled Victorian tubs and power showers and the bedrooms are wonderfully old-fashioned. Dinner here was always an event in Darjeeling society, and it still is if you enjoy such revered delights as bread and butter pudding and steak and onion pie. It is all owned by one remarkable Tibetan family, though they are often away. The best way to arrive is, of course, by the very slow 'toy' railway, taking in views of the impossibly beautiful five-peaked Kanchenjunga. A mellow Edwardian dream.

rooms	27: 25 doubles, 2 singles.
price	Full-board only. $119-$150. Singles $99. Plus 15% tax. Peak season: March-May; September-December.
meals	Included. Full-board.
closed	Rarely.
directions	Just above Chowrasta, the main square, on Observatory Hill. 500m from the train station.

	Tinkerbell
tel	+91 354 2254 041
fax	+91 354 2254 043
e-mail	reservation@windamerehotel.net
web	www.windamerehotel.com

Heritage Hotel

entry 9   map 7   C-D

Glenburn Tea Estate

Darjeeling, 734 101, Kolkata and West Bengal

Husna-Tara is a woman of charm, vision and flair. With these qualities she has created something of a dream – effortlessly stylish, mercifully comfortable and wickedly indulgent. A Scottish tea company established the estate in 1860, no doubt enticed by the luxuriant hillsides and cool climes reminiscent of the glens of Scotland. The spartan side of the Scottish inheritance has been left behind, however. The rooms are delightful – hand-printed fabrics from Delhi, matching cupboards delicately painted with Himalayan flowers, open fires, wicker chairs in bay windows. Every effort has been made to pamper: each of the four rooms has its own living area. You start the day with 'bed' tea – one of India's finest institutions – and end with hot water bottles. Sumptuous picnics are laid out on linen next to a burbling river and beneath the gaze of the misty Kanchenjunga: lashings of homemade jam and honey are doled out with homemade brown bread, washed down with pots of the Glenburn tea. I could go on... but see for yourself. An idyllic spot. *Fishing, tea tours, trekking and more.*

rooms	4 suites.
price	Full-board only, $250. Singles $160. Activities included.
meals	Included. Full-board.
closed	July-September.
directions	2.5 hours' drive from Mew Jalpaiguri station & Bagdogra station; a chauffeur-driven car will collect you from either. If you want to make your own way, call for more detailed instructions.

	Mrs Husna-Tara Prakash
tel	+91 33 2281 6795
fax	+91 33 2281 3581
e-mail	info@glenburnteaestate.com
web	www.glenburnteaestate.com

Homestay

B **map 7   entry 10**

Himalayan Hotel

Upper Cart Road, Kalimpong, 734 301, Kolkata and West Bengal

Still in the Macdonald family after all these years and going strong, with Himalayan oak ceilings, teak pillars, walnut and teak furniture, open fireplaces in most rooms and Tibetan memorabilia in the dining room. Tim's grandfather built it in 1920 and after a career in tea planting Tim and his Indian wife are now firmly rooted here. No wonder – Kalimpong is within sight of Kanchanjunga and is a centre for birdwatching, hill-walking and anything to do with mountains. Indeed, hardly a famous mountaineer has failed to stay here – Hillary and Tenzing, Mallory and Irving – let alone any author writing about Tibet and the mountains. It is a fine old hotel, airier than one would imagine, with delightful staff, solidly dependable food, red carpets and Nepalese rugs, whitewashed walls and deep peace. The cottages are fine, though less exceptional than the rooms in the main building; but they do have king-size beds. "A commonplace name for an exceptional place" – as the British writer, James Cameron, wrote. *Picnics by the river, and golf can be organised. Barbeques in winter.*

rooms	16: 4 doubles, 12 twins.
price	Rs2,200. Plus 10% tax. Peak season: September–January; March–May.
meals	Breakfast Rs160. Lunch & dinner Rs320.
closed	Rarely.
directions	Up the hill from town centre, about a 10-minute walk from 'Silver Oaks'.

Mrs Nilam Macdonald

tel	+91 3552 255 248
fax	+91 3552 255 122
e-mail	himalayanhotel@sify.com
web	www.himalayanhotel.biz

Heritage Hotel

Samthar Farmhouse

c/o Gurudongma Tours & Treks, Gurudongma House, Hill Top, Kalimpong, 734 301

On the edge of a remote Lepcha village with mountain views, this wood and stone farmhouse has an intimate feel and is a great starting point for treks. There's no electricity; a wood-fired Bhukhari heats the house, and kerosene-fired lamps light up the living area at night, when you can sip some Chang, the local tipple, or some of General Jimmy's brandy. Relax on the hand-woven cushion seats and yak-skin rugs and peruse the Lepcha musical instruments, Buddhist thankas and Sikh daggers lining the walls. Bedrooms are basic but comfortable – the heritage rooms are best for sunrise views, and there's a single room between them for children. You'll get hot water for a bucket bath – it's easy when you know how – and a hot water bottle at night, but it can get cold so bring warm clothing. Villagers staff the place under the expert supervision of Catherine, who is also a keen cook – food may be Goan, Indian or Tibetan, but it will always taste good. After a trek enjoy a foot bath on the terrace while your guides serve you tea, loll in the hammock or do yoga on the grassy terraces. *They run Gurugongma Tours for treks and more.*

rooms	6: 2 doubles; 2 cottages with 2 doubles.
price	Full-board only, $60. Transport & activities included. Plus 10% tax. Peak season: October-May.
meals	Included. Full-board.
closed	Rarely.
directions	80km from Kalimpong in a remote Lepcha village. Do not try to get there yourself.

Catherine Lobo

tel	+91 355 2255 204
fax	+91 355 2255 201
e-mail	gurutt@sancharnet.in
web	www.gurudongma.com

Guesthouse

Photography by Quentin Craven

himachal pradesh

Chapslee

Elysium Hill, Shimla, 171 001, Himachal Pradesh

If you have pottered up the mountainside in that splendid little train, filled with expectations of Shimla, you may have been underwhelmed by the town. Its glorious past and parochial present are at odds. But to find yourself in Chapslee is a rare treat. Some might describe it as decaying with dignity – it has been polished and scrubbed for many years. Others might think of it as 'upholding standards'. But there are some marvellous rooms and furniture, and an hour in the library will convince you that you are back in Scotland. Bedrooms are immensely comfortable: good reading lights, framed paintings or prints, white-painted Georgian-style doors, writing desks, perhaps a Victorian pitcher and bowl, and plenty of sparkling white paint and fine bathrooms, too. The sitting room is in Scottish-hunting-lodge style. It is all very old-fashioned – and not to be missed. The British will feel vaguely at home; others may be amused. (Note that the web site places the house, unnaturally, against a mountain backdrop, and there is a school, albeit a quiet one, in the old grounds.) *Lawn tennis, croquet and a fine library.*

rooms	6: 4 doubles, 1 single, 1 suite.
price	Full-board only, Rs5,250–Rs6,375. Single Rs3,700. Suite Rs7,400.
meals	Included. Full-board.
closed	January–February.
directions	Next to Aukland House Senior School, between Lakkar Bazaar & Longwood.

	Mr Kanwar Ratanjit Singh
tel	+91 177 2802 542
fax	+91 177 2658 663
e-mail	chapslee@vsnl.com
web	www.chapslee.com

Homestay

Fort Nalagarh

Nalagarh, District Solan, 174 101, Himachal Pradesh

Character, and stacks of it! Hidden turrets, deer on the dewy morning lawn, oleander and bougainvillea; the past very definitely there but kept from crumbling. Built in 1421 as the capital of the Hindur Kingdom, the Fort marks the point where the oceans of hot summer plains lap against the first folds of the Himalayan foothills. For many Indians and their families, it is an escape from the Delhi chaos. For travellers it is a wonderfully unstuffy, comfortable break in the journey between Delhi and the Himalayas (so there's a good mix of Indian and Western visitors). Nalagarh Fort has cast aside the regal stuffiness of its past, the constant battle to keep things in order leaving no time for grand pretence. The beds are comfortable and the rooms delightful in their pistachio tones and cotton throws, their large, cool spaces giving blessed relief from the heat. The hotel's popularity makes sure that the atmosphere never deadens and the dust never settles – the staff on always on their toes and unfailingly warm and attentive. A perfect stop-over.

rooms	22: 18 doubles, 3 suites, 1 family suite.
price	Rs2,200-2,500. Suites Rs2,990. Plus 10% tax. Family suite Rs5,900. Peak season: November-February.
meals	Breakfast Rs175. Lunch Rs275. Dinner Rs300.
closed	Rarely.
directions	60km from Chandigarh. At Nalagarh centre, turn right through the narrow streets & head up out of town towards the prominent fort.

	Mr Tikka Jayatendra Singh
tel	+91 1795 223 179
fax	+91 1795 223 021
e-mail	fortresort@satyam.net.in
web	www.nalagarh.com
res. no.	+91 11 2463 4139

Heritage Hotel

The Judge's Court Heritage Village

Pragpur, Kangra Valley District, 177 107, Himachal Pradesh

Pragpur is very beautiful, 1,800 feet up in the Kangra Valley and with views of the snow-tipped Himalayas. The village has cobbled streets, mud-plastered and slate-roofed houses and a very fine ornamental 'tank'. There is a strong whiff of aristocracy here, or ancestry. Vijai is proud of having had the village designated as 'heritage'. Justice Sir Jai Lal was educated in England and the house was built for him by a proud father. Vijai is his grandson and has returned to his roots with a passionate commitment to rebuilding the house. It is eclectic and surprising: butler service with pyrex dishes, touches of post-war affluence, cocktails before dinner, musicians – perhaps brought in from the village. All the staff are villagers and are still learning the ropes. The bedrooms are comfortable, even elegant, and have a mix of antique and more moderm furniture. If you are lucky enough to find Vijai and Rani living at home you will find a house full of bonhomie. It is all delightfully quiet, genteel almost, and there is much to do in this lovely countryside so fecund and fruitful – Pragpur means 'country of pollen'.

rooms	10: 6 doubles, 3 suites, 1 family room.
price	Rs2,300. Plus 10% tax.
meals	Breakfast Rs150. Lunch Rs250. Dinner Rs350.
closed	Rarely.
directions	Take train to Una & then 60km road journey. Or look at web site below.

	Mr Vijai Lal
tel	+91 1970 245 035
fax	+91 1970 245 823
e-mail	eries@vsnl.com
web	www.judgescourt.com
res. no.	+91 11 2467 4135

Heritage Hotel

Country Cottage

Chandpur Tea Estate, Palampur, Himachal Pradesh

Hemmed in by pine giants 5,000 feet up in the western Himalayas, just shy of the summer snow line and above an army cantonment, the Sarin family's huddle of blue mountain stone and knotted-pine cottages is a marvellous place for exploring and trekking in the Himachal interior. The first person to establish trekking proper in Himachal, Mr Sarin Snr, is a fount of perambulatory know-how and, with his son Navin, runs his own trekking company. Their passion for honest simplicity is evident in the basic but considered design of the huts and cottages that have all you need, and no more. All stone walls and wooden cladding, sisal flooring and slate roofing, these snug abodes sit among citrus and pine trees through which can be snatched tantalising glimpses of the mountains and the sprawling tea gardens. The more basic Forest and Eucalyptus huts are just that – a step up from camping, with a hot water bottle thrown in for chilly winter nights. The food is fresh, deliciously spiced, and entirely local – you get what's available and the concoctions are old family recipes. *Trekking & camping. Birdwatching and fishing for mahseer and trout.*

rooms	5: 3 cottages for 2, 2 huts for 2.
price	Cottages Rs1,100. Huts Rs1,500.
meals	Breakfast Rs140. Lunch & dinner Rs264.
closed	Rarely.
directions	Left through large cantonment gate 1km from Palampur on road to Kulu. Follow road to Chandpur; left just below helipad, then right. Country Cottage 800m down road.

	Mr Karan Sarin
tel	+91 1894 230 647
fax	+91 1894 230 041
e-mail	ksarin@sancharnet.in
web	www.countrycottageindia.com

Resort

F–G   map 2   entry 16

Norling Guesthouse

PO Sidhpur, Dist Kangra, Dharamsala, 176 057, Himachal Pradesh

The Institute to which the guesthouse is attached is built in traditional Tibetan style following a ground plan based on the proportions of Avalokiteshvara – the Bodhisattva of Compassion. It rises up the hillside from the entrance gate to the temple, through terraced gardens, pools, waterfalls and buildings housing the offices, workshops, museum and shop. It is a fascinating place – wander about and watch the craftsmen at work. The backdrop is the Himalayas; here 10 years only, it feels deeply rooted. It is a very special place, an oasis of peace and Tibetan culture. The guesthouse has the same charm, with a 'refectory' feel to the cool upstairs corridor, potted plants, cane easy chairs. All is simple, colourful, thoughtful and relaxing – very Tibetan. The bedrooms with high ceilings and a sense of air and space are perfect canvases for furniture, paintings, wall-hangings and bedcovers made by craftsmen at the Institute. Food is served in the café where you can eat on the rooftop – with views to the mountains – or in the garden, or inside. The Kangra valley, with its clear streams, old-style farming and green fields is a lovely foreground.

rooms	10: 8 doubles, 2 suites.
price	Rs1,150. Suites Rs1,800.
meals	Breakfast Rs60. Lunch & dinner Rs100.
closed	Rarely.
directions	In the valley 6km below Dharamsala.

	Mr Thenzin Lhamo
tel	+91 1892 246 402
fax	+91 1892 246 404
e-mail	normail@norbulingka.org
web	www.norbulingka.org

Guesthouse

Chonor House

Near Thekchen Choling Temple, McLeod Ganj, Dharamsala, 176 219, Himachal Pradesh

There is magic in the air here. Tibetan culture will never be lost while places like this continue to inspire and nourish visitors. Everything matters – from the way you are received to the tiniest detail. Tibetan wall-paintings on the bedroom walls, hand-embroidered cushions, attractive lightshades and brightly coloured exterior – everything is… respectful. Each bedroom depicts some aspect of Tibetan life in bold murals around which each room is individually furnished and named. The aesthetic voyeur in you will demand you enter each room. The artistry comes from the Norbulingka Institute. The bathrooms are dark but functional, with stone tiling and western-style loos. There's a library and a delightful restaurant serving Tibetan food and great pastries and a sun-dappled courtyard with marble-topped tables and wrought-iron chairs set among bushes and trees. Best of all are the Tibetans who look after you, and your money goes to the charity that owns Chonor and the Institute. One last, unexpected, bonus: an internet café called Cyber Yak. You would be wise to book in advance. *Wonderful crafts at the Norling Arts centre.*

rooms	11: 10 doubles, 1 suite.
price	Rs1,800–Rs2,200. Suite Rs2,500. Plus 10% tax. Peak season: March–November.
meals	Breakfast Rs120. Lunch & dinner Rs150.
closed	Rarely.
directions	Walking from Temple Road, take hairpin left turn up Thardoeling Road. No vehicular access.

Mr Dechen Namgyal Maja

tel	+91 1892 221 006
fax	+91 1892 221 468
e-mail	chonorhs@norbulingka.org
web	www.norbulingka.org

Guesthouse

 map 2   entry 18

Negi's Hotel Mayflower

Old Manali Road, Manali, District Kullu, 175 131, Himachal Pradesh

Handsome, unpretentious and comfortable – and a great place to retreat to in poor weather. There are log fires in your room and chairs to draw up and settle into. There is even cold-weather 'comfort' food such as bread pudding and apple pie. Hot water – in bath-fulls, and an open fire in the dining-room too, where you are in the sort of wood-lined rustic simplicity that reminds you of the Alps. The smell of pine is in the fabric of the building and the veranda is wide, comfortable and attractive. The backdrop is of tall pines and you may glimpse the snowy peaks. The little garden is on the other side and full of blossom in the spring. (You can hear the road and its miscellaneous noises in the day but not at night.) The wood-lined bedrooms are simple but amply comfortable, with good lighting, rough cotton-weave curtains and slightly elderly bathrooms that are immaculately clean. (A few rugs are UK-pub-style – but clean.) The staff are delightful and the food is excellent and cooked to order. *Mr Negi runs Himalayan Adventures – good trekking.*

rooms	18: 16 doubles, 1 single, 1 suite.
price	Rs625–Rs1,400. Single Rs500. Suite Rs1,600. Plus 10% tax. Peak season: May-mid September.
meals	Breakfast Rs150. Lunch & dinner Rs300.
closed	Rarely.
directions	From Manali Town go straight up towards old Manali Village for 1km.

	Mr Prem Negi
tel	+91 1902 252 104
e-mail	roopu@sancharnet.in

Hotel

are the leading upmarket specialist for tailor
made tour arrangements in India. Our expertise
and understanding of the country, its hotels
and destinations are reflected in the experience
of our staff. We have always been a strong
supporter of smaller heritage hotels as well as
the more established properties and have
worked with many of the owners since they first
opened to travellers. We travel to India regularly
to inspect hotels and seek out new properties
for our clients. The emphasis at Western &
Oriental is on providing informed personal
service supported by extensive knowledge and
research. When planning your tour to India
please contact us by telephone/e mail or visit
our website. We would be delighted to share
our knowledge with you to ensure your
experience of the subcontinent is unparalleled.

Western & Oriental

A W&ORLD APART

Indian Ocean | Caribbean | South East Asia | India | Africa | Australasia | Latin America

Telephone: 020 7313 6600 | www.westernoriental.com

Photography by Quentin Craven

uttar pradesh
uttaranchal

Mud Fort, Kuchesar

Village Kuchesar, Via BB Nagar, District Bulandhahr, Uttar Pradesh

The Mud Fort looms ochre-and-white like a beached battleship among gardens and palm trees. Looking at this idyllic spot, an isolated seven kilometres along a dirt track, you would never guess it saw internecine power struggles and battles against the British. Its seven turrets and battlements, built in the 18th century as defence against cannon, are now settings for dinner beneath the starry night. Colonial verandas overlook the gardens, in which a small pool is fed by a cascade of natural spring water. Peacocks pose decoratively among the neighbouring ruins — once a replica of Robert Clive's Calcutta house — and screech paeans to the moon, while green parakeets swoop and chatter by day. The bedrooms are simply furnished, and the periodic lapses of electricity are oddities to be enjoyed. The descendants of the original Jats still inhabit a wing of the Mud Fort, cultivating large mango groves nearby, and there is a working farm complete with water buffalo. You are surrounded by wheat and sugarcane fields; the only sound to compete with the birdsong is the distant toll of bells from a Hindu temple.

rooms	10: 2 doubles, 8 suites. Some a/c.
price	Rs1,500. Suites Rs1,650. Plus 5% tax. Peak season: September–March.
meals	Breakfast Rs150. Lunch Rs250. Dinner Rs250.
closed	Rarely.
directions	80km by road from Delhi.

	Mr Raju Singal
tel	+91 5736 273 039
fax	+91 11 2435 1112
e-mail	sales@neemranahotels.com
web	www.neemranahotels.com
res. no.	+91 11 2435 6145

Heritage Hotel

Oberoi Amarvilas

Taj East Gate, Agra, 282 001, Uttar Pradesh

Few hotels can say they have unbroken views of one of the world's seven modern wonders – from every room. The Taj Mahal rises out of the dusty woods just 600m from your balcony, the morning mist hangs over the trees adding to the ethereal mood. Shah Jahan's final extravagance was the main influence behind the design of Amarvilas. The high-domed marble entrance hall yields to a wide glass-sided atrium beyond which the Taj Mahal sits, as important as are the hotel's old oil paintings, bone-inlay chests and marble *jalis* to the overall sense of magnificence. Though the building may seem austere on arrival, with its wide geometric stone water gardens and cloistered courtyards, it takes on a new majesty at night when flaming torches throw leaping yellow light against high walls, and art-filled niches are picked out by discrete spotlighting. The feeling is grand and ineffably luxurious; care and expense is lavished even on the corners you don't see, and vast domed marble areas are embellished with beautiful hand-knotted carpets and geometric inlaid floors. *Rose-petal baths every evening.*

rooms	105: 98 doubles; 7 suites.
price	Doubles $375–$395. Suites $850–$2,250. Plus 5% tax. Peak season; October–March.
meals	Breakfast $12. Lunch $20. Dinner $25.
closed	Rarely.
directions	Follow the signs to the Taj Mahal. The hotel is 500m before the entrance to the monument.

Mr Visheshwar Raj Singh

tel	+91 562 231 515
fax	+91 562 231 516
e-mail	reservations@amarvilas.com
web	www.oberoihotels.com

Hotel

map 2   entry 21

Ganges View

B 1/163 Assi Ghat, Varanasi, 221 005, Uttar Pradesh

What a setting: the roof terrace overlooks the great Mother Ganga and all those bustling rituals of washers, bathers, buffalo herders and marigold sellers. This is a family-run guesthouse with a colonial feel, converted by Shar Shana 20 years ago – dark, cool rooms, marble floors, planters, portraits. *Trompe l'oeil* walls add an exotic touch and the rooftop rooms are the most inspiring (and, note, the hottest in summer). Your host could not be kinder or more charming. Instead of television he provides a lobby full of books and a delightful array of cultural events: traditional Indian music one evening, a talk from a Buddhist scholar another. This is a special retreat away from the Shiva energy of Varanasi that can be overwhelming - especially during festival time. You are on Assi Ghat, the southernmost *ghat* to which pilgrims flock for ritual bathing, and near the leafy area of the Benares Hindu University, popular with travellers and students of music and philosophy. The area teems with *chai* shops, round the corner is an excellent book shop and, a few blocks away, the funeral pyres - life and death on the doorstep. A rare treat.

rooms	12 doubles. Some on rooftop a/c.
price	Rs1,200-Rs2,000. Plus 10% tax. Peak season: July-April.
meals	Breakfast & lunch Rs150. Dinner Rs250.
closed	Rarely.
directions	7km from Varanasi train station, 26km from airport. A rickshaw from the train station to Assi Ghat costs about Rs70.

	Mr Prakash Kumar
tel	+91 542 2313 218
fax	+91 542 2369 695

Shiva Ganges View

B-14/24 Mansarovar Ghat, Near Andhra Ashram, Varansi, 221 001, Uttar Pradesh

Step through the door to this British-built four-storey family home and you'll instantly feel calm after the busy streets of Varanasi's old town. It has space aplenty but only six rooms, so it's best to book ahead. All are painted cream and green, have high ceilings, cool stone floors and sitting areas. The white-tiled bathrooms are basic but clean. Tandonjee and Ratna are your kind and peaceful hosts who will do almost anything to help you feel welcome in this enchanting city. Enjoy an Indian classical music recital in their inner courtyard, or one of Ratna's delicious vegetarian thalis, arranged in advance. Breakfast is extra, and can be taken in your room. There's a rooftop for yoga - or just to sit with an evening drink and people-watch; if you need a day off, stay up there. It's difficult to find such serenity and cleanliness in Varanasi unless you're in a five-star hotel – and better still, all of the rooms have balconies with fantastic views of life on the River Ganges. It's the tall red building on Monsarowar Ghat; don't let your rickshaw driver take you anywhere else! Long term stays are possible.

rooms	6 doubles.
price	Rs800–Rs900. Peak season: August–March.
meals	Breakfast Rs100. Lunch & dinner Rs150.
closed	Rarely.
directions	Right on the famous Kedar Ghat, near the Andhra Ashram.

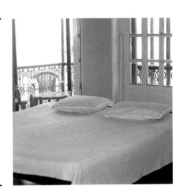

Mr Surendra Tandon	
tel	+91 542 2450 063
e-mail	saurabhrv2000@yahoo.com
web	www.varanasiguesthouse.com

Jain Paying Guest House

SN 14/3 A, Baraipur, Sarnath, 221 007, Uttar Pradesh

The Jain Paying Guest House, as it proudly announces itself, is run by Dr Jain and his wife who have, over time, converted more and more areas of their family home into rooms for guests... and introduced more and more guests to their delightful family. The food, which appears endlessly from the gently industrious kitchen, must be the most delicious in Sarnath, and the most suitable for delicate Western stomachs. (Being Jains, they serve kosher Hindu fare and exclude eggs.) It is a well-loved rest house for passing pilgrims to Sarnath, ancient cradle of Buddhism, and meal times are invariably stimulating with an eclectic gathering of people. The seven rooms are clean and modest; four have bathrooms, Indian-style – hot water is provided by the bucket. (The price reflects the simplicity.) The roof has one of the best panoramas in Sarnath: views swoop over the deer park and the ancient *stupa* that marks the spot where the newly enlightened Buddha gave his first sermon, aptly symbolised as the Wheel of the Dharma.

rooms	7: 5 doubles, 2 singles.
price	Rs250. Singles Rs200.
	Peak season: November–March.
meals	Breakfast Rs40. Lunch & dinner Rs50.
closed	Throughout the summer.
directions	10km from Varanasi train station.
	Near the Main Temple of Sarnath.

Dr Abhaya Kumar Jain

tel	+91 542 2595 621
e-mail	jpgh@rediffmail.com
web	www.visitsarnath.com

Guesthouse

Carlton's Plaisance

Near the L.B.S.N.A Academy, Happy Valley Road, Mussoorie, 248 179, Uttaranchal

In seven acres of fantastic gardens with camp fire spots, basketball courts and lazy areas, this 'place of peace' on the Mussoorie hillside sits dwarfed by towering pines. The whole area once belonged to the British East India Company, one of whose officials, Mr Forbes, built the house after falling in love with a French-Indian woman who persuaded him to stay. Anu and Ajit, an affable pair, have left much of the Victorian architecture and period furniture intact; the stables under the house, shoe-scrapers and bear rugs are small signs of an existence that has been all but lost in India. Famous feet have walked these corridors (you can read Sir Edmund Hilary's comments in the guest book) and aspiring writers, artists and thinkers still come to stay. The area is stuffed with places to visit and things to do — temples, churches, birdwatching and great walks — about which Anu and Ajit are well versed. A comfortable stay, and possibly the only place in northern India where you can find French sausages and Mississippi Honey Chicken. *Trekking can be arranged.*

rooms	8: 4 doubles, 4 suites.
price	Rs1,500. Suites Rs2,500–Rs3,000. Plus 5% tax. Peak season: 15 May–15 July.
meals	Breakfast Rs60. Lunch & dinner Rs150–Rs250.
closed	Rarely.
directions	From Library Bazaar (Gandhi Chowk) take road to Happy Valley. Carlton's Plaisance on right, down a clearly marked driveway.

Mrs Ajit & Anu Singh
tel +91 135 2632 800
e-mail carltons@rediffmail.com

Kasmanda Palace

The Mall Road, Mussoorie, 248 179, Uttaranchal

The only Mussoorie property still owned by royalty, Kasmanda was bought in 1915 as a summer retreat from the hot plains of Lucknow. Yet the Anglo-French house has had many reincarnations. Built in 1836 as part of the Christ Church complex, it became a sanitorium for British forces, a school, a private house and finally flung open its doors as a heritage hotel in 1992. Today territorial geese keep watch over its three acres of pine forest, terraced gardens and lawns up on one of Mussoorie's highest points – the hotel jeep now takes the strain out of the climb back from town. The colourful Nawab and his wife still live upstairs and bless you with their regal company over dinner – upon request – and the bedrooms are the staging ground for a silent battle between the antique and the modern. Tiger skins speak of the past; today the thrills come from sports offered here. Towering log fires fend off the winter chill and thick, whitewashed stone walls keep the summer heat at bay. *White-water rafting, trekking, paragliding and birdwatching.*

rooms	15: 9 doubles, 6 suites.
price	Rs1,700–Rs2,000. Suites Rs2,300. Plus 5% tax.
meals	Breakfast Rs100. Lunch & dinner Rs250.
closed	Rarely.
directions	From main road on past Padmini Niwas; 1st left up hill. Pass church on left. Kasmanda signed at top.

	Mr H Sharma
tel	+91 135 2632 424
fax	+91 135 2630 007
e-mail	kasmanda@vsnl.com
web	www.indianheritagehotels.com

Heritage Hotel

Padmini Niwas

Library, The Mall, Mussoorie, 248 179, Uttaranchal

Blessed with views over the Doon Valley to the Ganga (on a clear day) and in an enviable spot to catch the winter sun, Padmini Niwas is half-eco, half-regal 1920s bungalow. Passed down from the Maharaja of Rajpipla, the guesthouse has shaken off any erstwhile aristocratic stuffiness, replacing it with environmental resolve. Mrs Worah, a warm and generous host with a regal touch of her own, passionately recycles and has put in solar panels to catch a little of the Himalayan sun. She runs a nursery in the grounds with more than 400 varieties of plants, many of which adorn the flowery verandas and balconies, lily gardens and rose bowers – the perfect spots to laze with books and tea, drinking in the scents and colours, perhaps with large, hairy Reg the dozing Himalayan Bhutia dog for company. Mrs Worah and family are deeply involved in the local scene; daughter, Seja, whizzes between India and Africa for the WWF, weaving in local eco-tourism projects with wider work on environmental sustainability. Do chat to Mrs Worah about the area. *Indian cooking classes available, for groups of more than five. Good trekking.*

rooms	26: 24 doubles, 2 singles.
price	Rs1,400-2,600. Singles Rs1,000. Plus 5%. Peak season: 15 May-August; festival time.
meals	Breakfast Rs75. Lunch & dinner Rs130.
closed	Rarely.
directions	Halfway between the rickshaw stand at Rope Point and the library point. A 5-minute walk from the Library.

Mrs Harshada Worah

tel	+91 135 2631 039
fax	+91 135 2632 793
e-mail	harshada@vsnl.com
web	www.hotelpadmininiwas.com

Hotel

The Glasshouse on the Ganges

23rd Milestone Rishikesh-Badrinath Road, Rishikesh, District Tehri Garwal, 249 303

It is a fine thing to dip one's feet into the 'Ganga' at sunset – even finer to meditate on a rock by the water's edge. All this only a few metres from the Glasshouse, where luxury and good taste face the raw, tumbling vitality of the river as it flows through green hills towards Rishikesh. The main building, like a large modern cottage, still has – strangely – some ceilings of raw concrete, but the glass provides floor-to-ceiling views through the lush greenery to the river. Most of the bedrooms are huge and handsome, with big-tiled floors and a great sense of space. They are, on the whole, pretty, even if the odd detail is amiss. The dining area and veranda are comfortably set about with cane furniture and cloth-covered tables. There is a path that walks you along the river to the other cottages, whose bedspreads and curtains throw colour onto the white background of the walls. The one furthest away has a solid marble sink fed by spring water, and a bed of giant proportions. The food is good, the service impeccable, the management low-key and the setting unforgettable. *Camping and white-water rafting.*

rooms	16: 12 doubles, 4 suites. Some a/c.
price	Rs2,000–Rs2,500. Plus 5% tax. Peak season: September–March.
meals	Breakfast Rs100. Lunch Rs200. Dinner Rs250.
closed	Rarely.
directions	23km from Rishikesh on the road to Badrinath.

	Mr Neeraj Jain
tel	+91 1378 269 224
fax	+91 11 2435 1112
e-mail	sales@neemranahotels.com
web	www.neemranahotels.com
res. no.	+91 11 2435 6145

Heritage Hotel

Palace Belvedere

Awagarh Estate, Mallital, Nainital, 263 001, Uttaranchal

Great is the relief on tumbling into the shaded hall of the Belvedere. The Raja had to sell the rest of the hillside so houses press in on all sides, but the Palace stands firm. The great, pillared veranda sweeps round the sides and front, with a narrow garden and comfortable wicker chairs. The cavernous interior has a high, white-walled corridor below and another above, up a vast sweep of carpeted stair. Tigers hang on walls with bizarre Imperial prints. The lakeside rooms are vast and splendid, in that uniquely Indian way: it's the impression that counts, not the detail. The enclosed, wooden-ceilinged verandas with writing-desks and big windows look to the distant lake. Double beds are linked twins, there is space for yoga for two, the elderly bathrooms work well. The rooms to the rear are less impressive but large and with views over the back yard to the glorious hills. The dining room befits the grandeur of the palace, and there is a handsome sitting area stuffed with old armchairs. Everyone is helpful, including the owner and his son, Amrish. You are a minute from the market five from the lake. And do climb the steep hill behind for spectacular early-morning views.

rooms	21: 14 doubles, 7 suites.
price	From Rs1,900–Rs2,900.
meals	Breakfast Rs150. Lunch & dinner Rs250.
closed	Rarely.
directions	A 5-minute walk from Mall Road on the Mallital side, just above the Bank of Baroda. Well signed.

Mr Ambareesh Pal Singh

tel	+91 5942 237 434
fax	+91 5942 235 082
e-mail	belvederepalace@rediffmail.com
web	www.welcomheritage.com

Heritage Hotel

 E–F   **map 3   entry 29**

Ramgarh Bungalows

Ramgarh (Malla), Kumaon Hills, District Nainital, 263 137, Uttaranchal

The valley drops away, your eyes skim the fruit trees to the tree-covered slopes on the other side. At night only a few distant lights breach the darkness. Below some of the cottages is a little school that awakes you with its chant and chatter. The rooms are simple yet pretty, one with blue curtains and white walls and a modern bathroom. The veranda drops to a greenish patch of grass, wicker chairs and table and a row of irises, daisies and petunias. A brick path leads up to the dining room, a long, white-washed building set about with flowers, yellow curtains, paved floor, prints and plain colours. Indian music and scents mingle with the French mood to make a delightful space for delicious meals. Breakfast is European, with homemade local jams. The Old Bungalow, higher up, has a fine, pillared veranda and even prettier rooms. There are handsome chestnuts (and an avenue of them outside the gate) but less 'view'. Much is ill-kempt but the aesthetic is delightful overall. It is a place to spend several days in order to enjoy the magic, sit, write, walk, eat and read – far from the non-stop bustle of India.

rooms	10: 5 doubles, 5 suites.
price	Rs1,250–Rs2,000. Suites Rs1,750–Rs2,500. Plus 5% tax. Peak season: April–10 July.
meals	Breakfast Rs150. Lunch Rs200. Dinner Rs250.
closed	Rarely.
directions	15km from Bhawali town. Take the train from Delhi to Kathgodam, then a taxi for 2 hours.

	Mr K S Mehra
tel	+91 5942 81156
fax	+91 11 2435 1112
e-mail	sales@neemranahotels.com
web	www.neemranahotels.com
res. no.	+91 11 2435 6145

Heritage Hotel

Kalmatia Sangam Himalaya Resort

Kalimat Estate (near Kasar Devi), Post Bag 002, Almora, 263 601, Uttaranchal

The scattered houses in the valley below are slate-roofed and whitewashed with brightly painted doors and windows. The terraces produce wheat and vegetables, buffalos graze with goats, the women wear startling colours. It is not at all remote, for Almora is close – with a good market (woollens and jewellery), and the area feels prosperous. Geeta inherited this hilltop estate and after living in Germany she and Dieter took a deep plunge to create an Indo-European hotel. Dieter's style is German, Geeta bubbles with enthusiasm, the staff are impeccable, the manager is Austrian, the furniture is imaginative (modern, wrought-iron, Scandinavian, dhurries on the floor), the food delicious – a fusion of Indian and European. In winter you can light a fire in your bedroom and sleep in a cottage of your own; they are scattered among the pine trees, each with views and space galore, big beds and duvets, stone walls and good bathrooms. Practice yoga, have reflexology or meditate on a special terrace. The Reebs have a strong eco-policy: take a walk among the trees they have planted and collect herbs and mushrooms in season.

rooms	9: 7 doubles, 2 singles.
price	$60-$128. Singles $42-$61. Peak season: October-June.
meals	Lunch $6. Dinner $8.
closed	Rarely.
directions	Upper Binsar road towards Kasar Devi temple. Resort 1km before temple, on right. 380km from Delhi. 2.5 hours from Kathgodam train station. Pick-up possible.

	Dieter & Geeta Reeb
tel	+91 5962 233 625
fax	+91 5962 231 572
e-mail	info@kalmatia-sangam.com
web	www.kalmatia-sangam.com

Resort

 C-E **map 3   entry 31**

Photography by Toby Sawday

delhi

319 Panchsheel Park

S-319 Panchsheel Park, New Delhi, 110 017, Delhi

In a swish housing colony in south Delhi – eight kilometres south of Connaught Place – the first-floor flat has a distinctly Euro-Indian feel. The story is unusual – *Shirley Valentine* with a happy ending. Jill Lowe-Yadav left England to escape a grim English winter. She met her excuse to stay in the shape of her fine-looking taxi driver, Yadav, whom she married, beginning a new life that has seen them cover most of India in an Ambassador – you can read her book about it! Jill, quietly intelligent and unfailingly hospitable, was (and still is, on occasion) a tour guide in England, and Yadav is an excitable farmer-turned-taxi-driver from Haryana. They now run day tours of Delhi and further afield, Jill donning her guide hat and Yadav behind the wheel. The flat they share is cosy – this is urban Delhi life – though you get a bathroom to yourself. There's nothing formal about this homestay – you come and go as you please. The colours are muted, the Indian craft pieces few and delicate. Staying here plunges you into a more real part of Delhi life, with a lady who feels deeply for this difficult but fascinating sprawl. *Their Delhi Daytours unearth the city's hidden corners.*

rooms	1 twin. Air-cooled.
price	Rs800. Breakfast included.
meals	You can join in with their meals. Dinner Rs200.
closed	May-September.
directions	Off Outer ring road in south Delhi. Call or e-mail to ask for directions. 25-minute taxi ride from Connaught Place.

Jill & Lal Singh Yadav

tel	+91 11 2601 2637
e-mail	j_yadav@hotmail.com
web	www.delhidaytours.com

Homestay

Ahuja Residency

193 Golf Links, New Delhi, 110 003, Delhi

Wonderful – a peaceful oasis in the seething, sometimes overwhelming, capital. Delhi Golf Club is next door, and Khan Market – the city's High Street Ken – a powerful putt away. Marble staircases with wrought-iron railings twist through the six floors of this 50s giant, which you'll come to recognise by its rather bizarre white trestle frontage. Rooms vary in size and view; some have private balconies bursting with potted plants. Furniture is modern – mostly pine; floors are tiled and walls white. There's nothing over-patterned or mismatching here, just fresh blue stripes, or firey orange checks. Outside, carpets of creepers cling to the brickwork of the spectacular high walled garden – ensconce yourself in the greenery of it all. There's a homely feel here, but the place is run with an assured professionalism. Rashini is an impressive and highly educated woman, who knows her stuff and she has been taking guests since the Asian Games in 1982. The family live on the ground floor but join guests for breakfast in the gingham-clad dining room. They'll want to smooth out your time in Delhi; let them.

rooms	12 doubles.
price	Rs2,200. Plus 12.5% tax.
meals	Breakfast Rs60. Lunch & dinner Rs180.
closed	Rarely.
directions	In a small colony very close to Khan Market. Best to call when you arrive in Delhi & organise a pick up.

	Mrs Rashmi Ahuja
tel	+91 11 2461 1027
fax	+91 11 2464 9008
e-mail	info@ahujaresidency.com
web	www.ahujaresidency.com

Guesthouse

The Imperial
Janpath, New Delhi, 110 001, Delhi

Lutyens conceived the Imperial as the most luxurious hotel in his New Delhi, a blend of Victorian, colonial and informal Art Deco. It still works – an impeccable place, with an attention to detail that conquers the most sceptical visitors. Delhi has several fine hotels but this one stands out for its elegance and sheer grace. Italian marble, Burmese teak, the plushest plumbing – all is understated luxury. Have just a cup of tea in the Atrium and be made to feel like a Rajah. Dine in the Coffee Shop overlooking the gardens and be astonished by the furniture, the décor and the turbanned waiters. Prints of India's history add a country-house touch – and note that the Imperial has a huge collection of lithographs. The pool is a refuge from the heat and maniacal activity of Delhi. Although the bedrooms are big and luxurious with every detail considered, you'll be drawn to spend languid hours downstairs admiring the rare collection of 18th- and 19th-century art, the flights of fancy all around in the décor and the great and good of Delhi. A splendid hotel with panache.

rooms	234: 162 doubles, 27 twins, 45 suites.
price	$280–$340. Suites $400–$1,100. Plus 12.5% tax. Peak season: 15 September–15 April.
meals	Breakfast from Rs400. Lunch from Rs515. Dinner from Rs675.
closed	Rarely.
directions	In the city centre, a stone's throw from Connaught Place.

	Mr Pierre Jochim
tel	+91 11 2334 1234
fax	+91 11 2334 2255
e-mail	luxury@theimperialindia.com
web	www.theimperialindia.com

Hotel

Master Paying Guest Accommodation

R-500 New Rajinder Nagar, New Delhi, 110 060, Delhi

The luxury of having somewhere so small is that you can lavish attention on every corner. Avnish and Ushi's guesthouse is an expression of their principles and especially of their spiritual leanings – all encased in an unremarkable building in suburban north Delhi. Each room – choose from Mughal, Krishna, Ganesh or Lucky – has been decorated with spiritual calm in mind, the placing of every object carefully measured according to principles of balance and harmony. Ushi is a reiki master (her treatment room is on the roof garden) and Avnish is a genial man who spent years working for Taj Hotels – hospitality is in his veins – and now runs his own radio show offering hot business tips. The two rooms on the roof open onto a shaded, plant-scattered terrace where creepers climb the bamboo fence and spring evenings are easily lost to good conversation and books. The family live downstairs and occasionally eat with guests – Avnish and Ushi both talk fondly of past travellers who have become friends. Welcome relief from the mayhem of central Delhi, only 20 minutes away by rickshaw. *They run Offbeat Tours in and around Delhi, and Reiki sessions.*

rooms	4 doubles.
price	Rs900. Plus 12.5% tax. Peak season: July-April.
meals	Breakfast, lunch, & dinner Rs150.
closed	Rarely.
directions	Near the crossing of Shankar Road & Ganga Ram Hospital. 4km from Connaught Place. Entrance at back of house.

	Avnish & Ushi Puri
tel	+91 11 2574 1089
e-mail	urvashi@del2.vsnl.net.in
web	www.master-guesthouse.com

Guesthouse

Tikli Bottom

Manender Farm, Gairatpur Bas, P.O. Tikli, Gurgaon, 122 001, Delhi (Haryana)

Martin and Annie are true Delhi-ites, having been here for almost 20 years. Both have a profound knowledge of India and its machinations, and are immensely affable and generous hosts. Finished in 2000, their Lutyens-style farmhouse, an hour outside the craziness of Delhi, displays impeccable taste, every inch pondered over to combine elegance and taste. It is at once English and Indian – in winter a roaring fire blazes in the cosy living room where only the dormant fan above is a reminder of one's whereabouts. In summer you can sleep on *charpois* in one of the two garden temples, or in one of the elegant bedrooms, each of which opens onto the shaded, verandaed courtyard. The gardens, encircled by the only real hills around the capital, have been a labour of love – tiered lawns and flowerbeds bursting with colour, a discreet sunken pool – hewn from rough mustard plots. Martin will walk you round his manicured 16-acre organic farmstead, where mangos, oranges, gladioli and kitchen vegetables grow in neat rows. Peace, good conversation and the warmest of welcomes – the perfect soft landing.

rooms	4: 2 doubles, 2 twins.
price	Full-board only. $160. Singles $110.
meals	Included. Full-board.
closed	Rarely.
directions	Very difficult to find. They will pick you up from Delhi, or airport.

Martin & Annie Howard
tel +91 11 124 2066 556
fax +91 11 2335 1272
e-mail honiwala@vsnl.com
web www.tiklibottom.com
res. no. +91 11 2335 1272

Homestay

We dreamed that one day the whole world would want to fly the way Indians do.

NETWORK ● JA197-03

t all started with a few men, two aircraft and one dream.
ur mission was to make the world look up to the Indian skies.
Right from the start, international standards have always been
r benchmark. Put simply, we believe in offering you a little more
an what you would expect.
Of course, you've given us a lot more in return. In 2001, we won
e Air Transport World Award and joined the elite league of the
orld's best airlines. Last year, we received the ISO 9001:2000
rtification for the best in-flight service. Besides winning several
her distinguished accolades, we are also the first airline in India to
n the TTG Travel Asia Award.
t does feel wonderful to have reached so far. Though our mission
mains the same. To take India to the skies.

A decade that changed Indian aviation.

JET AIRWAYS

THE JOY OF FLYING

Photography by Michael Busselle

rajasthan

Neemrana Fort-Palace

Neemrana Village , District Alwar, 301 705, Rajasthan

If the marauding hordes descending on this maze of a palace got as lost I did, the inhabitants might never have been defeated. The warren spreads over 10 layers, the ramparts and colonnaded walkways leading to open courtyards are as confusing as an Escher sketch. A sensitive, modest yet beautiful restoration of near ruins, this 'non-hotel' is a powerful example of the triumph of good taste and moderation over standardised luxury. Built over 10 years, the rooms have slowly taken shape, reflecting the mindfulness of history that runs throughout this special place. Some have their own *jarokha* balconies facing out onto plains peppered with plots of bright mustard; others have bathrooms open to the skies. You can sleep in the old royal court, or in a tent on top of the highest turret. All are simply furnished with colonial and Indian antiques in the eclectic style so well executed here. This place embodies holiday calm – there are no TVs or phones in the rooms, just endless corners, courtyards and lush gardens in which to sit and read – one of the few hotels where you can always have a turret or courtyard to yourself. *Yoga and meditation.*

rooms	43: 21 doubles, 3 singles, 18 suites, 1 family room for 4. Some a/c.
price	Doubles Rs2,200-Rs3,300. Singles Rs1,100. Suites Rs4,400-Rs6,600. Family room Rs12,000. Plus 10% tax. Peak season: September-March.
meals	Breakfast Rs200. Lunch & dinner Rs400.
closed	Rarely.
directions	2 hours south-west of Delhi along NH8 to Jaipur. Right at the signs in Neemrana Village.

	Mr Ramesh Dhabhai
tel	+91 1494 246 006
fax	+91 11 2435 1112
e-mail	sales@neemranahotels.com
web	www.neemranahotels.com
res. no.	+91 11 2435 6145

Heritage Hotel

The Hill Fort Kesroli

Village Kesroli, via M.I.A., Alwar, Alwar, 301 030, Rajasthan

The architectural equivalent of a security blanket, the massive walls of this delightful 14th-century fort enclose pretty, flowered courtyards and are a retreat from the harsher world outside. Perched imposingly 200 feet above the plain, inside it has the feel of an intimate castle made for two. Each of the rooms is distinct. From the blue-and-white ceiling of the Hindola Mahal bedroom swings a large seat facing a window that frames the sunrise at dawn; the Mubarak Mahal suite is tucked away in one of the seven turrets. Rooms are reached by steep, narrow, stone steps leading to private terraces that overlook an agrarian landscape of mustard fields. In winter, the fort looks like a ship afloat in a yellow sea. There is a sense of total privacy and seclusion. Take tea on your arched veranda among the swooping parakeets, or dine among the ramparts in the glow of the setting sun – the sound of distant voices are the only reminders of the toil of village life below. *Visits to the Sariska Tiger Sanctuary and boating on the Siliserh Lake.*

rooms	21: 14 doubles, 7 suites.
price	Rs1,500-2,000. Suites Rs3,400. Plus 10% tax. Peak season: September-March.
meals	Breakfast Rs150. Lunch Rs300. Dinner Rs350.
closed	May-July.
directions	12km from Alwar train station. A 3-hour drive from Delhi.

	Mr Pramod Bist
tel	+91 1468 289 352
fax	+91 11 2435 1112
e-mail	sales@neemranahotels.com
web	www.neemranahotels.com
res. no.	+91 11 2435 6145

Heritage Hotel

 map 2   entry 38

Laxmi Vilas Palace

Kakaji Ki Kothi, Bharatpur, 321 001, Rajasthan

Set around a courtyard, this charming small palace was built in 1899 for the younger son of the Maharaja of Bharatpur. It had then the reputation for being one of the most impressive shoots in India – up to 90 guns would be lined up and guests would perform until the viceroy got bored. There are photos to prove it – heaps of birds piled at the feet of the happy party. These days you are encouraged to stalk with binoculars rather than a gun: rent a bike – or rickshaw – and spin off to Keoladeo, one of the most fascinating bird-feeding and -breeding grounds in the world. The rambling Laxmi Vilas combines both Mughal and Rajput architectural styles, and its rooms are furnished with a mixture of traditional and colonial pieces. Colourful Rajasthani murals adorn the walls and georgous tiles the floors. Bedrooms are comfortable, big and airy – the largest are upstairs – with gleaming white walls and wooden or brass beds. Food is colourful and good, and the landscaped grounds beautiful and full of interest. *Croquet and badminton.*

rooms	25: 12 doubles, 13 suites.
price	Rs2,450. Suite Rs3,300. Plus 10% tax. Peak season: October–March.
meals	Breakfast Rs175. Lunch & dinner Rs300.
closed	Rarely.
directions	27km from Udaipur, near the Bharatpur bird sanctuary. 5km from the train station & bus stand.

Mr Prem Prakash

tel	+91 5644 231 199
fax	+91 5644 225 259
e-mail	reservations@laxmivilas.com
web	www.laxmivilas.com

Heritage Hotel

 E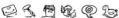

Alsisar Haveli

Sansar Chanrdra Road, Jaipur, 302 001, Rajasthan

Rajput interiors have a tendency to be unwelcoming: high ceilings, heavy furniture, grave ancestral portraits and an almost tangible stuffiness. Alsisar Haveli is a little different. Though not entirely free of dark wood, the rooms are hugely varied and show a more considered design approach. The block-printed covers and curtains match the newly painted arches, and the old inlay and mirror work has been scrubbed and polished to keep its original sparkle. However, it is the complete unstuffiness of the atmosphere that makes Alsisar stand out. The few common areas are inviting and comfortable and where there are antiques, they are uncluttered and attractive. The original 1892 building and its more recent additions stand in cosy grounds with great old shady neem trees and an inviting pool surrounded by high walls to cut out the main road. Proud stone elephants flank the steps up to the paved terrace where open fires flicker throughout the evening and turbaned waiters serve Rajasthani hotel food. Many people go out to eat, though the restaurant is adequate. *Daily Bhopa dance shows.*

rooms	36: 10 doubles, 21 singles, 5 suites.
price	Rs2,000. Singles Rs1,850. Suites Rs2,650. Plus 10% tax. Peak season: 1 October–15 April.
meals	Breakfast Rs150. Lunch & dinner Rs300.
closed	Rarely.
directions	Archway off Sansar Chandra Road, opposite Madawa Haveli.

Mr Shakti Singh

tel	+91 141 2368 290
fax	+91 141 2364 652
e-mail	alsisar@satyam.net.in
web	www.alsisar.com

Heritage Hotel

map 2   entry 40

Arya Niwas

Behind Amber Towers, Sansar Chandra Road, Jaipur, 302 001, Rajasthan

Arya Niwas is unusual among Rajasthani hotels and is prized by the wandering hoardes of smalltime international jewellery traders who settle in here for weeks at a time. The hotel is cheap, efficient and friendly. Tucked away down a side street, it's a relief after the Jaipur mayhem – and its green lawn and trails of potted plants are a rare sight in this dusty town. On the long veranda, weary wanderers sink into low wicker chairs to drink sweet tea, wipe the dust from their brows, and muse. The atmosphere is convivial and the guests mostly mature and involved – it would be hard to be lonely. You can rest free without fear of being 'touted' or 'hawked', eat cheap and cheerful food, and buy from a 'fixed price' craft shop. Plain and functional, the building is frill-free and simple rooms (some have no outside window) are always clean – crisp white linen, polished, tiled bathrooms, a separate bolt for your own padlock. The appeal lies in the rare feeling that you're getting just what you paid for. *Yoga classes.*

rooms	90: 60 doubles, 30 singles. Some air-cooled.
price	Rs450–Rs750. Singles Rs350–Rs550.
meals	Breakfast Rs75. Lunch & dinner Rs100.
closed	Rarely.
directions	Behind Amber towers, off Sansar Chandra Road.

Mr Tarun Bansal

tel	+91 141 2372 456
fax	+91 141 236 1871
e-mail	tarun@aryaniwas.com
web	www.aryaniwas.com

Hotel

Bissau Palace

Outside Chandpole Gate, Jaipur, 302 016, Rajasthan

Faded photos of past and present British royals take pride of place in the comfortable, wooden-floored sitting room where old weapons and vast portraits of steely-gazed ancestors remind you that peaceable Jaipur has seen more unruly days. The family were forced to build outside the Pink City walls because of their refusal to pander to the Mughal tormentors with whom the Maharaja of Jaipur had created a cosy alliance. The palace is therefore tucked away down an inconspicuous backstreet, off which you find the large driveway leading up to the austere edifice. Slightly scuffed around the edges, Bissau has an appealing informality – you can sit quaffing a cold beer in the living room without fear of upsetting etiquette, and feel unusually free of the old-world stuffiness that is synonymous with some heritage hotels. Juno, the present maharaja, is an affable, lively chap whose relaxed take on regal life infuses the hotel. The rooms have plain walls, delicately painted archways, heavy wooden beds and clean modern bathrooms. The suites are large and marvellous value. *Lawn tennis.*

rooms	45: 27 doubles, 18 suites. Some a/c.
price	Rs1,500-Rs1,800. Suites Rs2,100-Rs2,700. Plus 10% tax.
meals	Breakfast Rs150. Lunch & dinner Rs240.
closed	Rarely.
directions	Out of Chandpol Road & turn right. Keep right; hotel set back on left within a few yards.

	Mr Sanjai Singh of Bissau
tel	+91 141 2304 371
fax	+91 141 2304 628
e-mail	bissau@sancharnet.in
web	www.bissaupalace.com

Heritage Hotel

map 2   entry 42

Diggi Palace

SMS Hospital Road, Jaipur, 302 004, Rajasthan

Perhaps the garden – mature trees fringing the big lawn, hundreds of potted plants, flowers and birds – draws people here more than anything else and holds them for extra nights of rest from the hectic world outside. (It's a rickshaw ride to the main sights and shops.) But what the vivacious Diggi family also manage so successfully by sharing their home is to show guests a way of Indian life that is privileged and traditional yet neither pompous nor narrow-minded. Everyone who works here is either family or from one of the villages near their country property; there are no room phones, few TVs, no uniforms or anonymous service. There's a wide choice of rooms, from the simply functional with external bathrooms and no hot water, to the pretty swish, with their own bath and sitting rooms. There's choice, too, about where to sit and what to eat. Breakfasts are long, leisurely affairs with newspapers and organic coffee, fresh juice and bread, home-made from organic flour. Dinners, in the restaurant or on the candlelit terrace, are said to be excellent and mostly home-grown. Some people stay for months. *Golf arranged.*

rooms	43 doubles. Air-coolers.
price	Rs500–Rs1,210. Peak season: October–March.
meals	Breakfast Rs80. Lunch & dinner from Rs65.
closed	Rarely.
directions	Take Sawai Ram Singh Road, turning right into Shivaji Marg just after Maharani College, coming from Ajmeri Gate.

Mr Ram Pratap Singh

tel	+91 141 2373 091
fax	+91 141 2370 359
e-mail	reservations@hoteldiggipalace.com
web	www.hoteldiggipalace.com

Heritage Hotel

Jaipur Inn

B-17 Shiv Marg, Bani Park, Jaipur, 302 016, Rajasthan

Once across the cattle grid and through the Jaipur Inn arch everything changes. It all began as a campsite for backpackers in the 1970s and it still welcomes them; there's an open-hearted mood here, perhaps thanks to the ineffably generous Pushpendra's brilliant device of offering free rooms to anyone who has a special gift to bring, such as interior design, cooking, architecture or just good ideas. The wooden extension on the first floor is Dutch-designed and very attractive. The basic bedrooms are cheered by splashes of colour from Anokhi fabrics, bright blankets and bold paintwork. In some rooms there is Babul wood furniture and in others it is built-in – all a touch spartan but perfectly okay, and bathrooms are entirely functional, with marble floors, towels and flip-flops. The higher rooms have fine views over Jaipur and even higher there is the Amber Nectar roof café for sociable evenings. There's a simple good value buffet supper often served on the roof, overseen by Pushpendra. (Join in the cooking if you wish.) Cheap, cheerful, generous – and surprising. *Hire bikes (Jaipur is gratifyingly flat) or attend six-day pottery courses nearby.*

rooms	16 doubles. Some a/c.
price	Rs500–Rs600. Peak season: 15 October–15 March.
meals	Breakfast Rs80. Lunch Rs100. Dinner Rs200.
closed	Rarely.
directions	2km from train station on Shiv Circus at crossroads between Shiv Marg & Todarmal Road.

Mr Pushpendra Bhargava

tel	+91 141 2201 121
fax	+91 141 2200 140
e-mail	jaipurin@sancharnet.in
web	www.jaipurinn.net

Guesthouse

Hotel Madhuban

D-237 Behari Marg, Bani Park, Jaipur, 302 016, Rajasthan

A prancing elephant fresco, and probably one of their three dogs or two children, greet guests to the Singh's home. As they say, "Madhuban is not luxury. It is a comfortable way of life". You're about a kilometre from the old town, in a pretty, quiet, leafy residential area; there's a swimming pool in the sheltered garden, with the occasional partridge or peacock strutting between the tables and chairs dotted about the lawn – a good place to write and read. Digvijay, 'Dicky', is thoroughly at home with westerners, and understands their preoccupation with cleanliness and their desire for cornflakes and milder meals from time to time; his wife Kavita is welcoming though more reserved. The style here is quite sedate and proper: the sitting and dining rooms are formal, bedrooms come with traditional wooden furniture, heavy brocade drapes, curtains and bed covers, rugged, marble-chip floors and spotless bathrooms. Some rooms give on to a pleasant rooftop area with potted plants and easy chairs in the shade. A thoroughly reliable place – with free basic yoga sessions, from sunrise, in the next door ashram.

rooms	18: 15 doubles, 3 suites.
price	Rs590–Rs1,390. Suites Rs1,390–Rs1,890. 10% tax on rooms over Rs1,000.
meals	Breakfast Rs125. Lunch, & dinner from Rs225.
closed	Rarely.
directions	2km from both the train station and bus stand.

	Mr Dicky Singh Patan
tel	+91 141 2200 033
fax	+91 141 2202 344
e-mail	madhuban@usa.net
web	www.madhuban.net

Heritage Hotel

Hotel Meghniwas

C-9 Sawai Jai Singh Highway, Bani Park, Jaipur, 302 006, Rajasthan

The old Colonel is a genial man with a twinkle in his eye and a bear-like handshake, a man happy with his lot. Having spent many years travelling with the Indian army, he has returned to the roost to do what he loves most. The building is Forties-modern, not fancy, and sits gleaming white in green gardens that are neat but not fussy. Established 20 years ago as a functional base from which to explore Jaipur and the surrounds, the hotel is just this. Bedrooms are smartly, sedately furnished and come with all mod cons (including good lighting – which is a treat) and the suites have particularly good views. It is, however, the Colonel and his gentle wife, Indu, who make 'the house of the clouds' special – they thrive on having strangers around and love seeing people uncover the hidden nooks of Jaipur. The gardens are walled and private, and as green and as floral as can be. Croquet balls skim across the neat front lawn, and a deckchair-lined pool is sunk into the back lawn off which the Colonel's cosy travel bureau lies. The feeling is unfussy and without pretence; a hotel with all the western trimmings but a family feel.

rooms	27: 23 doubles, 4 suites.
price	Rs1,200-Rs1,800. Suites Rs2,000. Plus 10% tax.
meals	Breakfast Rs150. Lunch & dinner Rs250.
closed	Rarely.
directions	Approximately half-way down Jai Singh Highway, opposite ATM booth. A 15-minute auto-rickshaw ride from Jaipur station.

	Colonel & Mrs Indu Singh
tel	+91 141 2202 034
fax	+91 141 2201 420
e-mail	email@meghniwas.com
web	www.meghniwas.com

Hotel

Oberoi Rajvilas

Goner Road, Jaipur, 303 012, Rajasthan

Almost impossibly beautiful – fortunes have been lavished on getting it right, down to the traditional plaster mix and old tiles. The island temple is still used and the stunning spa is built in the old *haveli*, where a great tree trunk is respectfully allowed to soar through the roof. The gold leaf is real, the brass is polished and those uniformed pigeon-scarers do just that; such perfection underpins the luxury. Even the gardens are perfect – heir to the Mughal tradition: peaceful courtyard gardens, the gentle trickle of fountains, the turquoise sparkle of a reflection pool, moats with flowering water-lilies and lotus, pergolas entwined with climbing bougainvillea, emerald swathes of lawn, desert palms, neem trees, beds of jasmine and fragrant herb gardens. The genius is in the detail – the finest materials and craftsmen, ravishingly lovely interiors, not a square inch or member of staff that doesn't count. The subtle shift from Mughal to Oberoi is magical and breathtaking. The brochure and web site paint a genuine picture. Understated, sublime, sybaritic. *Gym, tennis, croquet, elephant safaris.*

rooms	54 + 17: 54 doubles. 13 tents, 1 tented villa, 3 pool villas.
price	$395. Tents $475. Tented villa $1,100. Pool villas $1,500-$2,250. Plus 10% tax. Peak season: October-March.
meals	Breakfast $15. Lunch $25. Dinner $35.
closed	Rarely.
directions	8km from Jaipur city. Take road towards Agra. Rajvilas is well signed.

Mr Paul Jones

tel	+91 141 2680 101
fax	+91 141 2680 202
e-mail	reservations@rajvilas.com
web	www.oberoihotels.com

Resort

Samode Haveli

Gangapole, Jaipur, Ajmer District, 302 002, Rajasthan

The Sheesh Mahal suites and spectacularly painted dining room deserve to be museums in their own right, even set against the Jaipur masterpieces of the Howrah Palace and Amber Fort. "A feast for the eyes", said our inspector, "and inspiration for any fabric designer" – the two main suites are wildly colourful and the crowning glory of the hotel, their rich fabrics and moody lighting unusual for Rajasthani hotels. The cheaper rooms are just as vibrant, their sumptuous bathrooms hung about with swathes of fluffy towelling. Built 150 years ago as an urban hangout for the regal Samode family, the building has not lost its air of luxury and indulgence. It has been beautifully restored and there are no cobwebs here. The floor-to-ceiling handpainted walls of the dining room are awesome, an unusually well preserved example of the arts that flourished under the Rajput rulers. Though the food is underwhelming, the atmosphere is blissfully and tranquil for somewhere as famous – there are no raucous coach parties. A real treat of a place. Ask to see the suites even if your budget won't allow you to sleep in them.

rooms	21: 12 doubles, 9 suites. Rooms 4,7,9,24 have no outside window
price	Rs3,650. Suites Rs5,050–Rs6,550. Plus 10% tax. Peak season: October–April.
meals	Lunch Rs425. Dinner Rs500.
closed	Rarely.
directions	In the north-east corner of Old City, within Pink City walls. 18km from airport, 10km from train station.

Mr K C Sharma

tel	+91 141 2632 407
fax	+91 141 2631 397
e-mail	reservations@samode.com
web	www.samode.com

Heritage Hotel

D   map 2   entry 48

Hotel Shahpura House

D-257 Devi Marg, Bani Park, Jaipur, 302 016, Rajasthan

One sighs with relief in India when sinking into a bed that is not like a marble plinth. Shahpura House has memorably soft beds. The seat of the head of the Shekhawat clan of Rajputs, the building stands in a residential enclave surrounded by high walls. It is relatively modern but has managed to avoid the worst of fifties Indian architecture by strictly following old architectural practices. Mixing Mughal and Indian styles, the facade with its domes lends a stately but not overbearing air. The Shekhawat influence is in the shape of hand-painted walls, stained-glass doors and skylights, and blown-glass-lamps – all set against pristine white walls and swathes of delicately inlaid marble. The place is immaculate and uncluttered, the bathrooms spotless and with a good supply of hot water, and the atmosphere inviting. People settle in for days, though the atmosphere is more hotel than guesthouse. Mr Singh is ex-military, a formal but pleasant man who keeps one foot in his past by parading his staff for a weekly check! It has to be seen to be believed. Excellent food. *Horse drawn carriages for sight seeing.*

rooms	34: 20 doubles, 14 suites.
price	Rs1,600. Suites Rs2,200. Plus 10% tax.
meals	Breakfast Rs140. Lunch Rs200. Dinner Rs250.
closed	Rarely.
directions	In residential area of Bani Park, to west of Chandpol Gate.

	Mr Surendra Shekhawat
tel	+91 141 2202 293
fax	+91 141 2201 494
e-mail	reservation@shahpurahouse.com
web	www.shahpurahouse.com

Heritage Hotel

Samode Palace

Samode Village, Jaipur, 303 806, Rajasthan

The landscape hides this glorious palace from all but the blue skies. Built on a hillock, it is a progression of courtyards of increasing height, conveying the exquisite aesthetic of the Rajput-Mughal era – effortlessly. Stately corridors, frescoed walls and ethereal audience halls reflect the skills of master craftsmen. A fountain bubbles in the central courtyard where you dine; sweet-smelling shrubs and climbers decorate the courtyard of the old 'women's quarters'; the pool and jacuzzi of marble and mosaic are to be found in a walled garden. Twisting staircases and painted corridors open to rooms at every level. Everything appears to be hand-painted and richly caparisoned, hand-woven and of cool marble. The luxury is ineffable. Service is attentive and charming. So beautiful are the Sheesh Mahal – the Hall of Mirrors – and the great painted Durbar Hall that groups of tourists may stand there in admiration. Otherwise it feels set apart and the sort of place that requires formal dress – though it doesn't. Massively impressive, and you can climb up to the fort for fine views of the arid but vital countryside.

rooms	43: 25 doubles, 18 suites.
price	Rs4,770. Suites Rs6,660–Rs16,650. Plus 20% tax. Peak season: October–April.
meals	Lunch Rs425. Dinner Rs500.
closed	Rarely.
directions	Head north off main Jaipur-Delhi highway at Chandawati (10km from Jaipur). Route is well-signed. 60km from airport, 55km from train station.

	Mr Yadavendra Singh
tel	+91 1423 240 014
fax	+91 1423 240 023
e-mail	reservations@samode.com
web	www.samode.com
res. no.	+91 141 2632 407

Heritage Hotel

Castle Pachar

Pachar, District Sikar, 332 729, Rajasthan

Not the easiest place to find but you arrive to a courteous, old-fashioned welcome from members of the same family to whom the Maharaja of Jaipur gave the village of Pachar as a reward for bravery in battle. Staying here may remind you of visits to affable but formal relatives. The grandeur is a little faded but the central *rang mahal* is impressive: a giant carpet on the decorated stone floor, sink-in sofas and chairs with brightly coloured patchwork throws, and a massive chandelier. Some of the best bedrooms, with painted pillars and garden or village views, lead off the first-floor gallery. They have a smattering of family photos and books, and genuine old furniture with the odd modern touch. Bathrooms were state-of-the-art a few decades ago. There's a pleasant dining room with more family-abilia, and the food is good, local and simply cooked – it's nice to see the papadums drying in the open air. A good place to relax around the tree-shaded swimming pool or gaze out across the flat, open Rajasthani countryside from the rooftop terrace, and gently observe an Indian way of life. *Bullock cart rides can be arranged.*

rooms	15 doubles.
price	Rs1,800. Plus 10% tax. Peak season: October–March.
meals	Breakfast Rs125. Lunch Rs225. Dinner Rs275.
closed	Rarely.
directions	Very difficult to find. Bikaner road north out of Jaipur to Chomu. Left to Renwal Station & Kishangarh. Pachar is 9km north of Kishangarh. Phone ahead.

	Mr Hanuman Singh
tel	+91 1576 264 611
fax	+91 141 373 671
e-mail	info@castlepachar.com
web	www.castlepachar.com
res. no.	+91 141 2382 955

Heritage Hotel

Roopangarh Fort
Roopangarh, Ajmer District, 305 814, Rajasthan

We can't promise all the delights of a 17th-century court but we can promise the luxury of space. Most bedrooms are bigger than those of your wildest fantasies, furnished with a rare individuality and an antidote to the magazine design culture. This was the abode of kings, a centre of culture and fine living and there is a lot to live up to – and somehow it happens. Where to begin? The sheer splendour of the scale, of course, but it is the sense of being somewhere very special that demands attention. Courtyards, decorated columns, green swards and courtyards, bougainvillea, cane chairs poised to receive you in marbled corners, a rooftop tennis court (why not?), bright red tables under decorated arches, a mad miscellany of marble in a bathroom. Then, lovely old mahogany desks against white walls, a chain mail suit on the wall above dining tables, polo sticks above the bed, an exquisite double/treble bed floating on a sea of white marble – on it goes. Yet this is not western luxury. Above it all looms the massively impressive fort, a comforting symbol of stability.

rooms	19: 18 doubles, 1 suite. Some a/c.
price	Rs1,300-Rs1,900. Suite Rs2,500. Plus 10% tax. Peak season: October-February.
meals	Breakfast Rs150. Lunch Rs250. Dinner Rs350.
closed	Rarely.
directions	Turn off Jaipur-Ajmer highway at Kishangarh; north for 22km along Highway No 8. Head into Roopangarh; fort entrance at far end of main street.

Mr Jasvir Singh

tel	+91 1497 220 444
fax	+91 1463 242 001
e-mail	roopangarhfort@yahoo.co.uk
web	www.royalkishangarh.com
res. no.	+91 11 2623 7000

Heritage Hotel

map 2   entry 52

Phool Mahal Palace
Kishangarh, 305 802, Rajasthan

By the old city gates and beneath its fort, this lakeside palace still feels like a grand and quirky family home. It appears in paintings of the Kishnangarh Miniature School and is home to India's version of the *Mona Lisa*, a beguiling 18th-century painting of sharp-profiled Radha. The Mararani is passionate about her new hotel venture, local arts and culture. She's keen to have small study groups come and paint, draw or take part in jewellery workshops, working with some of the many local artists. The bedrooms are all individual, with the essentials plus some early furniture, strong colours and ornate fabrics. All have murals reflecting the family's history, local plant and birdlife – this is a great place for birdwatching when the lake has been filled by monsoon rains. The deluxe rooms have the best views of the lake (and air-conditioning), but you can also gaze upon it from an armchair in the black-and-white marble-tiled sitting room. Kishnangarth is off the standard tourist trail, and a wander around the old buildings and the jostling market, where silversmiths and sweet-makers rub shoulders, is quite an experience.

rooms	16 doubles. Some a/c.
price	Rs1,350-Rs2,100. Plus 10% tax. Peak season: October-February.
meals	Breakfast Rs150. Lunch Rs250. Dinner Rs350.
closed	Rarely.
directions	On the lakeside by the gates into the old city beneath the fort.

Mr D D Purohit

tel	+91 1463 47405
fax	+91 1463 42001
e-mail	phoolmahalpalace@yahoo.com
web	www.royalkishangarh.com

Heritage Hotel

Bhanwar Vilas Palace
Karauli, 322 241, Rajasthan

The tiger stands facing the door, stuffed and splendid like so many of the ancestral figures that prowl the corridors of this house. Yet it was built in the 1930s because the Maharajah's City Palace was getting beyond repair; much of the furniture came across to Bhanwar Vilas and looks magnificent here. There's a lot of mahogany, some modern striped sofas under the portraits of ancestors, some beautiful spaces and gentle plain colours on the walls. The suites are somewhat colonial and elderly, while the other rooms are being brightened with colourful fabrics and white walls. The cottage rooms are more basic. Bathrooms are excellent, without being state-of-the-art. It's a place of wide verandas and cool places to sit – a family mansion with a strong whiff of splendour; the Maharajah and his wife are often here and are delightfully welcoming. They are also deeply committed to their area and people and have a lot of projects on the go. Karauli very alive and not at all touristy - so no touts. This is a lovely corner of Rajasthan and these interesting, unpompous people can bring it alive for you.

rooms	25: 21 doubles, 4 suites. All air-cooled. Some a/c.
price	Rs2,100-Rs2,400. Suites Rs2,750. Plus 10% tax. Peak season: October-April.
meals	Breakfast Rs175. Lunch Rs300. Dinner Rs325.
closed	Rarely.
directions	Karauli 60km of main Jaipur-Agra highway. Nearest train station is Gangapur City, 31km from Karauli. (Not the Old City Palace.)

H H Krishna Chandra Pal

tel	+91 7464 220 024
fax	+91 141 2292 633
e-mail	karauli@sancharnet.in
web	www.karauli.com

Heritage Hotel

E-F map 2 entry 54

Ranthambhore Bagh

Ranthambhore Road, Sawai Madhopur, Alwar, 322 001, Rajasthan

Whatever this place may lack in comforts is well compensated for by Aditya and Poonam. They are a vibrant, cheerful, hardworking couple, with natural smiles and endless energy. He's an amateur wildlife photographer and she a sculptress, so there is an artistic, eco-friendly mood. This is a great place for exploring the National Park; the station is nearby and there are bikes for hire. The building, on the outskirts of town, is around two small courtyards – not attractive – of concrete and stone, enlivened by plants and amusing, simple 'ethnic' decorations. The atmosphere is fun and friendly, the maps of the park are superb, the wildlife information also, and the game 'drives' are the main topic of conversation. Jeep safaris head out before breakfast or you can take a larger vehicle and book up a day or two ahead. The rooms are very basic but with crisp white linen, white-painted walls and traditional plaster. The tents are also basic, but on a solid stone base, with beds and good linen and a back section that is a 'bathroom'. (Sound travels well through canvas.) It is charming – and a place to unwind.

rooms	22: 12 doubles, 10 tents. All air-cooled.
price	Rs1,100. Tents Rs1,750. Plus 10% tax. Peak season: October–April.
meals	Breakfast Rs150. Lunch & dinner Rs250.
closed	July–September.
directions	From Sawai Madhopur train station take Ranthambhore Road towards the National Park. 4km from station.

Aditya & Poonam Singh

tel	+91 7462 221 728
fax	+91 7462 224 251
e-mail	tiger@ranthambhore.com
web	www.ranthambhore.com
res. no.	+91 11 2691 4417

Tented Camp

Sher Bagh

Sherpur-Khiljipur, Sawai Madhopur, District Sawai Madhopur, 322 001, Rajasthan

This is Jaisal's brainchild. He has known the Ranthambhore National Park since his infancy, is deeply drawn by its magic and, in Sher Bagh, created its first, truly comfortable tented site. Originally designed for turn-of-the-century hunting expeditions, the huge canvas tents sit on plinths, have specially designed beds, verandas with rattan chairs, proper bathrooms with hot water, electric heaters and hot water bottles. You are surrounded by jungle and there's a natural hillock from which to gaze at the lovely Aravalli hills... your sanctuary is also closer to the park entrance than others in the area, so, no long, cold morning drives in the back of the jeep. This is one of the finest places in the world for spotting wild tigers, so make the most of it – you have the keen eyes and the sharp ears of some highly experienced trackers at your disposal. Hunting was banned in 1971, Project Tiger was launched, and Jaisal, passionate about promoting constructive, sustainable tourism, is making his mark. There's a strong eco ethos here, and your food is as organic, locally grown and delicious as you might expect.

rooms	12 tents for 2.
price	Full-board only, $180. Plus 10% tax. Peak season: November-March.
meals	Included. Full-board.
closed	15 April-September.
directions	1km from Sawai Madhopur along the Ranthambhore Road.

	Mr Jaisal Singh
tel	+91 7462 52120
fax	+91 11 2331 2118
e-mail	sherbagh@vsnl.com
web	www.sherbagh.com
res. no.	+91 11 2374 3195

Tented Camp

map 5　entry 56

Oberoi Vanyavilas

Ranthambhore Road, Sawai Madhopur, 322 001, Rajasthan

Pretty much the last word in tented splendour. On the edge of the Ranthambhore National Park – with its population of tigers, leopards, crocodiles, bears and deer – is this extraordinary resort: 25 huge, air-conditioned tents with wooden floors, finely embroidered canopies, luxurious bathrooms and a private walled garden; each also has a sunbathing deck. Come for the tigers… or the luxury. There's a spa and fitness tent, full of the latest gym equipment if you want to work at it, or you can go with the range of holistic therapies. There are two elephants at your disposal for rides and picnics, a billiard room and a swimming pool (heated in winter). A small army of friendly, intelligent young staff from all over India make sure your every need is catered for at the drop of a hat. Eat Indian or 'international' indoors or in equal comfort under the stars, perhaps with a log fire. Then there are the library and bar with something of an olde English club atmosphere: armchairs by an open fire, gleaming woodwork, fresh flowers, plus a dramatic gold-on-blue mural by Oberoi's in-house artist. *Evening lectures or films on Indian wildlife.*

rooms	25 tents.
price	$475. Peak season: October–March.
meals	Breakfast from $12. Lunch $20. Dinner $25.
closed	July–September.
directions	Vanyavilas is well signed on the road between Sawai Madhopur station & the National Park.

Ms Lincy Mary Isaac
tel +91 7462 223 999
fax +91 7462 223 988
e-mail reservations@vanyavilas.com
web www.oberoihotels.com

Tented Camp

Brijraj Bhawan Palace

Civil Lines, Kota, 324 001, Rajasthan

A gorgeous palace, perched on the banks of the river Chambal, built as the British Residency in 1830. Today it belongs to the Maharaja of Kota and is run as a small hotel; the royal family live in one half, guests in the other. Ijyraj used to be a banker in Delhi and has brought stacks of energy to the place; he is also charming, and his style unusually 'hands-on'. Meet your host, and fellow guests, over dinner, held in the intimate dining room or on the terrace overlooking the river. Vegetables and herbs come from the kitchen garden, milk from the dairy, and there's a menu to please all tastes: Indian, Rajasthani, continental, Chinese. Whatever you choose you'll eat well. Then retreat to the drawing room, splendidly and comfortably furnished, or to your bedroom, which will be large and probably have a river view. Furniture dates back to the Raj, hunting trophies and photographs adorn the walls. You are on the edge of Kota but this is a marvellously peaceful spot... terraced gardens lead down to the river, birds trill in the shrubs and trees. *Trips to see the prehistoric etchings of the Alinia rock shelters.*

rooms	7: 4 doubles, 1 single, 2 suites.
price	Rs1,960. Single Rs1,450. Suite Rs1,450–Rs1,980. Plus 10% tax. Peak season: October–March.
meals	Breakfast Rs200. Lunch Rs325. Dinner Rs350.
closed	Rarely.
directions	Near to the Collectorate Circle, right next to the PWD office on the river Chambal.

Mr Ijyaraj Singh

tel	+91 744 2450 529
fax	+91 744 2450 057
e-mail	brijraj@datainfosys.net
web	www.indianheritagehotels.com

Apani Dhani Eco-Lodge

Jhunjhunu Road, Nawalgarh, 333 042, Rajasthan

Here your conscience and your corpus can be at peace. The principles are 'eco' and 'low impact', rooted in a deep concern for the local heritage and the damaging effects that tourism can have. Ramesh, the pioneer, lives here with his extended family, the sounds and smells of their lives providing a gentle backdrop to this beautiful setting. The rooms are a cluster of traditional huts with mud-rubbed walls, thatched roofs and ruddy, earthy colours. Wooden furniture and intriguing *objets* in russet-toned alcoves create an understated, minimalist feel. Everything you need is here, though luxuries are few. The bathrooms are all gleaming white tiles and polished chrome; you'll get no better at this price, anywhere. Seasonal, wholesome food is doled out on leaf plates under a bougainvillea-clad pagoda in the circular, crazy-paved courtyard that is the hub of the place. Ramesh is a pleasant, well-travelled man of principle, who believes strongly in the importance of harmonious living. Superb cafetière coffee! *Guided excursions to Shekhawati towns and villages. Great trekking. Ramesh has founded the 'Friends of Shekhawat' to preserve the disappearing local heritage.*

rooms	8: 4 doubles, 4 twins.
price	Rs750.
meals	All meals from Rs150.
closed	Rarely.
directions	Near Kisan Chatrawas off Nawalgarh bypass, on road from Sikar to Jhunjhunu.

	Mr Ramesh C Jangid
tel	+91 1594 222 239
fax	+91 1594 224 061
e-mail	enquiries@apanidhani.com
web	www.apanidhani.com

Ecolodge

entry 59   map 2   G

Hotel Mandawa Haveli

Near Sothaliya Gate, Mandawa, 333 704, Rajasthan

And so to bed: heavily-studded double doors clunk and creak; lower your head and step over the wooden sill into a mysterious and magical interior largely unadapted – apart from the bed and the fact they've managed to sneak in a startlingly modern bathroom. Rooms on each floor lead off the heavily decorated central courtyard, most have windows to the streetside, too, small and low; they were made for living at floor level. Cultivated, delightful Dinesh seems tireless in his appreciation of his wonderfully preserved 1890s merchant's *haveli*, the first frescoed building en route into the old town, and will tell you all about it. You approach up steps, through a formal garden – and more steps – then it's like stepping into a jewellery box, with inviting corners in which to sit in sun or shade and examine the architectural gems. It's all very relaxing and seductive, the floodlit house an unforgettable backdrop to starlit dinners. Food is local, sometimes from the owner's own farm outside town, and the style of cooking traditional. Camel rides, jeep safaris and an Ayurvedic massage on an authentic wooden Kerala table.

rooms	10: 8 doubles, 2 suites. Some a/c.
price	Rs1,100. Suite Rs1,750. Plus 10% tax.
	Peak season: October–January.
meals	Breakfast Rs125. Lunch Rs200. Dinner Rs275.
closed	Rarely.
directions	From central bus stop in Mandawa, towards castle; Haveli is set back form the road up a set of steps.

	Mr Dinesh Dhabai
tel	+91 1592 223 088
fax	+91 1592 224 060
e-mail	hotelmandawahaveli@yahoo.com
web	hotelmandawa.free.fr

Heritage Hotel

Piramal Haveli

Bagar Shekhavati, Village & P.O. Bagar, District Jhunjunu, 333 023, Rajasthan

Of the famous, frescoed mansions that punctuate the Shekhawati region, the Piramal Haveli is among the most gracious, its grandeur tempered by a touch of tongue-in-cheek kitsch. Once past the imposing entrance tower, built to honour the visit of the Maharajah of Jaipur in 1928, and beyond the green, wisteria-trailing façade, you enter a private world. Lovingly restored, the house gives you a taste of the life of a wealthy Marwari merchant in the early 20th century. Eight bedrooms with heavy doors and massive padlocks surround the pillared courtyards, which are decorated with friezes of flying cherubs and gods in motorcars. Rooms are large and dark against the heat, decorated with 1930s colonial furniture and ageing portraits of British royalty. Facilities and service are basic, and language can be a bar, but staff are friendly and helpful. Meals take the form of lashings of vegetarian *thali*, with local herbs and spices. You can dine on the rooftop, serenaded by Rajasthani musicians and watch the exclusively male peacocks prance among the balustrades. *Picnics in the surrounding Thar desert, and treasure hunts can be arranged.*

rooms	8: 2 doubles, 6 suites. Some a/c.
price	Rs1,500. Suites Rs2,000. Plus 10% tax. Peak season: September–March.
meals	Breakfast Rs100. Lunch & dinner Rs200.
closed	Rarely.
directions	In the main gate of Bagar. Haveli on left, set back from the road, beyond the gardens.

	Mr Sibhash Rai
tel	+91 5972 221 220
fax	+91 11 2435 1112
e-mail	sales@neemranahotels.com
web	www.neemranahotels.com
res. no.	+91 11 2435 6145

Heritage Hotel

Ajit Bhawan

Ajit Bhawan Palace, near Circuit House, Jodhpur , 342 002, Rajasthan

Everyone loves Ajit Bhawan – it is one of India's earliest heritage hotels and a delightfully well-run place. Originally built for the maharaja of Jodhpur's younger brother, Maharaj Sir Ajit Singhji, the hotel was the former Maharaj Swaroop Singh's brainchild; an MP who pioneered the jeep safari, he would accompany tourists and dispense assistance to the needy at the same time. He's still around today, but tends to leave the running of things to the younger members of the family. There is a slight theme-park feel to the place, as the original eight rooms in the old house have become 50 or more themed huts, rooms and suites scattered around the grounds. But you have all you need for a comfortable stay: two restaurants to choose from, a curvaceous pool, several musicians. Bedrooms sport pictures on bright walls, fringed bedspreads, Rajput rugs and furniture and ceilings fans, there's masses of greenery outside, a compound of cattle even, and endless places to sit, including a charming courtyard where you can dine in the evening. *Horse safaris can be arranged.*

rooms	55: 50 doubles, 5 suites. Some a/c.
price	Rs2,400–Rs3,000. Suites Rs3,500. Plus 10% tax. Peak season: October–March.
meals	Breakfast Rs195. Lunch Rs250. Dinner Rs350.
closed	Rarely.
directions	Right in the centre of Jodhpur, 2km from the train station.

	Mr Chetan
tel	+91 291 2510 410
fax	+91 11 2622 1419
e-mail	ajitbhawan@rediffmail.com
web	www.ajitbhawan.com
res. no.	+91 11 2622 1420

Heritage Hotel

E map 4   entry 62

Haveli Guest House
Makrana Mohalla, Jodhpur, 342 002, Rajasthan

Haveli Guest House is so good you should beware of commission-hungry rickshaw wallahs who may take you to one of three imitations. *Ours* is a five-storey, 350-year-old golden sandstone building with a single glass door entrance and reception on the right. You'll find a friendly, unassuming place in the thick of Jodhpur's atmospheric old Blue City. Bedrooms are simple but spotless – tiled floors, carved wooden doors and headboards, cheerful printed cotton bed covers – all with decent bathrooms. Front rooms are best, all have window seats/balconies, with plump cushions to lie on, and fantastic views of the Meharangah Fort. Others open onto a sunny pink-and-yellow courtyard filled with plants. Treat yourself in the roof terrace restaurant, lit by sandstone lamps at night; it has the best fort views and massive, mouthwatering vegetarian *thalis*. Owner Upendra Shrimali and his family are full of enthusiasm for their NGO, promoting education and self-sufficiency in local communities; take one of Haveli's village safaris to really learn something about life in Rajasthan, and check out the web site www.nativeplanet.org.

rooms	22 doubles.
price	Rs200–Rs800.
meals	Breakfast Rs95. Lunch Rs125. Dinner Rs150.
closed	Rarely.
directions	Do not be fooled: there are 3 other guest houses using variations on the name 'haveli' to ride on the real one's success. You want the tall golden sandstone building opposite a stepwell in the centre of the blue old city, beyond the clock tower.

	Upendra Shrimali
tel	+91 291 2614 615
e-mail	havelighj@sify.com
web	www.haveliguesthouse.net

Indrashan Guest House

593 High Court Colony, Jodhpur, 342 001, Rajasthan

A lush, flower-filled garden surrounds this neat, pretty house in one of Jodhpur's quietest neighbourhoods. You might walk by and wonder enviously who lives here, never dreaming you could be ensconced inside. Your hosts are keen to emphasise this is a homestay, not a hotel; they take all meals with their guests, and often join them on sightseeing expeditions. Bedrooms, all a decent size, are spotless; much of the furniture belonged to Chandrashekhar's grandfather. One light, bright suite with its own garden entrance and two double bedrooms would be ideal for families. Food is fresh and home-cooked to order by Bhavna, who wins the gong of 'Best Meal Eaten in India' from satisfied guests. But you're also encouraged to help yourself in the kitchen – and from a generously stocked bar in the living room. The Singhs' tour company, Rajputana Discovery, does something few others do, sending you on week-long tours through Rajasthan, staying with aristocratic relations of the family and being drawn into the heart of Indian households. The guest book bears testament to the magic of the trips. Genteel Indian hospitality at its finest – don't rush it.

rooms	5 doubles. Some a/c.
price	Rs900.
meals	Breakfast Rs95. Lunch Rs190. Dinner Rs225.
closed	Rarely.
directions	No English sign or number on house. Best to request a pick-up from train station or airport, 3km away.

	Mr Chandrashekhar & Bhavna Singh
tel	+91 291 2440 665
fax	+91 291 2438 593
e-mail	rajdisk@datainfosys.net
web	www.rajputanadiscovery.com

Guesthouse

 map 4   entry 64

Ratan Vilas

Loco Shed Road, Ratanada, Jodhpur, 342 001, Rajasthan

Brijraj Singh's great-grandfather built this dignified red sandstone villa; a hundred years of family memories — including four generations of championship polo teams — line the walls of the cosy drawing room. Now Brijraj, his wife Namrata, and his spry parents are immensely kind, sharing hosts. Rooms are big and pleasingly simple: mosaic stone floors, crisp Indian print bedcovers, spotless bathrooms. The Singhs' hobby is buying and restoring antiques; each piece of furniture has its own story. Ask for a delectable buffet dinner; everything will be chosen from a local market on the day. A family cow provides not only fresh milk but homemade yogurt and cottage cheese and when the rains return to drought-stricken Rajasthan, the Singhs will grow vegetables again. A cheerful courtyard in the middle of the house is filled with red and white hibiscus — Brijraj's favourite flower — and the heavenly scent of jasmine. A swing seat and deckchairs in the sun, armchairs under a shaded patio, and a fire in winter; no need to bring your own good books — there are plenty here. A very friendly and environmentally-friendly guest house. *Jeep safaris.*

rooms	12: 11 doubles, 1 suite. Some a/c. Others air-cooled.
price	Rs750–Rs950. Suite Rs1,500. Plus 10% tax on rooms over Rs900.
meals	Breakfast from Rs100. Lunch & dinner from Rs200
closed	Rarely.
directions	2.5km from train station.

	Mr Brijraj Singh
tel	+91 291 2613 011
fax	+91 291 2614 418
e-mail	ratanvilas_jod@rediffmail.com

Guesthouse

Shahi Guest House

City Police Gandhi Street, Opposite Narsingh Temple, Jodhpur, 342 001, Rajasthan

Small, original and endearingly ramshackle, Shahi Guest House attracts those who don't mind swapping luxury for a friendly place with lashings of character. It's down a tiny cobblestoned alley in the middle of Jodhpur's Blue City, the mighty Meharangah fort towering above, and has bird's-eye views onto neighbouring roof terraces and brightly coloured sarees hang from washing lines against a riot of blue. Your host is a charming and sociable young man; nothing is too much trouble. Ask for the Queen Palace room, the best of the three, where the women of the house used to meet in purdah: mosaic-tiled floors, stained-glass windows and loads of atmosphere. An upstairs balcony has an extra sleeping area which kids would love. Shelves are filled with family curios; rose oil sprinkled on curtains keeps the room smelling delicate. You'll eat home-cooked *thalis* with Bantu on the sunny, plant-filled roof terrace; he picked up English from his first guests three years ago. A backpackers' favourite – understandably. *Palm reading and classes on yoga, meditation and Hindu traditions.*

rooms	3: 2 doubles, 1 family room for 5. All air-cooled.
price	Rs400–Rs800. Peak season: July–March.
meals	Breakfast Rs95. Lunch & dinner from Rs150.
closed	Rarely.
directions	In city centre 2km from train station & 2.5km from bus station.

	Mr Vimlesh 'Bantu' Soni
tel	+91 291 2623 802
e-mail	shahigh@rediffmail.com

Fort Chanwa

VPO Luni, Dist. Jodhpur, Luni, 342 802, Rajasthan

The impressive, slightly austere fortress, carved out of the famous red sandstone of Jodhpur, is a fine example of the architecture of 18th-century Rajasthan. Here are ornately carved lattice work friezes, intricate *jharokas*, courtyards, towers, little passages, unexpected stairways and secret pavilions that lead to rooftops with shimmering views over the village to the desert beyond. Owned by the son of one of the uncles of the current maharaja of Jodhpur, Fort Chanwa was in a state of disrepair before its reincarnation as a luxury hotel – hard to believe today! Bedrooms are cool, high-ceilinged, all different: here a beautiful tiled floor, there a splash of coloured glass, a decorative wall hanging, an antique bed. A bar and a bazaar lend bustle and colour to the evenings, and there's a serene pool. Come to escape Jodphur; jeep safaris can be easily arrranged, and the village of Luni is fascinating in itself – a centre for metal, clay and wood workers, it is utterly traditional and unspoilt. *Folk music. Massage. Croquet.*

rooms	31 doubles.
price	Rs1,800–2,600. Plus 10% tax.
meals	Breakfast Rs175. Lunch Rs300. Dinner Rs375.
closed	Rarely.
directions	35km (30 minutes) from Jodhpur towards Udaipur.

	Mr Rajvir Singh
tel	+91 2931 284 216
fax	+91 291 432 460
e-mail	info@fortchanwa.com
web	www.fortchanwa.com
res. no.	+91 291 432 460

Heritage Hotel

Rohet Garh

Village P.O., Rohet, District Pali, Rajasthan

An established heritage hotel, and very much a family affair. Your hosts are keen and accomplished riders and are proud to take guests out on horseback 'village safaris' to discover the Bishnoi tribal lands, where blue bull roam free and unthreatened, and to meet local farmers and weavers in their own homes. This is is a rare opportunity and not something the ordinary tourist can easily do (and for the less equestrian-minded, there are camel and jeep safaris, too). The fortified desert home of the Rathores' descendants, on the banks of a birdlife-rich lake, has been beautifully restored in the traditional style of the region. Lounges are decorated with trophies and artefacts; bedrooms, some large, some less so, are bright and airy with colourful furnishings and views over garden or lake... peacocks perch under finely carved archways and strut among the neem tree groves. Take a massage, hone your croquet skills, dine by the lovely pool at night as musicians serenade you. Make the most of the safaris and the wonderful riding, or just stay put a day or two – Rohet Garh is a relaxing stopover on the way from Jodhpur south to Udaipur.

rooms	30: 26 double, 2 singles, 2 suites.
price	Rs2,000. Singles Rs1,450. Suites Rs3,000. Plus 10% tax. Peak season: 1 October–31 March.
meals	Breakfast Rs190. Lunch Rs350. Dinner Rs400.
closed	Rarely.
directions	40km from Jodhpur.

Mr Sidharth Singh

tel	+91 2936 268 231
fax	+91 291 2649 368
e-mail	rohet@datainfosys.net
web	www.rohetgarh.com
res. no.	+91 291 2649 368

Heritage Hotel

map 4   entry 68

Rawla Narlai

Village Narlai, Pali District, Rajasthan

This small 17th-century fortress, tucked between the desert and the rolling hills, was once the favourite hunting lodge of the Jodhpur royal family. It is still owned by an uncle of the maharaja, and he and his wife often visit; in their absence you are looked after by excellent staff and a fine cook. This is an exceptionally peaceful place: Narlai is barely a village, and you are in the middle of it, at the foot of a huge, granite rock. The inner courtyard, round which rooms cluster, is vivid with bougainvillea, while inside all is comfortable without being lavish. Bedrooms, not huge, make the very most of the given space; walls are colour-washed, traditional beds have lovely quilts and bathrooms are simple (and work). Explore the countryside by foot, or even better, by Marwari horse; the scenery is spectacular and there's a beautiful stepwell nearby, just right for a picnic. Brush up on your Hindi before you arrive: it will go down well with the local people; the younger generations are no longer taught English. Don't miss the vertiginous climb to the hermits' caves, or the elephant statue at the very summit – fabulous.

rooms	25: 21 doubles, 4 suites. Some a/c.
price	Rs2,400–Rs2,900. Suites Rs3,000. Plus 10% tax. Peak season: September–March.
meals	Breakfast Rs195. Lunch Rs250. Dinner Rs350.
closed	Rarely.
directions	Midway between Jodhpur & Udaipur, 25km from Ranakpur temples.

Mr Ajay Pal

tel	+91 2934 282 425
fax	+91 11 2622 1419
e-mail	ajitbhawan@rediffmail.com
web	www.ajitbhawan.com
res. no.	+91 11 2622 1420

Heritage Hotel

Deogarh Mahal

Deogarh-Madaria, District Rajsamand, 313 331, Rajasthan

Beautiful, rambling, yellow-and-white Deogarh Mahal dominates an unspoilt little town deep in the Aravalli hills. It is a 400-year-old, fairy-tale castle, owned and run – with charm – by the former ruling family. The food is excellent, the rooms are gorgeous, there's lashings of hot water – a rare treat – and a glassy, circular pool in the place where the elephants once stood. Shatran Jai and his wife, Bhavna, his father and his brother attend to every detail, and genuinely enjoy their active role. There's masses to do: a bike trip to the local villages, a picnic by a lake, a bullock-cart safari to one of the many majestic forts in the rugged, rocky hills. By special request they will also arrange for you to see over 200 original paintings owned by the Rawatsahib, a historian and art connoisseur. The bedrooms are elegant and special; one has a parrot motif in memory of the children's parrots that lived here, another a low dado of richly coloured elephant processions and walls shimmering with plant motifs. An exquisite place that epitomises luxury on a budget – and the views are unforgettable.

rooms	43: 19 doubles, 5 singles, 14 suites, 5 family rooms. Some a/c.
price	Rs2,999. Singles Rs2,200. Suites Rs3,999-Rs4,995. Plus 10% tax. Peak season: October-February.
meals	Breakfast Rs225. Lunch Rs350. Dinner Rs450.
closed	Rarely.
directions	3 hours from Udaipur on the Jaipur Highway.

Mr Veerbhavra Singh
tel	+91 2904 252 777
fax	+91 2904 252 555
e-mail	info@deogarhmahal.com
web	www.deogarhmahal.com

Heritage Hotel

map 5   entry 70

Devi Garh

Village Delwara, Tehsil Nathdwara, District Rajsamand, Rajasthan

Absorbed into the state of Rajasthan in the Sixties and subsequently abandoned, this 18th-century palace-fort has risen from ruin to become one of the most exciting heritage hotels of India. Lines are simple, mosaic floors are bold, walls are wax-treated, marble and semi-precious stones glisten: Davi Garh is a modern take on Rajput design, and the Indian industralist family who own it have achieved something rare and special. Immerse yourself in your garden or palace suite, where ultra-cool lines are offset by the occasional flash of silver inlay or amber silk... or go native and camp under the stars. The views are magnificent, and the higher you go the better they become, sweeping over the village to the hills beyond. Dine on sophisticated food in the courtyard filled with banana trees and spider lilies – the thali and rose petal ice cream is worth leaving home for... then laze by the black marble rooftop pool and gaze out over the Udaipur valley. All is exemplary, from the Ayurvedic massage and yoga to the staff who chauffeur you around. In the exotic land of maharajas and nawabs, a thrilling touch of modern India.

rooms	29: 23 suites, 6 tents for 2.
price	Suites $325-$725. Tents $150. Plus 10% tax. Peak season: October-March.
meals	Breakfast $10. Lunch $18. Dinner $20.
closed	Rarely.
directions	26km (45 minutes) North East of Udaipur on National Highway 8.

	Mr B Venkatesh
tel	+91 2953 289 211
fax	+91 2953 289 357
e-mail	reservations@deviresorts.com
web	www.deviresorts.com
res. no.	+91 11 2372 2200

Heritage Hotel

Castle Bijaipur
Bijaipur, District Chittorgarh, 312 001, Rajasthan

In a gloriously remote spot in southern Rajesthan, this 16th-century castle was built to defend the Mewar empire from the Mughals and Marathas. The multi-layered, icing-white building, still in the family, has recently opened its doors to guests... yet little has changed! Facilities are basic, the hot water and electricity can be erratic, and the choice of menu is limited. Yet the views are breathtaking, your host, the thakur, and his family are charming, and the bedrooms, though small and simply furnished, look over the colourful inner garden. Meals are served in the open-air dining room – vegetarian or non-vegetarian, as you wish – and cooked by the family's retainers. Afterwards, recline with an evening drink and watch tribal folk dances in the garden. It feels amazingly cut off here, amid the serene Vindhyachal ranges, and yet Chittorgarh, former capital of the state of Mewar, is really not too far. Do consider a horse or camel safari into the neighbouring state, and don't miss the fascinating towns of Begun and Menal. A wonderfully relaxing, hospitable place.

rooms	22: 10 doubles, 5 singles, 7 suites. Some a/c.
price	Rs1,435. Singles Rs1,350. Suites Rs1,810–Rs1,890. Peak season: October–March.
meals	Breakfast Rs130. Lunch Rs230. Dinner Rs345.
closed	Rarely.
directions	40km from Chittorgarh train station, 150km from Udaipur.

Mr Rao Narendra Singh

tel	+91 1472 240 099
fax	+91 1472 240 099
e-mail	hpratapp@hotmail.com
web	www.castlebijaipur.com

Heritage Hotel

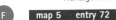

map 5   entry 72

Amet Haveli

Outside Chandpole, Udaipur, 313 001, Rajasthan

First came the restaurant, dominating the shaded terrace that juts out into the water. It has become an institution in its own right, with fabulous, unfussy food and views that rival those from any lakeside in the world. A huge mango tree casts its shade over the wrought-iron chairs and marble-topped tables — more Provençale than Mewari, though certainly with a touch of India. The old handlebar-moustachioed owner saw that his spot was the envy of Udaipur, and renovated a few of his collapsed rooms. The result is five bedrooms done with admirable restraint and taste. They have a low-ceilinged, airy, almost mediterranean mood, with bare white interiors that can only work in a hot country. Any heritage touches are subtle: where there are coloured lines they accentuate the curves of the arches, and where patterns are used they are modest. Neither hotel nor homestay, this is one of Udaipur's most intriguing places to stay — the luxury lies not in opulent furnishings or obsequious staff, but in that wonderful feeling that you have found somewhere genuinely special. Come to eat if you do not stay.

rooms	5: 3 doubles, 2 suites. Some a/c.
price	Rs1,250. Suites Rs1,650. Plus 10% tax. Peak season: November-February.
meals	Lunch Rs250. Dinner Rs300.
closed	During Holi Festival in mid-March.
directions	Outside Chandpole on Hanuman Ghat, 2km from main town. Opposite City Palace.

Mr P P Singh

tel	+91 294 2431 085
fax	+91 294 2431 085
e-mail	regiudr@datainfosys.net

Guesthouse

Fateh Prakash Palace

City Palace, Udaipur, 313 001, Rajasthan

How often can you stay in the rooms of a royal residence that anywhere else in the world would be cordoned off? Walking along the heavily tapestried gallery that looks down into the mighty Durbar Hall to find your suite feels like sneaking about behind the scenes in a museum. Heavy, worn, woollen rugs and oil paintings of growling Mewar ancestors line the corridors to the suites, yet the atmosphere verges on the cosy, unusually so for a region where architects were inclined to create open, cool spaces to combat the challenges of Rajasthani summers. The fabrics are dark and rich and the spaces smaller, more European castle than Indian palace – a welcome change. The new rooms in the Dovecote are more standard – black-and-white chequered marble floor, *jarokha* balconies, marble bathroom – though less scuffed than Shiv Niwas next door and each with commanding views out over the lake. Perhaps it is being in a working, living palace that appeals most. The present maharaja is creating his utopia, the 'city within a city', and his aim is to re-establish the City Palace as the epicentre of creativity, learning and welfare.

rooms	28: 21 doubles, 7 suites.
price	$175. Suites $200-250. Plus 10% tax. Peak season: October-March.
meals	Breakfast $10. Lunch & dinner $20.
closed	Rarely.
directions	In the centre of the City Palace complex.

tel	+91 294 2528 016
fax	+91 294 2528 006
e-mail	gmfpp@udaipur.hrhindia.com
web	www.hrhindia.com

Heritage Hotel

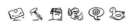

map 4   entry 74

Jagat Niwas Palace Hotel

23-25 Lal Ghat, Udaipur, 313 001, Rajasthan

You know you're onto something good when you see local families eating in the restaurant. It usually suggests that the food is good, and in this case it is wonderful: simple, generous, and enjoyed with wonderful views through the *jarokha* arches to the Aravalli hills beyond. Rarely do you see people sitting in *jarokhas* – they serve more to decorate than to entice – yet here, clutches of folk recline in the overhanging balconies three storeys above the lake. Jagat Niwas is more like a hotel than its next door neighbour, Kankarwa Haveli – there are shops, an internet café and a travel desk – but this more formal set-up doesn't dampen the easy atmosphere. It's fine to lounge about. The building is large, dominated by the central split courtyard around which run the wide, marbled verandas dotted with pot plants and the odd antique. The rooms are less cluttered than most, with the usual dark wooden beds and miniatures in alcoves, and Rajasthani bedspreads to add colour. A perfect place in which to organise yourself, and if you don't stay here, at least come and eat. *Camel trips and boating on the lake.*

rooms	29: 25 doubles, 4 suites. Some a/c.
price	Rs1,250–Rs1,400. Suites Rs1,895–Rs2,395. Plus 10% tax. Peak season: October–March.
meals	Breakfast Rs135. Lunch Rs275. Dinner Rs300.
closed	Rarely.
directions	Right on the Lal Ghat. Enter through a covered alley on right of entrance to Kankarwa Haveli.

	Mr Devraj & Veerendra Singh
tel	+91 294 2420 133
fax	+91 294 2418 512
e-mail	mail@jagatniwaspalace.com
web	www.jagatniwaspalace.com

Heritage Hotel

Kankarwa Haveli

26 Lal Ghat, Udaipur, 313 001, Rajasthan

Mustiness has been banished but the essence is maintained – this is heritage as it should be. There is nothing extra here, no tat and no plastic, and, above all, no hassle – an atmosphere that stems from the family's presence. The rooms are 'to die for', intelligently renovated to show the simple majesty of the architecture. Cushioned *jarokhas* hang over the Lal Ghat steps, delicately stitched lace-work curtains stretch across the arched windows and Rajasthani block-printed bedspreads provide the only real dose of colour. The interiors, though sparse, seem close to perfection; the old building is a handsome structure in which it would have been sacrilege to go for fuss. There is a refreshing absence of mirror-work, glass inlay or coloured walls that can go so 'wrong'; this way it feels more genuinely authentic. Your host is a delightful man, intelligent, easy and earnest. His weakness is magazines, and there's a huge collection of weird and wonderful glossies. Those who return each year – having happened upon a place so close to ideal – often add to the pile.

rooms	13 doubles.
price	Rs750–Rs1,200. Plus 10% tax on rooms over Rs1,000.
meals	Breakfast Rs110. Lunch & dinner from Rs125–Rs180.
closed	Rarely.
directions	Right in Lal Ghat. You can't miss it.

	Mr Janardan Singh
tel	+91 294 2411 457
fax	+91 294 2521 403
e-mail	kankarwahaveli@hotmail.com
web	www.indianheritagehotels.com

Guesthouse

Rang Niwas Palace Hotel

Lake Palace Road, Udaipur, 313 001, Rajasthan

It's rare to find a Rajasthani heritage hotel with such an informal atmosphere. There are no liveried, turbaned doormen, no hushed attendants, no rules and no fusty managers. You can splash in the pool and lounge in the grassy courtyard – people 'hang out' here. Run by the affable Vikram, whose regal past is all but hidden by liberal charm, the hotel is an odd mix of 'backpacker' and 'heritage'. There's a dark austerity that comes from heavy rosewood furniture and low lighting. One suite has a massive bathroom with two loos, wooden screens, an Oxford bath and swathes of marble. Its adjoining bedroom is cool and dark, with double doors that swing open to the marbled balcony over the courtyard. It is grand, a feeling created by dark, colonial wooden furniture and high ceilings, though the delicate glass inlay and handpainted lotus flowers soften the mood. The main rooms are charming: those upstairs have cosy *jarokha* balconies and plenty of space, the downstairs ones are geared more towards younger travellers. Slightly Victorian in design, Rangniwas is easy, perfectly comfortable and without pretence.

rooms	24: 18 doubles, 6 suites. Some a/c.
price	Rs660–Rs1,100. Suites Rs1,500–Rs,500. Plus 10% tax.
meals	Breakfast Rs175. Lunch Rs300. Dinner Rs350.
closed	Rarely.
directions	On the Lake Palace Road. Well signed – it's impossible to miss the leafy entrance.

	Mr I C Shrimali
tel	+91 294 2523 890
fax	+91 294 2527 264
e–mail	rangniwas75@hotmail.com
web	www.rangniwaspalace.com

Heritage Hotel

Shiv Niwas Palace

City Palace, Udaipur, 313 001, Rajasthan

The old royal guest house, a crescent-shaped building wrapped around an 1880s marble swimming pool and courtyard, has an almost European air and most rooms are free from the fussy mirror-work and spindly furniture used in every royal palace in Rajasthan. The best rooms are around the pool, raised on a wide marble terrace that runs round the half-moon of the courtyard, and with truly regal views across Lake Pichola. Yet it is not the bedrooms you come for (silver beds and trickling bedroom fountains in the suites may be too much for some) but the feeling of sleeping within the walls of a living, working palace, the main focus of arguably the most romantic city in India. Entered through huge, two-storey wooden doors and with a ceiling designed with giraffes in mind, the bar's stately home-cum-Rajput palace interior suggests, wrongly, of the close ties between imperial Britain and Udaipur's royal family. Though the counter is padded leather, the footrail polished brass and the chandeliers of European fluted crystal, the walls are hand-painted and inlaid in traditional Mewari style. A refreshingly vibrant, fascinating palace. *Solar-power boats.*

rooms	31: 14 doubles, 17 suites.
price	$125. Suites $300-$600. Plus 10% tax. Peak season: October-March.
meals	Breakfast $10. Lunch & dinner $20.
closed	Rarely.
directions	In the centre of the City Palace complex.

tel	+91 294 2528 016
fax	+91 294 2528 006
e-mail	gmsnp@udaipur.hrhindia.com
web	www.hrhindia.com

Heritage Hotel

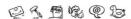

C   map 4   entry 78

Oberoi Udaivilas

Haridasji Ki Marg, Udaipur, 313 001, Rajasthan

If maharajas could still afford to build without restraint, they might well concoct something as luxurious and lavish as Udaivilas, where every square inch has been pondered over and each nook is filled with art. It is very beautiful. Set on the far bank of Lake Pichola, looking across the floating Lake Palace to the City Palace beyond, the rambling building extends its cuppola-ed embrace through 30 acres of manicured gardens and rocky mounds that run down to the lake's edge. Vast open courtyards of reflecting marble pools are tranquil and majestic – spaces that serve no purpose other than to create beauty. Designed to capture the splendour of traditional Mewari palaces, the building is a triumph of modern architecture in its resurrection of old crafts: ethereal, candlelit sheesh mahals throw soft, mirrored light from soaring domes; hand-painted Mewari scenes cover whole walls; gold leaf and cobalt-blue domed ceilings create awe-inspiring lobby areas. The food is scrumptious, the infinity pools and spa more than first class and the service better than regal. An outstandingly luxurious hotel. *Gym, health spa, lake cruises.*

rooms	90: 85 doubles; 5 suites.
price	$395-$475. Suites $1,500-$2,250. Plus 5% tax. Peak season: October–March.
meals	Breakfast $15. Lunch $30. Dinner $45.
closed	Rarely.
directions	Catch private launch from just below City Palace complex to Udaivilas.

Mr Joseph Polito

tel	+91 294 2433 300
fax	+91 294 2433 200
e-mail	reservations@udaivilas.com
web	www.oberoihotels.com

Resort

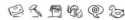

Karni Fort Bambora

Bambora Village, Tehsil Girva, Udaipur, Rajasthan

The terraced gardens of the 18th-century fort slope down to a marble pool (which is particularly magnificent at night), peacocks strut the grounds, sunsets can be arranged from every window. The old Sisodia outpost has been recently restored from a ruinous state, and the comforts are princely. Towels are laid out by the pool, Ayurvedic massage with aromatic oils is yours for the asking. You are high up overlooking the village, with views to the rolling Aravalli hills, and each bedroom has a bay window. The interiors of the hotel are, by western standards, vibrant, sumptuous even, and every room dramatically different. Dine in style at night – perhaps on your balcony, if you are fortunate enough to have one; picnic by the reservoir by day, bright with tree-pies and bee-eaters, kingfishers, swallows and kites. When the pampering palls, browse round the village bazaar – or be adventurous and go on a horse safari to meet the local tribes. Udaipur is a drum–beat away, a one-hour drive by car – a fairy-tale city of lakes, ghats and temples, it is dominated by the labyrinthine City Palace, the largest in all Rajasthan.

rooms	30: 24 doubles, 6 suites. Some air-cooled, others a/c.
price	Rs1,900-Rs2,700. Suites Rs2,900. Plus 10% tax. Peak season: October-March.
meals	Breakfast Rs150. Lunch Rs275. Dinner Rs350.
closed	Rarely.
directions	50km from Udaipur airport & train stations.

	Mr Vikramaditya 'Viku' Singh Sodawas
tel	+91 294 2398 220
fax	+91 294 2512 105
e-mail	karnihotels@satyam.net.in
web	www.karnihotels.com
res. no.	+91 291 2512 101

Heritage Hotel

Udai Bilas Palace

Dungarpur, 314 001, Rajasthan

It dates from the mid-19th-century and remains a royal residence today. Lying on the banks of the Gaibsagar Lake – a paradise for birds – and for those who spot them – the hilltop palace has a deliciously serene setting and a pleasantly faded grandeur. The exquisite tile and fresco work is in near-perfect condition and is among the finest examples of its kind; two stone elephants guard the limpid pool. The inside comes as something of a surprise: Scottish hunting lodge circa 1940. The dining room is lined with stags' heads (Maharawal Udai Singhji II was a keen hunter and often travelled to Africa in search of large game) and the bedrooms are traditional and floral; some have balconies. Fine bathrooms sport fluffy white towels – there's a good deal of comfort here. But this is more home than hotel, a convivial place with minimal staff where you all eat together at a long table (with your cosmopolitan host, when he's at home). A perfect place to stay for those keen to discover southern Rajasthan, with plenty to do nearby – boating, cycling, birdwatching and more.

rooms	20: 7 doubles, 3 singles, 10 suites.
price	Rs2,650. Singles Rs2,000. Suites Rs3,250-Rs3,800. Plus 10% tax. Peak season: October-March.
meals	Breakfast Rs200. Lunch Rs390. Dinner Rs410.
closed	Rarely.
directions	120km from Udaipur & 175km from Ahmedabad.

Mr Harshvardhan Singh

tel	+91 2964 230 808
fax	+91 2964 231 008
e-mail	contact@udaibilaspalace.com
web	www.udaibilaspalace.com
res. no.	+91 11 5151 4120

Heritage Hotel

   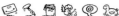

Bhairon Vilas

Next to Junagarh Fort, Bikaner, 334 001, Rajasthan

How to do justice to this funky, fabulous guest house? An oasis-like walled garden filled with birdsong and bougainvillea leads to an opium den of a reception room. Harshvardhan 'Harsh' Singh is a charming host; you're treated as honoured guests at a very special house party. His two passions in life are entertaining and decorating, both executed with warmth and flair. Unexpected steps lead to hidden doorways and terraces; there's a small Hindu temple in the garden. Décor is decadent – lots of vibrant colours and creative reupholstering using old saree material. Everywhere are amusing, quirky pieces; some family heirlooms, others hand-picked from markets. All bedrooms are delightful, but Room 101 (what a contradiction in terms) is the best, and the size of a suite. Pink walls are inlaid with dozens of small mirrors; peacock feathers sprout from vases beside sinfully comfortable armchairs. Outside a sofa suspended from gold chains makes an irresistible swing seat. Staff are faultless: kind and attentive, humorous and relaxed, in keeping with the spirit of the place. All this and excellent food too. One-of-a-kind perfection.

rooms	16 doubles.
price	Rs500–Rs1,000.
meals	Breakfast Rs120. Lunch Rs220. Dinner Rs250.
closed	Rarely.
directions	500m from Bikaner train station, just behind Junagarh Fort in front of main post office.

	Mr Harshvardhan Singh
tel	+91 151 2544 751
fax	+91 151 2209 932
e-mail	hbhairon@rediffmail.com
web	hotelbhaironvilas.tripod.com

Heritage Hotel

Bhanwar Niwas

Rampuira Street, Bikaner, 334 005, Rajasthan

This elegant family mansion is in Bikaner's most atmospheric quarter, among the narrow alleys and terracotta-and-pastel buildings of the old city. Look for an ornately carved red sandstone front, a smart doorman and a splendid 1927 Buick sitting at the entrance. Much of the furniture would look at home in a Parisian townhouse. The Rampuria family still occupies the top floor; Sunil Rampuria, the owner, is an occasional artist who painted the flowers on the walls of the 20-foot-ceiling dining room. Each room is different, all have high ceilings, antique teak furniture and Belgian tiled bathrooms with huge tubs. A beautiful cloth-bound book on some of the writing desks, *An Indian Miscellany of Wise Nuggets*, is written by grandmother Chandra Rampuria; one of many family mementos. There's a luxurious sofa swing seat in an outdoor upstairs gallery, lit by soft lamps at night. Close your eyes and you'll hear nothing but birdsong and the faint tinkling of a courtyard fountain. A secluded slice of old-fashioned opulence close to the delights of Bikaner. *Traditional painting classes, 'Desert Nights' of music and dinner on the dunes.*

rooms	24: 19 doubles, 2 singles, 3 suites.
price	Rs2,500. Singles Rs2,200. Suites Rs3,000. Plus 10% tax. Peak season: October–April.
meals	Lunch & dinner Rs400.
closed	Rarely.
directions	In the centre of Bikaner's old city, a 2-minute walk from City Kotwali Police Station.

	Mr Bhagwan Singh
tel	+91 151 2201 403
fax	+91 151 2200 880
e-mail	bhanwarniwas@rediffmail.com
web	www.bhanwarniwas.com

Heritage Hotel

Hotel Palace View

Lallgarh Palace Campus, Bikaner, 334 001, Rajasthan

Down a quiet, dusty desert road, this unassuming terracotta guesthouse is tucked away outside Bikaner's town centre. It's a good place in which to unwind, only a rickshaw ride from the sights. The front walled garden has bright flowerbeds and lush splashes of bougainvillea; long, lazy meals can be taken here. Inside, you'll find spotless, cheerful bedrooms with crisp sheets, bright cotton rugs on cool tile floors and good table lamps. All rooms have French windows onto terracotta verandas. Those upstairs have views of red sandstone Lallgarh Palace and its clock tower next door. Owner Vikram Singh is gracious and kind; nothing is too much trouble. His wife Nirmala is a strong, confident woman and an excellent cook. They love looking after people, and it's reflected in guests' comments, such as: "Best family we've encountered in India". The Singhs run their guest house as a partnership of equals – particularly refreshing in male-dominant Rajasthan. Two charming teenage daughters are on hand to entertain children (toys, games and teddies provided). A good choice for women travelling alone, or for young families.

rooms	16 doubles.
price	Rs400–Rs800.
	Peak season: October–February.
meals	Breakfast Rs100. Lunch Rs200.
	Dinner Rs250.
closed	Rarely.
directions	Next to Lallgarh Palace, on right-hand side when entering palace complex from Jaisalmer Road. 3km from train station & walking distance from bus stand.

	Mr Vikram Singh
tel	+91 151 2543 625
fax	+91 151 2522 741
e-mail	opnain_jp1@sancharnet.in

Hotel

Fort Rajwada

1 Hotel Complex, Jodphur-Barmer Link Road, Jaisalmer, 345 001, Rajasthan

Fort Rajwada does a fine job of looking and feeling like a 17th-century maharajah's palace – though it was finished in 2000. Every detail, from the carved sandstone balconies in the atrium lobby to the staff's turbans and sarees, was created with a palace in mind. The whole place feels classic but contemporary – no stuffiness here. It was designed not by architects but by the owner, Dilip Singh Rathore, according to the Indian principle of 'vastu shastra' so, for example, the infinity swimming pool is in the north-east corner of the hotel grounds; water works best at the point of sunrise. The elegant interior is the work of a French-German opera designer; bedrooms are big, stylish, with raw silk upholstery, marble floors and fresh flowers in the bathrooms. The hotel has a no-plastic rule, hence the bamboo wardrobes and laundry baskets. Sip an aperitif in the gorgeous bar – light, white and cream, with one wall lit at night by dozens of tiny lamps in alcoves. The staff are gracious and attentive. The sights and smells of Jaisalmer and 'real India' are just down the road. *Camel safaris, or even camel polo! Desert treks and dinner on the dunes.*

rooms	69: 65 doubles, 4 suites.
price	Rs3,900. Suites Rs6,500-8,500.
meals	Breakfast Rs250. Lunch Rs450. Dinner Rs550.
closed	Rarely.
directions	3km from Jaisalmer fort, 2km from train station.

Mr Aji Alex

tel	+91 2992 253 233
fax	+91 2992 253 733
e-mail	sales@rajwadafort.com
web	www.fortrajwada.com

Hotel

Hotel Killa Bhawan

On Fort, 445 Kotri Para, Jaisalmer, 345 001, Rajasthan

Killa Bhawan has gained quite a reputation since it opened eight years ago, winning a coveted *Harpers & Queen* travel award and hosting a raft of visiting dignitaries. Perched on the edge of Jaisalmer fort's ramparts and with unparalleled views, it's the baby of a French designer and European and Indian influences are mixed with irresistible flair. Bedrooms are gorgeous, everything carefully chosen, from antique four-poster beds to wrought-iron lamps. Most have dreamy views of the golden fort ramparts and the old city merging into the distant desert. Sunrises cast warm rays onto window seats piled high with silk cushions; later in the day the romance is enhanced by candlelight. Two rooms with en suite bathrooms are in a separate annexe of the hotel with its own private courtyard, dining room and roof terrace; great for families and honeymooners. Bathrooms are white marble and polished sandstone with luxuriously thick towels; funky printed cotton robes guarantee you'll actually want to be seen in the communal bathroom. Achingly romantic, and an unbelievable bargain. Miss this delightful mini-hotel at your peril.

rooms	7: 3 doubles; 4 doubles sharing 1 bath. Some a/c.
price	Rs1,600–Rs2,200. Plus 10% tax. Breakfast included. Peak season: November–February.
meals	On request only.
closed	Rarely.
directions	Inside Fort, near Little Tibet Restaurant. 1-minute walk from the main square/grand palace.

Mr Bharat

tel	+91 2992 251 204
fax	+91 2992 254 518
e-mail	kbhawan@yahoo.com
web	www.killabhawan.com

Heritage Hotel

Nachana Haveli

Goverdhan Chowk, Jaisalmer, 345 001, Rajasthan

A golden sandstone *haveli* inhabited by the Bhadi family for 300 years, it feels much more like a funky home than a hotel, with a touch of Bikaner's marvellous Bhairon Vilas about it. Deluxe rooms are big and high-ceilinged, all with silk-canopied four-poster brass beds and massive, dignified old bath tubs. Other rooms are smaller but no less stylish. Family portraits hang on the walls next to ancestral hunting trophies: a tiger skin in one room, a bear in another. Vikram and Divya are as relaxed and hip as their home; young, beautiful and charming, they put everyone at ease. They love entertaining, and often bring friends and guests together – lavish barbecues in the central courtyard are especially popular. Divya's treatments – herbal facials, henna applications or perhaps a hot turban head massage – are spoiling. Despite being in the main market district all is peace and quiet within, as Nachana is set well back from the street. Jaisalmer Fort is a five-minute walk away, so eco-conscious visitors can rest assured they're not contributing to an unfortunate side-effect of tourism – subsidence damage – by staying outside walls.

rooms	13: 11 doubles, 2 suites.
price	Rs900–1,500. Suites Rs2,100. Plus 10% tax. Peak season: October–March.
meals	Breakfast Rs110. Lunch Rs225. Dinner Rs250.
closed	Rarely.
directions	In Jaisalmer's main square, 5-minutes' walk from the fort.

	Mr Vikramaditya Singh
tel	+91 2992 252 110
fax	+91 2992 252 778
e-mail	nachana_haveli@yahoo.com

Guesthouse

entry 87   map 1   F–G

Shahi Palace

Shiv Road, Jaisalmer, 345 001, Rajasthan

Owners of budget guesthouses take note: a cheap room doesn't have to mean dingy, dirty or nondescript, as the Lal family have proved. Friendly Jora and his three brothers designed theirs like a 500-year-old *haveli*, although the building's only a year old; the place feels bright, fresh and modern, and has stacks of character. Jora visited hotels all over Britain picking up tips – including bathroom ones! The attention to detail shows: bedrooms are cheerful and comfortable, with polished sandstone floors, wicker chairs and soft uplighting. And bathrooms are wonderful: squeaky clean, all polished sandstone and gleaming fittings, they wouldn't look out of place in a top-end hotel. Rooms upstairs are small, but open onto a big, sunny roof terrace and have the best views. A Nepalese cook serves excellent multinational dishes; if guests want to eat with a family, Jora will happily escort you to his nearby village home for dinner with his. An excellent budget option. *Camel safaris available.*

rooms	9 doubles. Some air-cooled.
price	Rs150-Rs550.
meals	Breakfast Rs60. Lunch, & dinner around Rs100.
closed	Rarely.
directions	A 5-minute walk from fort along Shiv Road. 2km from train station. Opposite Government Bus Stand & State Bank.

	Mr Jora Lal
tel	+91 2992 255 920
e-mail	shahipalace@yahoo.co.in

Photography by Michael Busselle

gujarat

House of MG - Metro Heritage Hotel

Opposite Siddi Saiyad Mosque, Lal Darwaja, Ahmedabad, 380 001, Gujarat

Mr Manga Girdhardas, a successful Ahmedabad business man and philanthropist, had a vision and built this grand house for his family. He died in 1928, not long after its completion. Now his grandson is realising another vision and ten years into the project, work is almost complete. The aim was to preserve and restore this extraordinary Gujarati home with its Italian mosaic marble flooring, stained-glass windows, courtyards and passages and to establish a Heritage complex, showcasing the culinary skills of Gujarat. Now there's the Green House café on the ground floor, the open kitchen described as "our food theatre" and the more formal Agashiye restaurant on the terrace. The food is excellent. There's also a banquet 'facility', and a Life Style Store (so many people asked after the traditional décor used at the House of MG that it was logical to start selling similar items...), a movie and a reading club and more. Work on the 10 big rooms with all mod cons, and balconies, around an inner courtyard will be completed by 2004 – and the six we saw were shaping up well. *Heritage walks.*

rooms	10 doubles.
price	Rs3,000–Rs6,000.
meals	Lunch Rs150. Dinner Rs200.
closed	Rarely.
directions	In central Ahmedabad near old town, opposite Siddi Saiyad Mosque.

	Mr Chirag Kayasth
tel	+91 79 2550 6899
fax	+91 79 2550 6535
e-mail	customercare@houseofmg.com
web	www.houseofmg.com

Heritage Hotel

Bhavani Villa

Danta Bhavangadh, District Banaskantha, 385 120, Gujarat

The old, colonial villa sits high above the palace and the town. Maharana Mahipendra Singh, the 129th descendant of the founder of the Rajput dynasty, is passionate about animals and keeps a stud farm down below; he also breeds basset hounds at the villa. The quaint interiors have period furniture, plastic ceiling fans, the odd antique or hunting trophy and animal pictures galore. Guest bedrooms are in a new building separate from the villa: five big rooms with balconies and views, to scrubland hills on three sides, the town on the other. If you're lucky, you'll spot a panther in the hills. Dine on the terrace with the family – they're the nicest hosts and happy to serve the Rajput dishes that most guests prefer (you can have western food here, too). The produce comes from their farm and is as fresh as can be: chickens, milk, carrots, gourds, tomatoes, eggplant, beans. Then explore the jungle and hills – on foot, bike, horse or by jeep. Your host will be only too happy to place you in the saddle of one of his fine Marwari mares, and you're bound to spot a partridge or peacock, antelope or bear. It's a terrific place for wildlife.

rooms	5: 3 doubles, 2 suites.
price	Rs1,200-Rs1,400. Suites Rs1,800.
meals	Breakfast Rs100. Lunch, & dinner Rs200.
closed	Rarely.
directions	40km from the Abu Road train Station, 40km from Palanpur, 170km from Ahmedabad Airport. On the Palanpur-Ambaji Road, 20km from Ambaji.

	Mr Mahipendra Singh
tel	+91 2749 278 705
fax	+91 2749 278 759

Balaram Palace

Chitrasani Village-off Abu-Palanpur, Highway No.14-Banaskantha-Gujarat, Gujarat

The neo-classical treasure is easily the best preserved of the Gujurat palaces, yet it was wrested from marauders and saved from ruin in the fairly recent past. Now it is a jewel in the heritage tourism crown. The original family – who used the place as a weekend and hunting retreat – has long since gone and the professional Gopi group have taken over. The beautiful marble galleries and wooden staircases have been preserved and modern luxuries – air-conditioning, helipad – have been added. The hotel's descriptions of the traditional uses of rooms and grounds give a fascinating insight into its past. Balaram sits on a hilltop overlooking the river, with views stretching over green fields to the Aravalli hills and the borders of Rajasthan. Most people come here to indulge and be spoiled – an entire staff is at your beck and call – but for the more energetic there are camel-cart rides in the grounds, the Moghul gardens to explore, a Nawabi period swimming pool and an indoor gym. Visit Patan, famous for its weavers, the hilltop temple of Taranga for its carvings, and the temple of Ambaji, most holy at full moon.

rooms	17: 16 doubles, 1 suite.
price	Full-board only, Rs2,100. Suite Rs5,600. Plus 15% tax. Peak season: September-February.
meals	Included. Full-board.
closed	Rarely.
directions	167km from Ahmedabad airport; 15km from Palanpur train station. By road from Ahmedabad go via Mehsana & Palanpur. Well-signed on way to village.

	Mr Dilip Thakkar
tel	+91 2742 284 278
fax	+91 2742 284 278
e-mail	gopigroup@icenet.net
web	www.gopigroup.com

Heritage Hotel

Garden Palace

Kheda, Balasinor, 388 255, Gujarat

You hear about the food long before you reach Balasinor and you may even get a whiff of it as you sweep down the driveway from the lake. The nawab's wife is renowned for her cooking and after the family's initial warm greeting they will probably press Indian and Mughlai morsels on you, insisting that "one more piece won't do any harm"! The soft-pink balconied 19th-century palace was originally built for a senior minister of state; now it is the home of the royal family of Balasinor. Louis XIV-style chairs line the drawing room where the family entertains; guest bedrooms comfortable furnished with antiques are on the ground floor. You are surrounded by fields and vegetable gardens where they grow wheat and maize, custard apples and coconuts, chillies and chickoo – most of which end up, deliciously, on your plate. The well-worn phrase "people come as guests and leave as friends" fills the guestbook; repeat visitors endorse this. The Babis are lovely people and may well join you for dinner – or take you on a jaunt by jeep to the 65-million-year-old dinosaur fossil park or despatch you with a picnic to the Wanakbori dam.

rooms	8 doubles. Some a/c.
price	Rs2,200. Plus 15% tax. Peak season: September-February.
meals	Breakfast Rs150. Lunch Rs250. Dinner Rs300.
closed	Rarely.
directions	86km from Ahmedabad airport; 45km from nearest train station, Godhra.

	Mr Salauddin Babi
tel	+91 2960 266 786
fax	+91 2960 267 786
e-mail	gopigroup@icenet.net
web	www.gopigroup.com

Heritage Hotel

map 4   entry 92

Palace Utelia

Via Lothal-Burkhi, Utelia, District Ahmedabad, 382 230, Gujarat

Chakoresahibji, the owner, has a walking cane and a bad knee but it doesn't stop him climbing the steep stairs to the first and second floors to show off the views. The terracotta rooftops and rural fields are lovely and so is the leafy courtyard below with its spilling bougainvillea and shady areas – cool even in summer. Chakoresahibji is not always here but his wife and son are in high season, and couldn't be more friendly. His family founded Utelia in 1786 and built the palace in Indo-Saracenic style around the turn of the century. It is best seen from a distance as you approach the village; it is quite a sight, and, indeed, impossible to miss with its commanding position and many domes and porticoes (and it is the only place to stay). Bedrooms have heavy wooden doors with carvings and big terracotta-tiled floors. You can sit and ponder on each floor – on period furniture or swing chairs – and admire some strikingly orginal stained-glass windows. And take a moment to enjoy the cushioned alcoves by the bedroom windows, with their long and peaceful views.

rooms	20 doubles.
price	Rs1,990. Plus 15% tax.
meals	Breakfast Rs200. Lunch, & dinner Rs400.
closed	Rarely.
directions	80km from Ahmedabad towards Badodara and Bhavnagar.

	Mr Bhagirat Singh
tel	+91 2714 262 222
e-mail	uteliaad1@sancharnet.in
res. no.	+91 79 6445 770

Heritage Hotel

Nilambag Palace
Bhavnagar, 364 002, Gujarat

It takes 20 people to lift one of the rugs – that's the scale of things here. The chandeliers are from Czechoslovakia, the tigers and panthers on the walls from India and the architect was from Germany. It is a magnificent palace, completed in 1895 – arguably the finest in Gujarat, though the family no longer lives here. The position is stunning and the building seems to soar on two layers of Rajula stone and pillars. The bedrooms are vast, with beds to match. The King's original suite is five feet higher than the rest – lest anyone forget he was King. Original carpentry decorates the rooms and there are two bedrooms, two bathrooms (one with stairs down to it) and a private balcony from which you can view most of the palace. The Queen's suite has two rooms, the beds have canopies and there's space for a writing desk, lounge chairs *and* room to dance; bathrooms are big. There is a central courtyard with small fountain into which all the rooms look from upstairs balconies. Outside: a lawn tennis court and a round pool in Roman style surrounded by red columns. Luxury and deep aristocratic elegance in one.

rooms	20 doubles.
price	Rs2,000-Rs3,800. Plus 15% tax. Peak season: September-March.
meals	Breakfast Rs175. Lunch Rs350. Dinner Rs400.
closed	Rarely.
directions	2km from Nilambag railway station. 8km from the airport.

Mr M H Triverdi

tel	+91 278 2424 241
fax	+91 278 2428 072
e-mail	info@nilambagpalace.com
web	www.nilambagpalace.com

Heritage Hotel

Old Bell Guest House

Sayla Circle, Ahmedabad-Rajkot Highway, P.O. Sayla, District Surendranagar, Gujarat

The colonial villa drips with remnants of British India with its overhanging creepers, sweeping drive, wide staircase and stately gardens. It was built in 1890 to house special guests of the state of Sayla; sepia-stained photographic evidence of the original family's life, hunting parties and cherished vintage cars line the veranda. Animal heads hang above doors, brass locks and old doorknobs still shine and bougainvillea splashes its colour among the garden greenery – it is very Raj but gently so. The bedrooms are generous: an extra room for luggage, four pillows of different colours, music and modern phone systems, comfort and charming simplicity. You may play tennis on the vintage court, practise your cricket at the nets or your chess on the outdoor board. The food is dependable and the staff bursting with good will. In the evening you see the Old Bell at her best – the turbaned guard at the gate, the lady by the flower pots greeting you with a *tikka*, high tea on the veranda, watching the sun set. Magic. *Latura-Katura wildlife sanctuary 45km.*

rooms	10 doubles.
price	Full-board only, Rs1,500. Plus 15% tax. Peak season: September-February.
meals	Included. Full-board.
closed	Rarely.
directions	35km from Surendranagar train station. By road from Ahmedabad through Limdi to Sayla, where the guest house is signed.

	Mr Bhavan Singh
tel	+91 2755 280 017
fax	+91 2755 280 357
e-mail	gopigroup@icenet.net
web	www.gopigroup.com

Guesthouse

Royal Oasis

Wankaner, 363 621, Gujarat

When the family's palaces grew too hot the family would retreat here to the cool of the Oasis, only two miles away. Much rebuilding has been going on and when finished the rooms will have their own bathrooms and dressing rooms. One will be blue, with blue furniture; another green, and so on. There will be Art Deco plastering around the door frames and along the walls. Rajasthani quilts will go on the beds. But the deepest lure of the Oasis is the stepwell, or Vaav, the last to be built in India in the 20th century and superbly preserved. It has three stories underground, with fountains, some fantastic sculptures and carvings. There is also a big, Art Deco, indoor pool. The food is western but this has its benefits: a grand opportunity to eat bread and butter pudding, maybe! This was – is – a remarkable family; after Independence their members were frequently elected to the state and national legislatures. If the Prince is here he often shows visitors around the palaces. All this and richly interesting Gujarat, too. *India's first land-sailing outfit will be up and running by December 2003.*

rooms	14: 8 doubles in main house, 6 doubles in annexe.
price	Full-board only. Rs2,100. Plus 15% tax. Peak season: September-February.
meals	Included. Full-board.
closed	Rarely.
directions	The nearest airport & train station are 50km away in Rajkot.

	Mr Anirudh Nayak
tel	+91 2828 220 000
fax	+91 2828 220 001
e-mail	gopigroup@icenet.net
web	www.gopigroup.com

Heritage Hotel

 map 4   entry 96

Royal Residency
The Palace, Wankaner, 363 621, Gujarat

There are three palaces – one for the King, one for the Prince and one for the Princess and any other women. The King's is vast and imposing, part museum and part king's domicile. The formalities of separate living are still observed, as are the memorabilia and paraphernalia of royal life: animal heads from all over the world, huge ceilings, shadowy rooms, heavy furniture, billiard tables and a collection of vintage cars. The Residency, built in 1882, is not much less grandiose and palace guests often stay there. Only some of the rooms are yet ready for paying guests but things look promising. The style is Art Deco, the quilts on the bed are Rajasthani, the furniture wooden and the bath tub a satisfyingly old tin one with ancient plumbing and shower above. There is a wonderful sense of space, an engaging mix of formality and laissez-faire and much to see. Where else can one sleep in such splendour, at the heart of such historical and architectural magnificence? Luxury is not the word – for it has been corrupted by western gadgetry – but this is elegance indeed, with a very modern royal family across the way. *Horse riding and land sailing.*

rooms	26: 23 doubles, 1 single, 2 suites. Some a/c.
price	Full-board only Rs3,700. Singles Rs1,850. Suites Rs4,000. Plus 12% tax. Peak season: November–March.
meals	Included. Full-board.
closed	Rarely.
directions	50km from Rajkot Airport; 230km from Ahmedabad.

	Mr Yuvraj Digvijay Singh
tel	+91 2828 220 000
fax	+91 2828 220 002
web	www.indianheritagehotels.com

Orchard Palace

Palace Road, Gondal, 360 311, Gujarat

The present owner is the descendant of that enlightened maharajah who transformed Gondal into a progressive princely state (out with purdah, in with roads, schools, drainage and electricity). The 19th-century villa is imposing, surrounded by orchards, gardens and lawns – enjoy an early-evening chat on the upstairs terrace with the sociable Maharani, and watch the peacocks (and cuckoos, sunbirds and herons if you're lucky) strut around the lotus pond. Your hosts share the same driveway as their guests and, happily for you, the same excellent chefs. Other members of the family manage the place and your stay not only includes meals but tours of the town (don't miss the intricately carved Naulakha Palace) and viewings of the family's classic and vintage car collection. Huge bedrooms have 1940s décor and plumbing with a heritage feel; some have canopy beds, four are air-conditioned. There are sitting areas on both floors dotted with family photos, big glass ashtrays, the odd stuffed cheetah, a collection of miniature paintings. Trek off on a long-distance safari; birdwatching is excellent when the lake refills.

rooms	19 doubles. Some a/c.
price	Full-board only, Rs4,400. Plus 15% tax. Peak season: October-March.
meals	Included. Full-board.
closed	Rarely.
directions	A short walk from Gondal bus station.

Mr Kanak Singh

tel	+91 2825 220 002
fax	+91 79 6300 962
e-mail	nwsafaris@hotmail.com
web	www.ahmedabadcity.com/gondal

Heritage Hotel

Maneland Jungle Lodge

Gir Lion Sanctuary & National Park, Sasan, District Junagadh, 362 135, Gujarat

Sometimes a brochure is well worth quoting: 'You will find yourself waking up to crispy mornings and the chirping of birds. Let the staff pamper you with lemongrass tea on sit-out jharokas. Listen to wild stories around a warm bonfire in the dead of night. Hear the night come alive with only the rustling of eight-feet high grass and fire flies. Yet feel the comfort of home in the midst of a jungle.' The jungle is very real – lions come to the water-hole nearby and, for a fee, you can set off for a proper safari with sightings of jungle cats and antelope and other beasts possible. You are on the edge of the Gir Sanctuary and National Park, run by the Forest Department. The Lodge has several unconventional cottages – arches, balconies, 'kutchi' designs – built of local stone. Cane chairs and bright bedspreads set the tone and all is cool and restrained, with white-painted walls and exposed stone, oxide-red floors and mosaic tiles, statues, bronze objects, wrought-iron lamps. Each cottage has a sitting room. An unusual and lovely place, deeply peaceful, even in the company of peacocks.

rooms	15 doubles.
price	Full-board only, Rs3,000. Plus 15% tax. Peak season: 15 October–March.
meals	Breakfast Rs50. Lunch & dinner Rs130.
closed	Rarely.
directions	60km from Junagadh, 160km from Rajkot Airport.

	Mr Hemant Sharma
tel	+91 2877 285 555
fax	+91 22 2619 2578
e-mail	info@maneland.com
web	www.maneland.com
res. no.	+91 22 2618 4014

Safari Lodge

Hotel Sao Tome Retiro

Next to Diu Museum, Firangiwada, Diu, 362 520, Gujarat

Only three whitewashed churches remain in Diu from Portuguese times. If you would like to sleep – in perfect simplicity – in one of them, here's your chance. You can even dine, or barbecue, on the roof, with unforgettably lovely views over the town, the fort, the other two churches and the sea. Extraordinary – an unforgettable experience. The Retiro occupies the two upstairs floors of the church while downstairs is a museum full of saintly statues. The bedrooms are simple but clean, with black and white chequered floors, blue walls and fluttering curtains. There is an apartment-type place with attached bathroom and sitting area and a tiny kitchen. The Retiro is run by the immensely friendly and laid-back George D'Souza, who speaks excellent English and welcomes you into his Goan-born family. His sister cooks delicious meals and his brother, Almondo, has a taxi (reasonably priced). It is quirky and delightful, with pigs and chickens in the garden – definitely worth a visit for the open-minded. The word has got around so book well ahead. *Seafood barbecues on request.*

rooms	5 doubles.
price	Rs250–Rs300.
meals	Breakfast Rs50. Dinner from Rs75.
closed	Rarely.
directions	Above Diu museum inside Sao Tome Church. About 500m from town centre in direction of fort.

	Mr George D'Souza
tel	+91 2875 253 137
e-mail	georgedsouza@hotmail.com

Guesthouse

Garha Safari Lodge

Rudranimatadam, PO Kunariya, Bhuj, Gujarat

In drought-stricken Gujarat it is a pleasure to see water, which is why this position high above the dam is such a relief to the weary traveller. Pelicans may circle above you while you eat; there are bougainvillea and green lawns (perfect for moonlit picnics), swing chairs in the garden and a few arty statues scattered about the place. Randy, the golden retriever, appears to be permanently asleep on the veranda. Come with an open heart, for they lost much during the terrible earthquake of 2001 and are rebuilding vigorously. But they are already pretty well back on their feet and the residents of Bhuj often come out here to dine. Manhendra (aka Mike) used to work in travel and was educated in the USA; he's full of enterprise and ideas, such as jeep safaris and Kutchi and African (many Africans have settled here) dance events. The bedrooms in the kooba-style huts are attractive and simple, with carved wooden charpoy-style beds, your own little kitchen and lattice windows that let in the breeze. You can slip into the pool after a day exploring and learning about the Kutch.

rooms	9 doubles. Some a/c.
price	Rs2,300. Plus 15% tax. Peak season: October–February.
meals	Breakfast Rs175. Lunch Rs250. Dinner Rs300.
closed	Rarely.
directions	14km from Bhuj Township. 9km from airport.

	Mr Mike Vaghela
tel	+91 2832 269 467
fax	+91 79 6583 952
e-mail	gbglad1@sancharnet.in

Safari Lodge

Rann Riders

Dasada, Surendranagar, 382 750, Gujarat

The sea receded a few hundred years ago and left this fascinatingly barren land of salt and desert called the Little Rann of Kutch. Many of the villages were once ports and you can see the old port walls, forts and entrances. It's hard to imagine making a living here, but the area provides much of India's salt and the people, many of them nomadic, bring survival skills and traditions from Rajasthan and as far away as Afghanistan: exquisite embroidered textiles, silver jewellery and pottery, and colourful festivals. There is also, astonishingly, a vast variety of bird and animal life: pelicans, flamingoes, nilgai, gazelle, wolves, jackals and wild asses. The 13 huts were created in traditional Kutchi style, of mud and with roofs of terracotta tiles or grass. Inside are paintings on the walls and mirror-work on the wooden beams or doors, many of which are ornately carved. There are cane chairs and a writing desk, rugs on the floor – ample space; bathroom and open-air showers. The staff are formal, helpful and charming, and the surroundng area rich in interest and history. *Spend a night camping with a nomad community.*

rooms	13 cottages for 2.
price	Full-board only. Rs2,100. Includes safari. Plus 15% tax. Peak season: September–February.
meals	Included. Full-board.
closed	Rarely.
directions	135km from Rajkot airport; 35km from Surendranagar train station. Clearly signed just before entering Dasada.

	Mr Amit Thakore
tel	+91 2757 280 257
fax	+91 2757 280 457
e-mail	gopigroup@icenet.net
web	www.gopigroup.com

Resort

map 4   entry 102

Desert Coursers

Zainabad, Via. Patdi, District Surendranagar, 382 765, Gujarat

Dhanraj Malik has entertained National Geographic film crews, French photographers and Japanese equine researchers at his camp on the edge of Kutch; you, too, will be made welcome. A member of the ruling family that once governed this former princely state, Dhanraj grew up in Zainabad and is a gracious and knowledgeable host. Set off by camel or jeep to discover the wildlife of Rann: wild asses, black bucks, desert cats, flamingoes, cranes, waterfowl. Or visit the nomadic tribes – cattle-hunters, hunters and musicians – for an insight into their colourful cultures. Camp Zainabad has been running for 20 years; it's ethnic, well organised and the local guides look after you with minimum fuss. You sleep on spotless linen in thatch-roofed kooba huts (shower rooms attached) and there are concrete dormitory blocks for bigger groups. The restaurant – open sided with mud-coated seats and bright cushions – does hot meals served buffet-style; then get cosy round the camp fire when darkness falls. Dhanraj will take you on as many safaris you like – and you'll tire long before him.

rooms	22 doubles. Some a/c.
price	Full-board only, Rs3,800. Peak season: October–March.
meals	Included. Full-board.
closed	May–August.
directions	45km from Viramgram train station. Frequent State Transport buses run to Zainabad from Viramgram.

Mr Dhanraj Malik
tel +91 2757 241 333
fax +91 2757 241 334
e-mail zainabad@hotmail.com

Safari Lodge

E

HOW TO USE THIS BOOK

explanations

sample entry

① rooms

All rooms, in this example, are 'en suite'.

② room price

The price shown is for one night for two people sharing a room. A price range incorporates room differences. We say when price is per week.

③ meals

Prices are per person for a set two-course meal. If breakfast isn't included we give the price.

④ closed

When given in months, this means for the whole of the named months and the time in between.

⑤ directions

Use as a guide; the owner can give more details, as can their web sites.

⑥ map & entry numbers

Map page number; entry number.

⑦ type of place

⑧ price band

Price ranges, see last page of the book.

⑨ reservation number

⑩ symbols

See the last page of the book for fuller explanation:

🚭 smoking restrictions exist
💳 credit cards accepted
🍷 premises are licensed
🍴 food served
🐑 working farm
❄ air-conditioning
@ internet connection available
🏊 swimming pool

RAJASTHAN

Neemrana Fort-Palace
Neemrana, 301 705, Rajasthan

If the marauding hordes descending on this maze of a palace got as lost I did, the inhabitants might never have been defeated. The warren spreads over 10 layers, the ramparts and colonnaded walkways leading to open courtyards and as confusing as an Escher sketch. A sensitive, modest, yet beautiful restoration of near ruins, this 'non-hotel' is a powerful example of the triumph of good taste and moderation over the evils of standardised luxury. Built over ten years, the rooms have slowly taken shape, reflecting the mindfulness of history that runs throughout this special place. Some have their own jarokha balconies facing out onto plains peppered with plots of bright mustard, while others have bathrooms open to the skies. You can sleep in the old royal court, or in a tent atop the highest turret. All are simply furnished with colonial and Indian antiques in the eclectic style so well executed here. This place embodies holiday calm – there are no TVs or phones in the rooms, just endless corners, courtyards and lush gardens to sit and read – one of the few hotels where one can always have a turret or courtyard to oneself. *The smaller rooms are very cosy. Yoga, meditation.*

rooms	43: 21 doubles, 1 single, 18 suites, 1 family room for 4. Some A/C.
price	Doubles Rs2,200-Rs3,300. Singles Rs1,100. Suites Rs4,400-Rs6,600. Family room Rs12,000. Plus 10% tax. Peak season: September-March.
meals	Breakfast Rs200. Lunch, & dinner Rs400.
closed	Rarely.
directions	2 hours southwest of Delhi along NH8 to Jaipur. Turn right at the signs in Neemrana Village.

Mr Ramesh Dhabhai

tel	+91 1494 246 006
fax	+91 11 2435 1112
e-mail	sales@neemranahotels.com
web	www.neemranahotels.com
res. no.	+91 11 2435 6145

⑦ Heritage Hotel

⑥ entry 37 map 5   ⑨ E-F ⑧   ⑩

①
②
③
④
⑤

Photography by Robin Hamilton, Kipling Camp

madhya pradesh
maharashtra

Ahilya Fort
Maheshwar, 451 224, Madhya Pradesh

Few come to this region – they are missing much! Ancient Maheshwar, with its many-tiered temples and sacred river, is stunning. And the Ahilya Fort, perched high above the Narmada where there's always a breeze, is an enchanting place to stay. More home than fort, the building has been perfectly restored: pale old stone floors, ancient shuttered doors, an exquisite bathroom peeping through a carved arch, a white bloom in a glass vase. The tents – there are two – are the grandest ever. Richard Holkar is the driving force behind Ahilya and the Holkars are the kings of Indore; the family is more westernised today, indeed, Richard is married to an American. Thanks to the Holkar Trust they set up, the saree-weaving for which Maheshwar was once famous is back in full, glorious swing; don't miss the handloom centre nearby. Ahilya is special and full of intimate corners: lounge on silk cushions on the *jarokha* overlooking the water, dine amid greenery on the terrace (the food is good), dream in the soft-lit magic of the courtyard in the evening. *Two-day boat trips down the Narmada & organic farms trips on request.*

rooms	11: 9 doubles, 2 tents. All air-cooled.
price	Full-board only, $200. Activities included. Peak season: November–March.
meals	Included. Full-board.
closed	Rarely.
directions	Indore Airport: 45-minute flight from Bombay; 2 hours by car. Difficult to find. Call in advance if you are planning to find your own way.

	Mr Richard Holkar
tel	+91 11 2462 9592
fax	+91 11 2464 4547
e-mail	mail@ahilyafort.com
web	www.ahilyafort.com

Heritage Hotel

Kipling Camp

Mocha Village, Kanha National Park, Mandla District, 481 768, Madhya Pradesh

Herds of spotted deer mingle with blackbuck and barasingha in the Kanha meadows… in the jungle, there's the thrill of an unexpected encounter with a tiger. In spite of being one of the most inaccessible places on the planet, Kipling Camp, created by Anne and Bob Wright in 1990, has become a magnet for conservationists from all over world. The lodge and tents – you can sleep in either – sit in a clearing of *Jungle Book* jungle (hence the name). You may not live in the lap of luxury, but the cottages have a simple elegance: tiled roofs, whitewashed mud walls, traditional floors, wooden shutters. They stay coolish thoughout the day, and have bathrooms and electricity. Young British workers help create a house-party feel, dining at long tables is a convivial affair and you eat leisurely and well. Then it's round the camp fire to swap stories… and a chilly, exciting dawn rise to see and photograph the wildlife from your 4x4. (The tigers have been on the move long before sunrise.) The camp is also home to Tara, star of Mark Shands' *Travels On My Elephant*, and watching her bathe is one of the highlights of this trip.

rooms	24 doubles.
price	Full-board only, Rs9,000 including activities. Peak season: November-April.
meals	Included. Full-board.
closed	Mid-May-October.
directions	3 hours from Jabalpur; 5 hours from Nagpur.

	Ms Gemma Hyde
tel	+91 7649 277 218
fax	+91 7649 277218
e-mail	info@kiplingcamp.com
web	www.kiplingcamp.com

Safari Lodge

map 6   entry 105

Gordon House Hotel

5 Battery Street, Appolo Bunder, Colaba, Mumbai, 400 039, Maharashtra

You'd never guess what lies behind the façade of this unassuming white tower block: two buzzing street-level restaurants, three floors of 'themed' bedrooms, and an easy-mannered young staff in white suits and brightly coloured shirts. Everything about Mumbai's only boutique hotel oozes trendiness. If the idea of a fashionable themed hotel fills you with dread, fear not – the place doesn't take itself too seriously, and the themes won't make you cringe. A tapestry in the Versailles suite reads "It ain't easy being King", and the Mediterranean, Country and Scandanavian rooms differ only in clever twists on the interior detail; a ruffled curtain instead of a wicker blind, or plain white bathroom tiles rather than colourful floral ones. All the rooms are a good size, and are full of little treats: a bowl of sweets by the bed, 'smellies' in the bathroom. Rooms are on three levels around the central atrium, which floods the jazzy reception with natural light. Stylish and immaculate, this place won't give you the most Indian of experiences, but an indulgent continental one. India Gate is just round the corner. Great fun.

rooms	29: 28 doubles, 1 suite.
price	Rs5,000. Suites Rs10,000. Plus 6.3% tax.
meals	Lunch from Rs300. Dinner from Rs350.
closed	Rarely.
directions	Right behind Colaba's Regal Cinema, very near The Gateway of India.

Ms Gayle Almeida

tel	+91 22 2287 1122
fax	+91 22 2287 2026
e-mail	dutymanager@ghhotel.com
web	www.ghhotel.com

Boutique Hotel

The Verandah in the Forest

Barr House, Matheran, District Raigarh, 410 102, Maharashtra

Deep in primary forest, reached only by foot, palanquin or on horseback, the Verandah in the Forest is well named. This is a most opulent veranda, framed in decorative white wooden balustrades and tiled in large floral-shaped terracotta tiles — perfect camouflage for the pervasive red dust of the forest. Here you may lounge on planters' chairs, lime soda in hand, and stretch your eyes over the view. Dine out here, or indoors, sharing the long table with other guests. The food is delicious. The airy drawing room echoes beneath a huge vaulted ceiling and is decked with coffee-table books about the history of the region. Matheran is the last pedestrian hill station in Asia, and the house — the second one in Matheran - was built in 1852 by a British colonel, to escape the heat of Bombay — only an hour's drive but many worlds away. The hire of a horse, whether pony or local racehorse, can be arranged by the hotel, and there are beautiful walks. Retire to your four-poster bed in the large, simple but tastefully-furnished rooms and sleep soundly... you may be woken by monkeys scrabbling over the rooftop at dawn.

rooms	11: 6 doubles, 1 single, 4 suites.
price	Rs2,500. Singles Rs2,000. Suites Rs3,000-Rs4,000. Plus 6% tax. Peak season: September-March.
meals	Lunch Rs275. Dinner Rs325.
closed	Rarely.
directions	150km from Mumbai.

	Mr Kiran
tel	+91 2148 230 296
fax	+91 11 2435 1112
e-mail	sales@neemranahotels.com
web	www.neemranahotels.com
res. no.	+91 11 2435 6145

Heritage Hotel

E   map 4   entry 107

Photography by Toby Sawday

goa

Fort Tiracol

Tiracol, Perney, 403 524, Goa

You expect a fort to be austere and uncluttered, but not elegant like this one. Although it is a national monument, with all the restrictions on change that implies, they have managed to repaint and refurbish every corner, with yellow walls and wrought-iron furniture giving the most delightful mood to the building. Each room has its own balcony, with the best views in all Goa. The Fort is on a river estuary and you can see down into it and along a length of coast and out to sea – breathtaking. You can even see the fishermen at work on the sandbanks, and you can take dolphin-watching trips out to sea. From the rooftop restaurant/café there are those same, eye-stretching views. Within the fort's compound is an old chapel to which the townspeople still retain the keys and where Mass is held on weekends and Wednesdays. The whole place is open to tourists so there are people coming and going all the time. The owners live away but the manager is extremely friendly and helpful. A busy and unusual place, more like a Portuguese pousada than anything you might expect in India.

rooms	7: 4 doubles, 2 suites, 1 family room for 4.
price	Half-board only $110. Plus 10% tax.
meals	Included. Half-board. Lunch $10-$20.
closed	Rarely.
directions	From Panjim you go to Calangute then Siolim on your way to Tiracol.

Mr Vivek Tiracol

tel	+91 832 2276 793
fax	+91 832 2276 792
e-mail	nilaya@sancharnet.in

Heritage Hotel

Olive Ridley

Vithaldas Vaddo, Morjim, 403 512, Goa

The best way to spot the endangered Olive Ridley turtle nesting on the Morjim beach in November is to stay at the guesthouse of the same name. Delightful, Belgian Isla (known as Lulu), convent-educated in Surrey and in Bombay, brims with interest and talent: she likes art, design, poetry, yoga. Cooking is another love, and she buys food daily from the market for her restaurant. The whitewashed little house by the beach has a garden bursting with white bougainvillea and palms, while inside is as stylish as can be: big beds on stone platforms, curving passageways, plants, books, shutters and shells. Lulu designs with natural materials and uses concrete in bathrooms "for convenience" – the effect is stunning: huge sinks, delightful showers, pebbles for foot massage set in the floor. Shuttered doors open on to a cool veranda with chairs; at the back is the much used herb garden. You beakfast at Lulu's renowned beachside restaurant; lunch on organic salads, French sauces, crayfish, pasta. Come to meet like-minded people, and book in for courses on yoga and meditation, theatre, poetry, cookery. Monsoon retreats, too.

rooms	2 doubles.
price	Rs3,000. (Price may increase).
meals	Breakfast, lunch & dinner from Rs100.
closed	May-October.
directions	On the beach front on the Mandrem road out of Morjim.

	Ms Isla 'Lulu' Polak
tel	+91 832 2246 732
fax	+91 832 2246 733
e-mail	islapolak@hotmail.com

Guesthouse

E **map 9   entry 109**

Laguna Anjuna

Soranto Vado, Anjuna, 403 509, Goa

Lazy days! This unconventional, architect-designed hotel is the ultimate, laid-back place to stay. It sits in a coconut grove verdant with bamboo, frangipani, banana and mango, there's an intimate central courtyard, rustic cottages to hide away in, and a delightful, meandering pool. The cottages, made of local laterite stone, differ in shape and size; all have whitewashed walls, wooden rafters, pillars, arches, domes, split levels and masses of space. Furniture is wrought-iron, colours are bright, materials natural. The hands-on owner-manager Farrokh is as relaxed as they come, and guests an eclectic mix: motorbike riders in studded leather, international chefs, visiting DJs (welcome to play their music in the bar). There are views onto a bowl of paddy fields that stretch to the hills, and a sociable restaurant with old-world style and grace. Don't miss the Thai buffets at weekends! The whole place blends in perfectly with Anjuna, Goa's hippy heart, and should you tire of the easy living at Languna, the beach is a sprint away. Ideal for those who thrive on informality and spontaneity. *Water sports, cycling, casino trips.*

rooms	24: 17 cottages for 2, 7 cottages for 4.
price	Rs6,000. Cottages Rs8,400. Peak season: 20 December– 5 January.
meals	Lunch & dinner Rs250.
closed	Rarely.
directions	Ask anyone in Anjuna village to direct you.

	Ms Sheela Pillai
tel	+91 832 2274 305
fax	+91 832 2274 305
e-mail	info@lagunaanjuna.com
web	www.lagunaanjuna.com

Resort

Palacete Rodrigues

Mazal Vaddo, Anjuna, Goa

Mrs Iria Da Costa celebrated her wedding here; 40 years on she lives with her grandson and shares their much-loved home with guests. She is a watercolorist (her paintings decorate the corridors), proud of the 200-year-old Portuguese mansion and full of stories about the old days – the place resonates with family history. High-ceilinged bedrooms have polished red floors and soft lighting; some have four-posters with canopies, others their own bit of veranda. Large living rooms are busy with carved and polished pieces, and small collections to take your fancy – shells, pottery hot-water bottles, old terracotta jars. There are plants everywhere, an inner courtyard garden, a lawn with plastic chairs, and an imposing 'conference room' for dinner parties on busy nights. You are in a quiet part of town, yet the famous beaches are a walk away. It is a homely and comfortable place to stay, and 'Madam' and her staff are the icing on the cake. Make sure you spend some time with this gentle elderly lady: it will be both educational and entertaining.

rooms	15: 11 doubles, 3 suites, 1 single. Some a/c.
price	Rs650. Single Rs550. Suites Rs750–Rs850. Peak season: December–March.
meals	No meals. Anjun's cafés are a short walk.
closed	Rarely.
directions	9km from Mazal. 1.5km from Anjuna beach.

	Mrs Iria Da Costa
tel	+91 832 2273 358
e-mail	palaceterodrigues@hotmail.com
web	www.palaceterodrigues.com

Guesthouse

map 9   entry 111

Hotel Bougainvillea/Granpa's Inn

Gaumwadi, Anjuna, Goa

It doesn't matter what you call this place, it will soon feel like home – thanks to your lovely hosts, Lucindo and Bettina. He is a direct descendant of the family that built this 200-year-old, Portuguese-styled Goan mansion and you can see the ancestral portraits inside; Lucindo knows all the history. The house has recently been modernised but the old terracotta tiles, lofty rooms and stained-glass windows remain. It's a cool, rustic, one-storey hotel, with good-sized rooms clustered around a central courtyard; bedrooms are light and airy, with cheerful bedspreads and plants and each with its own piece of veranda. There's no one to rush you – breakfast lasts as long as you like – and the food is good, with much coming from the Farias' farm: chickens and cashews, avocados and almonds, fruits and spices. On some days there are barbecues with a band. Cool off with a cocktail by the pool, lounge in the lovely, lush gardens, wander indoors for billiards or yoga. Then spin off on a bike (they'll lend you one) to discover Anjuna's flea-market - and the heady, hippy delights of the coconut-palm-fringed beach.

rooms	10: 8 doubles, 2 suites.
price	Rs1,800. Suites Rs2,500. Peak season: October–March.
meals	Lunch & dinner Rs150.
closed	Rarely.
directions	3km from Anjuna Church on the Mapusa-Anjuna Road. 7km from Mapusa town.

	Mr Lucindo & Bettina Faria
tel	+91 832 2273 270
fax	+91 832 2274 370
e-mail	granpas@hotmail.com
web	goacom.com/hotels/granpas

Guesthouse

F

Nilaya Hermitage
Bhati, Arpora, 403 518, Goa

An exquisite retreat on the crest of a tropical hill. The hotel was designed by Goan architect Dean D'Cruz; German-born designer Claudia added the final touches. Cosmically themed with fantasy elements, bedrooms have vibrant colours, white muslin, bathrooms of mosaic; some are air-conditioned, all are large and cool and connect around a curving central pool. Be charmed by bowls of floating flowers, sun-shaped lamps, teak columns from a temple in Kerala… and glorious views over paddy fields and wooded hills to the glittering sea. Hari and Claudia Ajwani are not always present, but you are cared for by young, friendly staff in blue kurtas and white sarees. Food is a subtle blend of eastern and western flavours, masterminded by a French chef. There's no starched formality and the atmosphere is more house party than hotel; dine in your sarong, or by the pool, or in your room. Breakfast lasts as long as you like. And should you finally tire of the pleasures of the gym, steam room, sauna and Ayurvedic treatments – or sunning yourself by the heavenly decked pool – the coast is a 10-minute drive. *Children over 12 welcome.*

rooms	12 doubles. Some a/c.
price	Full-board only $280. Over Christmas & New Year up to $450.
meals	Included. Full-board.
closed	Rarely.
directions	Pick-up from Arpora is included in the price.

	Mr Ramakant Pal
tel	+91 832 2276 793
fax	+91 832 2276 792
e-mail	nilaya@sancharnet.in
web	www.nilayahermitage.com

Boutique Hotel

  map 9   entry 113

Casa Palacio Siolim House

Waddi, Siolim, Bardez, 403 517, Goa

Much-travelled Varun Sood, a businessman from Delhi, discovered the neglected, 300-year-old villa on one of his travels, then transformed it into a haven of luxury. Once belonging to the Governor of Macau, the *casa de sobrado*-style building has been properly renovated with walls of shell and lime plaster, and windowpanes of oyster shell. It's a spoiling place – seven big suites named after 17th-century trading ports, fabulous food, solicitous staff. Terracotta pots sit under shapely white pillars in the central courtyard with fountain and bougainvillea; more pots nudge the pool. Bedrooms, two on the top floor, some around the courtyard, have white walls, dark wooden or tiled floors, rosewood cupboards and wrought-iron beds hung with muslin. There's a sitting room and a library with chess, a restaurant with glass-topped tables. Dine on caught-that-day fish: pomfret, snapper, bass, mussels, crab and the biggest prawns ever seen. Siolim is a small village with a large Catholic church (services are in English at weekends), bustling Anjuna is three kilometres away, Calangute beach ten. *Tailor-made tours to see the local areas.*

rooms	7 doubles.
price	$125-$155. Plus 8% tax. Peak season: 19 December–10 January.
meals	Lunch & dinner $15.
closed	Rarely.
directions	At entrance to Siolim village just north of Chapora river in north Goa.

Mr Varun Sood
tel +91 832 2272 138
fax +91 832 2272 941
e-mail info@siolimhouse.com
web www.siolimhouse.com

Guesthouse

B-C

Goofy's Countryside Hermitage

Sal Village, P.O. Assonora, Bardez, North Goa, 403 503, Goa

Godfrey 'Goofy' Laurence discovered these 20 acres while scouting for film locations in an earlier life. Now he has his own inland paradise, or 'paddy bowl', minutes from beaches and at the end of a red dirt road. The cluster of one-storey cottages blends quaintly into the landscape (at its lushest and most peaceful in the monsoon months). Comfort is ethnic within these four mud walls, with hessian curtains, terracotta lamps, beds "big enough for foreigners" and blue-tiled bathrooms. The *machhan* (treetop house) – perfect for honeymooners – has dreamy views. Goofy oversees the cooking: choose your favourite spices from your garden and he'll toss them in. Then dine in the grass-roofed restaurant with a safari feel… on okra, rice, king fish and prawns. Much of the food comes from the farm, including the Jersey milk. Goofy sorts plastics, returns organic waste to the soil, redirects water to the gardens and has made sure the pool is chlorine-free (it's ionised instead). No loud music, no TV, just peace, the odd piping of the flute as you sip a cool beer. When you leave, plant a sapling in memory of your stay.

rooms	12 cottages for 2. 1 a/c.
price	Full-board only Rs3,600–Rs4,800. Peak season: 15 October–15 April.
meals	Included. Full-board.
closed	Rarely.
directions	12km from Thivim train station, 20km from Mapusa.

Godfrey Laurence
tel +91 832 2389 228
e-mail goofyscounty@hotmail.com
web www.goofyshermitage.com

Ecolodge

Corjuem Island, Bardez, Goa

Though we were missing some details, including a name, as we went to press we could not leave this wonderful place out of the book. The choice of setting is inspired and a 40m-long covered veranda is the place to sit and dream to the sweet smells of jasmine and frangipani. Unfussy decorative touches – copper pots, bowls of floating flowers, cane lampshades – sooth, as do the views of the river, buffalos grazing and distant forest. You can breakfast on homemade strawberry jam, lashings of real coffee and Goan bread. Goan-born of a Belgian family, Lulu grew up in England and her approach to guests is very warm; nothing is too much trouble and her new venture looks set to be a real success. Only traditional materials have been used (apart from in the bathrooms): laterite stone, high wooden ceilings and tiled roofs. All the new furniture, divans and charpoys, is copied from old designs, to preserve those techniques. Bedrooms, each with a private balcony, sit around an inner courtyard where four fountains play so there is a constant, restful sound of flowing water. There are plans for cookery courses, concerts, a library and star-gazing.

rooms	6 doubles.
price	From Rs5,000.
meals	Breakfast, lunch & dinner from Rs150.
closed	May–October.
directions	Turn right off NH7 North from Panjim, opposite turning to Mapuza. Continue for 6km to Aldona village, from where you catch the tiny ferry to Corjuem Island. It's a 10-minute rickshaw journey from here.

	Ms Isla 'Lulu' Polak
tel	+91 832 2246 732
fax	+91 832 2246 733
e-mail	islapolak@hotmail.com

Guesthouse

Kerkar Retreat

Gaurawaddo, Calangute, 403 516, Goa

A little dose of culture in the big beach party that is Goa. Subodh Kerkar gave up medicine to pursue his passion for art – sculpture, furniture, painting, pottery, architecture – and here are the results. On the ground floor of the elegant, Indo-Portuguese-styled house are a gallery – a showcase for his work – and a café, all blue walls and metal chairs, inspired by the sea. Upstairs the generous, colourful bedrooms have big beds on glazed floors, soft lights, paper lanterns, gauze curtains and art by Subodh and his father. The staff are kind, the fish and vegetable curry truly local, and there's a kitchen should you choose to rustle up your own king prawns and crabs (fresh from unpolluted Goan waters, they're as good as can be). Get stuck into philosophy or art with a book from the library; relax with a drink from the honesty bar; salute the sun on the rooftop terrace under the shady palms. There's even a studio where you can hone your pottery or painting skills and, in summer, open-air performances of music and dance. No matter if the electricity fails, they'll carry on by candlelight! The bustling, beautiful beach is a walk away.

rooms	5 doubles. Some a/c.
price	Rs3,500.
	Peak season: 20 December-10 January.
meals	Breakfast Rs250. Lunch & dinner Rs250.
closed	Rarely.
directions	40km from airport; 15km from Panaji; 300m from beach.

	Dr Subodh Kerkar
tel	+91 832 2276 017
fax	+91 832 2276 509
e-mail	subodhkerkar@satyam.net.in
web	www.subodhkerkar.com

Guesthouse

Marbella Guesthouse

Sinquerim-Candolim, 403 515, Goa

The search for authencity is serious. Dian and Monika collected the white borders on the roof from old houses, as well as pillars and furniture. The ceramic tiles on the courtyard table are from North Goa and the flooring was done by a company that still uses old stencils from houses that were built at the turn of the last century. It is unashamedly romantic, with six luxurious suites individually decorated and named (Bougainvillea, Moghul etc). The Penthouse is especially lavish – with marble floors and huge views. The house itself was built not long ago, to resemble an old Goan mansion. There is plenty of space, but you can mingle with other guests in a central courtyard entirely screened by greenery. There is no official reception area and cats and dogs doze in and around the house. The kitchen is a French-style live-in one where you can watch the chefs prepare your meal. This whole wonderful place is down a quiet lane at the edge of Candolim village and away from the tourist hum. The touch of the exotic may stem from Dian's half-German background and his passion for the guitar – rock, jazz and blues. Come and play.

rooms	6 suites.
price	Rs1,300-Rs2,300.
	Peak season: December-February.
meals	Breakfast Rs150. Lunch & dinner Rs250.
closed	Rarely.
directions	Turn right at Joe Joe's on the main road towards Fort Aguada Beach Resort. Guesthouse 500m along, one of the last properties on the right. Take a taxi.

	Dian & Monika Singh
tel	+91 832 2247 9551
fax	+91 832 2276 509
e-mail	shrisai@goatelecom.com

Guesthouse

Panjim Inn & Panjim Pousada
E-212 31st January Road, Fontainhas, Panjim, 403 001, Goa

These two are perfect if you want a taste of Panjim's colourful Portuguese past. They're close to each other, in Fontainhas, the throbbing heart of the Latin Quarter; an area of sleeping dogs and gonging chapels. The Inn is Goa's first, and only, official Heritage Hotel, a 300-year-old mansion built by the current owners' family. It's filled with handsome colonial rosewood furniture; most rooms have four-poster beds with colourful covers, and curtains billowing from wooden lattice window frames. Two upstairs rooms have private balconies and there's a large veranda restaurant; the cooking is Goan or international, and good. The nearby Pousada – choose this for greater peace and quiet – is a Hindu house (in a largely Catholic area), also recently renovated by Mr Sukhija and in a similar style with carved rosewood cupboards and four-poster beds. Downstairs rooms can use the garden and also open onto the inner courtyard – an eclectic art gallery; upstairs rooms share a balcony overlooking the garden. Mr Sukhija is as interesting as his houses; you're likely to find him sipping a watermelon juice with guests on the first-floor veranda of the Inn. *Dolphin watching & bird spotting.*

rooms	22 doubles. Some a/c.
price	Rs720-Rs2,000. Plus 10% tax. Peak season: 20 December-20 February.
meals	Breakfast Rs150. Lunch & dinner Rs200-Rs250.
closed	Rarely.
directions	In Fontainhas (Latin Quarter of Panjim) next to People's High School.

Mr Ajit Sukhija

tel	+91 832 2226 523
fax	+91 832 2228 136
e-mail	panjimin@sancharnet.in
web	www.panjiminn.com

Guesthouse

Coconut Creek

Bimut Ward, Bogmalo, 403 806, Goa

Paradise, says the brochure – not far off if your paradise includes cottages among swaying coconut palms beside the water, and being lulled to sleep by the rustle of the wind. It is ineffably lovely, state-of-the-art and yet respectful of the environment and the essence of Goa. Lynne and Agnello are a Scottish-Goan couple who have thrown everything at this place. It is a 'resort', so you must expect such things as quiz nights and activities, but it is exquisitely done and some of the profits go to a local orphanage. Each house has two storeys, the ground floor air-conditioned and the upper floor with ceiling fans and big French windows. The taste is minimalist and exotically eastern. One bedroom has a mattress on a raised wooden platform stretching across the room, simple white bed linen and pale yellow walls with niched arches for candles and flowers. You cross the pool on little wooden bridges, and the sea, and Bogmalo beach – a few hundred yards long, and little-spoiled – is only minutes away. Lynne is wonderfully friendly and down to earth and can give you Baskins & Robbins ice cream.

rooms	20 doubles. Some a/c.
price	$65-$85. A/c rooms $80-$100. Prices rise considerably for Christmas & New Year.
meals	Breakfast from Rs80. Lunch, & dinner from Rs200.
closed	Rarely.
directions	20-minute drive from Vasco railway station, 2-minute walk from the beach.

Lynn & Agnello D'Cruz
tel +91 832 2538 100
fax +91 832 2538 880
e-mail joets@sancharnet.in

Guesthouse

entry 120　map 9　 D–E

Joet's

Baillichal Ward, Bogmalo, 403 806, Goa

Right on the beach at Bogmalo with Coconut Creek a few yards down (owned by the same delightful Lynne and Angello), an unusual meeting of Scotland and Goa. His family are fishermen so there is a constant supply of prime fish to the restaurant: fresh prawns, shark, kingfish, crab. People come from far and wide to eat here: the reputation for food is enviable. Joet's is a guesthouse, on a more modest scale than Coconut Creek – though you may share the pool if the sea isn't enough – and one of the few signs of tourism in the area. But it's where it all began and it has been a huge success, starting from truly humble beginnings as a fisherman's shack. It still stands alone among battered fishing boats and wind-bent palms, and the beach is pretty much yours – a treat in Goa. It is light and colourful, simple and charming – with blue tiles in the restaurant, blue bedspreads, tiled floors, fans and mini-bars and little balconies for the rooms. The noise of giant waves tumbling onto the sand will lull you to deep sleep.

rooms	12 doubles.
price	Rs1,200. Suite Rs1,500. Peak season: 19 December-3 January.
meals	Breakfast from Rs50. Lunch & dinner from Rs150.
closed	May-September.
directions	20-minute drive from Vasco railway station, 2-minute walk from the beach.

Lynn & Agnello D'Cruz

tel	+91 832 2538 036
fax	+91 832 2538 880
e-mail	joets@sancharnet.in

Guesthouse

 map 9 entry 121

Bhakti Kutir

296 Patnem, Colomb, Canacona, 403 702, Goa

Ute has started a school on the premises for her children; yours may want to pop into a class. She is German, and has become engagingly Indian after so many years here. She and Panta have created a remarkable place: 22 thatched huts, eight of them two-storey, in leafy surrounds teeming with birdlife at the southern end of Palolem beach, five minutes' walk from the town. There are candles and mosquito nets, hessian curtains and low divans, stone floors inlaid with shells; all have their own bathrooms, some outside but private. Ute and Panta are serious about environmental sensitivity: the loos use a biodegrading system, much to the delight of visitors, the bathrooms are 'bucket bath', vegetables are organic and home-grown, fish is caught that day. There is a tailor on site and handwork shops for clothes, a mud bath, a steam bath, Ayurvedic massage, a library and a concert area. Everything is made from natural and local materials – mud, coconut wood, eucalyptus, bamboo – to keep it natural, simple and comfortable. It works brilliantly. *Dolphin watching and fishing.*

rooms	22 doubles.
price	Rs1,200-2,500. Plus 8% tax. Peak season: 15 December-March.
meals	Breakfast, lunch & dinner from Rs80.
closed	During monsoon.
directions	By taxi from Canacona train station. Regular trains & buses (every 15 minutes) leave Margoa for Canacona.

Ute & Panta Ferao
tel	+91 832 2643 469
e-mail	bhaktikutir@yahoo.com

Hotel

Casa de Morgado

House 115, Sontrant, Cortalim, 403 710, Goa

This 'house of friendly spirits' is just that: beaming Beulah runs it with her mother, two small cricket-mad sons, and friends as backup. She does everything – scooter pick-ups, housework, room design. There's a lovely family feel at Morgado... Beulah, a traditional Catholic, likes quiet after 11pm, but you really can come and go as you please. This is also a rare chance to experience one of the oldest houses in Goa; the 400-year-old ancestral home – part Portuguese, part Moorish – has been declared an official heritage house. It sits at the foot of a hill, overlooking an expanse of green paddy fields, and is a mile from the village where friendly locals take your hand and wish you well – in Konkani! You'll get a real taste of Goan village life. Bathrooms are modern; bedrooms are a good size with white walls, red-oxide floors, plain wrought-iron beds and share the veranda that wraps itself around the place. Breakfast is fruit and eggs several ways; there's home-cooking for dinner, red wine and fruit. Beulah, kind and helpful, provides excellent daily itineraries. *Boat rides on the river.*

rooms	3 doubles.
price	Rs990. Peak season: 1 September–30 March.
meals	Breakfast Rs50. Lunch & dinner Rs250.
closed	Rarely.
directions	12km from Dabolim International Airport, midway between Panjim & Margao. Call for directions.

	Mrs Beulah Athayde Gomes
tel	+91 832 2550 216
e-mail	beula_h@yahoo.com

Homestay

Photography by Toby Sawday

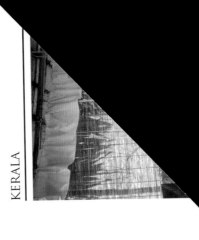

KERALA

Taj 28th
hin Taj 29th, 30th
N Taj 31/12 - 2/1
2/1 Cruise
8

kerala

⊙ Old Harbour 2 + 3 Jan £78
✱ ⊙ Hotel Kadaltheeram Res 3-5 Jan
3km from Varkala
Not avail 90 BBP

Villa Jacaranda
Swaswara ✱ ⊙ Taj Garden £115
Marari Beach Resort Theh.
Taj Garden Retreat Th. 31/12 - 2/1
Pollethai Beach
Taj Garden Retreat Varkala
Kovalan
Spice Village
Paradisa Plantation

Green Magic Nature Resort

Thalipuzha, Lakkidi (P.O.), Vythiri, Wayanad District, 695 001, Kerala

The stuff of dreams. Real tree houses reached by rope bridges and wicker baskets on pulleys, 30 metres up in the forest canopy where running water, electricity, clean linen, double beds and a sitting room make the Swiss Family Robinson look like amateurs. You bumble off the main road into real Indian jungle – towering giants almost devoured by vines, a mess of green and birdsong – part of the mystical Western Ghats. The ethos is 'eco' and deeply so – local tribes have been involved in the gradual crafting of this place, the materials are mostly from the forest and the visible impact on the area is barely discernible. The food is simple, delicious and utterly Keralan – almost all of it is organic and is served on banana leaves to minimise the need for wasteful washing. You can be as active as you please: nature trails criss-cross the forest, designed partly to show you the huge bio-diversity; the river (for swimming) is right there; guides are at hand to help make sense of the incredible bird life. Not all the rooms are in tree houses. The eco-lodges down on the forest floor are delightful, though less awesome. *Great trekking.*

rooms	10 doubles (4 treehouses, 6 eco-lodges).
price	Full-board only. Treehouses $180. Eco-lodges $110. Plus 15% tax. Peak season: 15 December–15 January.
meals	Included. Full-board.
closed	Rarely.
directions	From Vythiri (2 hours from Calicut) 3km to Thalipuza. A jeep will pick you up from the Gandhi Gramam spice shop to take you the last 6km.

Mr V K Moorthy
tel	+91 471 2330 437
fax	+91 471 2331 507
e-mail	tourindia@vsnl.com
web	www.tourindiakerala.com

Ecolodge

Rain Country Resorts

Lakkidi, Wayanad District, 637 576, Kerala

Swirling mists and echo-ing monkey calls weave through the majestic Wayanad valley, and low lamps illuminate the dirt trail that carves its way through this wonderfully un-resorty 'resort'. In a splendid departure from the world of 'pack 'em in': Rain Country's 20-acre valley is shared by just four cottages and you'd have to yodel to be heard by your neighbours. Tiled roof cottages are simple and comfortable 'heritage' affairs with either one, two or three double rooms. Although less private, the triple cottage makes interesting use of the space; there are semi-open bathrooms and a porch, a *charupadi*, juts out from the veranda. Potter across a wooden bridge to the small thatched dining room – the kitchen will spice up any successful catches from the natural pool, which is also good for swimming. Stroll undisturbed through the grounds or attempt one of the stunning walks. Die-hard trekkers should try the Chembra peak; at 2,100m it's the highest in Wayanad. It's impossible to rush here; just pause and take a deep breath – and what good air it is! Spectacular.

rooms	8 doubles.
price	Rs2,000-Rs2,500. Peak season: October-May.
meals	Breakfast Rs100. Lunch & dinner Rs150.
closed	Rarely.
directions	60km from Calicut. Pick up will be arranged from Lakkidi, 3km from resort.

	Mr E K Anil
tel	+91 4936 255 286
fax	+91 4936 255 286
e-mail	resorts@raincountryresort.com
web	www.raincountryresort.com

Resort

 map 9 entry 125

Vythiri Resort

Vythiri, Lakkidi P.O., Wayanad District, 673 576, Kerala

A deep, cool relief from the oppressive heat of the plains is provided by the misty green of the Wayanad forests. The Paadi rooms were once watering holes for plantation workers; they have now been cleverly converted to create cossetting bedrooms, with a bed raised off the floor and a small arch with overhead beams leading to the bathroom. The huts and cottages have been recently built, but the surrounding forest has been left undisturbed – polished bamboo doors lead into wonderfully comfortable rooms you may share with a tree or huge slab of rock. Local, naturally tinted mud dresses each cottage in vast orange swirls, all rustic 'designer'. There's no plastic here, just terracotta water jugs and mugs and bamboo light fittings. Cottages have vast balconies where monkeys tumble with gay abandon. The 'resortiness' is subtle and unobtrusive; yes, there is a health club, plus business centre and TV room, but this cannot detract from the arresting beauty of the place. There are wonderful walks to natural pools and waterfalls – just don't forget the leech socks. *Serena Spa treatment.*

rooms	32 cottages for 2.
price	Full-board only, $75-$90.
meals	Included. Full-board.
closed	Rarely.
directions	25km from Calicut airport. A jeep will take you the few bumpy km from Vythiri town to the resort, or pick-up can be arranged from the train station or airport.

	Mr Roy Chacko
tel	+91 4936 255 366
fax	+91 4936 255 368
e-mail	vythiri@serenaspa.com
web	www.vythiriresort.com
res. no.	+91 484 2356 249

Resort

Tranquil, Plantation Hideaway

Kuppamudi Coffee Estate, Kolagapara P.O., Kolagapara, Wayanad District, 673 591, Kerala

Three thousand feet up in the Western Ghats, this unusually comfortable homestay sits hidden away among the coffee bushes and rainforest of the Kuppamudi Coffee Estate. Many people consider this one of the most unspoilt Keralan regions; the true magic is only beginning to be realised by travellers. Undulating hills, wild jungle, and cardamom and tea plantations roll away from this 70-year-old plantation bungalow, which has been beautifully restored. Each of the eight rooms is different, imaginatively decorated and wonderfully cosy. The breezy veranda runs around the house, where cane planters beg to be lounged in; trekking and plantation walks are there for the more active and the Edakal Caves are within walking distance. Both Victor and Ranjini sweep you into their lives: this is a working plantation. More luxurious than most family homes, this special place has brought true professionalism to a rather informal accommodation scene, and has just won the 2003 state prize for the best homestay, which it surely deserves. *Trekking and birdwatching in the Wild Life Sanctuary.*

rooms	8: 7 doubles, 1 family room (double plus sofabed).
price	Full-board only, $225. Family room $325. Peak season: December–March.
meals	Included. Full-board.
closed	Rarely.
directions	260km (5 hours) from Bangalore. 117km (2 hours) from Mysore. 130km (3 hours) from Calicut Airport. 105km (2 hours) from Calicut train station.

	Victor & Ranjini Dey
tel	+91 4936 220 244
fax	+91 4936 222 358
e-mail	tranquil@satyam.net.in
web	www.tranquilresort.com

Homestay

  map 9   entry 127

Costa Malabari
Near Adikadalayi Temple, Kannur, 670 007, Kerala

Absolute bliss. If you want somewhere off the tourist trail, and are a fan of 'small is beautiful', you'll love Costa Malabari – hemmed in by cashew and coconut plantations and an idyllic five-minute amble from empty beaches. Once a power shed, then a coconut-oil processing outfit, this unpretentious guest house still has a lofty warehouse feel, so don't come looking for luxury. Pastel pink walls soften the cavernous dining hall, and a warm yellow washes the four snug and simple bedrooms. Kurien is intelligent and welcoming and his inventive twists on traditional recipes make every meal a feast – the tropical fruit ice creams are delicious. All ingredients are bought locally, staff are from the neighbouring village, and the guesthouse hasn't expanded in its six years – the result is a respectful, easy, and unobtrusive relationship with the community. You may get invited to local events or weddings, and are well placed to find out about Keralan festivals; Kurien has written a book on them and has clocked up visits to thousands of temples. A getaway in the best possible sense, wonderful people, and a great ethos.

rooms	4 doubles.
price	Full-board only, Rs2,000. Peak dates: 15 October–14 February.
meals	Included. Full-board.
closed	June–July.
directions	8km south of Kannur train station. Please call.

Mr P J Varghese

tel	
e-mail	touristdesk@satyam.net.in
web	www.costamalabari.com
res. no.	+91 484 2371 761

Guesthouse

Ayisha Manzil

Court Road, Telicherry, 670 101, Kerala

The house on the hill was built by an English colonel-turned-cinnamon-planter in 1862. In 1900 it was bought by Mr Moosa's grandfather. The house itself is neither large nor exceptional, though the bedrooms and bathrooms are on a grand scale, and it is stuffed with the original colonial furniture. Come for Mr Moosa – a lovely man, passionate about Keralan culture and proud of the martial dance displays (for which the area is famous) that he arranges for guests. He is a hugely resourceful and engaging host, so make the most of him. You'll eat well here, too: Faiza, the lady of the house, serves delicious food and specialises in Mapalla cuisine, the local Muslim cooking. This coastal area, surprisingly overlooked by travellers, is where the old British trading ports used to be; now Mr Moosa and his heritage homestay are beginning to put the region back on the map. Ayisha overlooks the vast Arabian sea, with a glorious stretch of unpopulated virgin beach nearby. Make time, too, for the 1750 Protestant church, and the 450-year-old mosque, owned by the Moosa family, built of rosewood and copper. *Cookery courses available.*

rooms	6 doubles.
price	Full-board only, $150.
meals	Included. Can be arranged for non-residents. Lunch & dinner from $15.
closed	Rarely.
directions	Close to Telicherry town. 90km from Calicut airport.

	Mr C P Moosa
tel	+91 490 2341 590
fax	+91 490 2341 590
e-mail	cpmoosa@rediffmail.com

Harivihar Ayurvedic Heritage Home

Bilathikulam, Calicut, 673 006, Kerala

Inviting lawns tumble around this horse-shoe-shaped house and if you can resist the charms of the natural rocky pool there are plenty of shady reading spots under jackfruit and mango trees. Inside, an oasis of calm: oceans of gleaming red oxide floors swell beneath fresh white walls, and the veranda oil lamps spill light onto huge bright canvases of temple icons and dancing forms. Simple, almost monastic bedrooms, some with great garden views, a high-ceilinged dining room that opens to the lawn, and a meditation and yoga room that presides serenely over all, from the top of the house. All is tranquil here; it's easy to forget that you're in the centre of Calicut – and hard to believe that until the early 1980s almost 60 members of Neethi's extended family called this home. She returned here with her husband Srikumar three years ago, and they have carved out a little sanctuary – a committed centre of treatment and learning. Join talks on Indian culture and philosophy, and dabble, or immerse yourself, in Ayurveda. Just be prepared for the pristine living rules that go with it. Balm for the soul.

rooms	8: 6 doubles, 2 singles. Some a/c.
price	Full-board only, $90. Singles $65.
meals	Included. Full-board.
closed	Rarely.
directions	In central Calicut about a 15-minute drive from the train station.

	Dr G Srikumar
tel	+91 495 2765 865
e-mail	admin@harivihar.com
web	www.harivihar.com

Guesthouse

Jamshad & Suchi's Place

33/457 Koyapathody Bungalow, Malaparamba, Calicut, 637 009, Kerala

You'll be struck by the energy of the place before you're over the threshold. Jamshad and Suchi's creative flair has transformed an unremarkable 70s building in suburban Calicut into a remarkable home. There are two stylish living rooms, the bedrooms are swimming in space and have charming balconies, beds are huge and very comfortable. There is art from all over India; ask about the story behind Jamshad's grandfather's Mahoot stick. Unusual antique pieces are inventively displayed: a cabinet is made from a family cot, and a carved full-length mirror partitions off a dressing room. Jamshad and Suchi are well-travelled and natural hosts, as is their young daughter Ayra. Friends and relatives encouraged them to go 'official', and their unconventional union (his background is Muslim, and hers Hindu) makes for interesting meal-time chat over exquisite Keralan recipes. You'll love the place as much as they do. Plenty of places to relax, too, maybe in the veranda-cum-open-air living room with its low-slung divans and bright cloth lanterns, or in swing seats in secluded corners of the undulating garden lawns. *Leave the city for walks and a tour round Jamshad's plantation.*

rooms	2 doubles.
price	Full-board $70; half-board $60.
meals	Included. Full & half-board available. Dinner from $6.
closed	Rarely.
directions	38km from Calicut airport, 5km from the city centre.

	Mr K C & Ms Sucharita H Jamshad
tel	+91 495 2371 389
e-mail	jamshad@vsnl.com

Homestay

E   map 9   entry 131

Kasa Marina

Telephone Exchange Road, Elathur, Calicut, 673 303, Kerala

Gerhard, a German carpenter and musician, chose this rocky seashore spot to build his family chalet by the sea. There's lots of wood: the modern spiral staircase and much of the stylish furniture are his own creations, and you may find the odd guitar lying around; Gerhard hooks up with his old band whenever he's back in India. In his absence Kasa Marina is enjoying a renaissance as an intimate and informal guest house. You could cartwheel across the rough wooden floor panelling of the top-floor suite – it's vast, and its deep balcony looks over the rocky Arabian shore. A U-shaped balcony wraps around the Dolphin suite, and you may catch sight of the real dolphins over long breakfasts in the wicker chairs. It's worth the extra for the bigger rooms, but the more snug ones are fine too; all are excellent value although this is a family house and none have their own bathrooms. Best known to locals as a dining spot, the bright-yellow open-air restaurant shacks give the place quite a buzz in the evenings. You can join in, or eat in the chalet dining room, which is yours alone. A great place for little groups.

rooms	4 doubles with separate bathrooms.
price	$20-$35. Plus 7.5% tax. Peak season: September-April.
meals	Lunch Rs200. Dinner Rs300.
closed	Rarely.
directions	Right on the beach in Elathur, 10km from Calicut city centre.

Mr K P Mayan

tel	+91 495 2462 162
fax	+91 495 2462 162
e-mail	salkaram@sify.com
web	www.silknspice.com

Guesthouse

Tasara, Centre for Creative Weaving

North Beypore, Calicut, 673 015, Kerala

Piles of plush bright fabrics are strewn over tables and floors, the weaving factory clatters with activity, and fantastical completed pieces are showcased in the new whitewashed exhibition building. (Their weavings are sold worldwide to hotel resorts and European offices, even to Blair Castle in Scotland.) The atmosphere is one of easy work, the ethic was clear long before Vasudevan explained (tongue only slightly in cheek) that "we don't really like idle people here". He shares the house with his five siblings, two children, a pair of bounding dogs, and any number of artistically inclined guests. Rooms in the exhibition building are less bustling than those of the family house, but all are simple and vary considerably in size. Things here may be a bit too shambolic and high energy for some and it's definitely not the spot to tick 'quality lazy time' off your holiday wish list. But, if you love people, creativity, and hussle, you'll relish carving out a happy niche in this busy family den. If not to weave, come to write, paint, play and create in what must be one of the most truly unique of Keralan homestays. Eccentric and intriguing. *Weaving courses, including Christmas.*

rooms	4: 2 doubles, 2 singles. 2 more doubles to be completed by Jan 2004.
price	$20. Singles $15. Peak season: 1 December–30 April.
meals	$10 per day for all meals.
closed	Rarely.
directions	21km from Calicut airport & 7km from Calicut train station. Ferok is the nearest train station.

	Mr V Vasudevan
tel	+91 495 2414 233
e-mail	tasara@eth.net
web	www.tasaraindia.com

Homestay

 F–G map 9 entry 133

Tharavad

Kandath Tharavad, Thenkurussi, Palakkad, 678 671, Kerala

Nearly all the agricultural land you'll pass on the way here from Palakkad belonged to the Kadath family. Their impressive ancestral home was built on part of the estate in 1794 using mud and teak. Much of the land has been redistributed but the Tharavad seems unwilling to relinquish the splendour of its glory days. However, renovation has added creature comforts, and the presence of Mr Bhagwaldas and his family memorabilia gives it a homely air. Bulbous carved teak pillars frame the colourful naturally dyed tiles of the striking 'purathalum', or raised seating area. Here perched Bhagwaldas's grandfather to conduct his money lending. Little carved wooden doors draw you to a smaller purathalam which was traditionally the female domain. Although only 20 feet apart neither group had to mince their words, for it was acoustically contrived that not a word could be heard between the two. Conversation is still important here, and you'll enjoy shared meals with your quietly intelligent host, in the dining room or on candlelit tables on the lawn. A fascinating home.

rooms	4 doubles.
price	Full-board only, $125. Peak season: October-March.
meals	Included. Full-board.
closed	Rarely.
directions	In Palakkad call to be picked up. Tharavad about 10km from Palakkad.

Mr Bhagwaldas Sudevan

tel	+91 492 2284 124
e-mail	tharavad15@yahoo.com
web	www.tharavad.com

Homestay

Kadappuram Beach Resort

P.O. Nattika Beach, Trichur, 680 572, Kerala

From the air, Kadappuram is indistinguishable from the fishing villages scattered along the coast; like many other dwellings, its cottages are long and low, made of coconut-palm thatch, wood and bamboo, all set back among the coconut trees. In 'The Land of the Coconut', there's little reason to build any other way. The six cottages sprawl across a sandy four acres; this is a place for easy beach living and there's enough space to really enjoy it. The bamboo-mat walls are a restrained backdrop to the simple luxury of the rooms – in some, the cascading mosquito net hangs over the crisp white sheets of a dark wooden four-poster, and polished wooden steps either side of the bed add further grandeur. Small details have been thought through: incense wafts through your room each evening, palm leaf origami figures hang from verandas and dance on the warm evening air, and the sweet smell of Ramachan roots stuffed into the thatched cottage walls snakes its way around the room when the rains and winds come. *There is a strong Ayurvedic focus, and any diet can be catered for.*

rooms	13 doubles.
price	Full-board only, $85. $120 from 20 December-3 January. Plus 7.5% tax. Peak season: October-30 April.
meals	Included. Full-board.
closed	Rarely.
directions	25km from Trichur train station on the National Highway from Kochi to Calicut. Well signed from Nattika Junction. 65km from Kochi airport.

	Mr M R Gopalakrishnan
tel	+91 487 2394 988
e-mail	kadappuram@sancharnet.in
web	www.kadappurambeachresorts.com

Resort

E   map 9   entry 135

The Brunton Boatyard

1/498 Fort Kochi, Kochi, 682 001, Kerala

Permission to build in this preservation area is tightly controlled which says something for the architectural integrity of the Casino brothers. The hotel is at once big, grand and simple – like a huge colonial plantation owner's house. This is history recreated: the large, beautiful rooms like a museum of Dutch colonial living, though far more comfortable, and the lobby walls are like a gallery of the major players in Cochin's life. 'Punkas' hang from the lobby ceiling and work, though there are no 'wallahs'; instead, old Bakelite switches turn on 10kg restored electric fans. There's a vast slate billiard table and open walkways circle the central courtyard with its vast, serene rain tree. In contrast, behind this, every room's balcony faces out over the busy shipping channel, where tankers cross wakes with beaten ferries and fishing canoes, on their way to the islands beyond. The pool area is hotel-standard and large, and the restaurants not as remarkable as the hotel. The real appeal of Brunton lies in its dignified, handsome dominance of the waterfront and its bustling setting near the Chinese fishing nets.

rooms	26: 14 doubles, 8 twins, 4 suites.
price	$190. Suites $250. Plus 15% tax. Peak season: 21 December-20 January.
meals	Breakfast $8. Lunch & dinner from $12.
closed	Rarely.
directions	At the mouth of the harbour next to Fort Kochi bus station.

	Mr Erine Louis
tel	+91 484 2215 461
fax	+91 484 2215 562
e-mail	brunton@vsnl.net
web	www.casinogroup.com

Hotel

Fort House

2/6A Calvetty Road, Fort Kochi, Kochi, 682 001, Kerala

The harbour, one of the grand sights of Kerala, is right there, lapping against the edge of the hotel's jetty. All that remains of the old trading company building where Fort House now stands are the whitewashed walls of the jetty and the grand old wooden front door. Scattered in between, where traders used to haul their wares from boat to roadside, is a haphazard mess of trees, plants, sculptures and bright floral blooms. Don't expect luxury here: the bamboo-and-brick huts are basic but immaculate. They are also wonderfully free of hotel frippery – just a big bed, crisp white sheets and a clothes rail – all you need but nothing more. Each hut shares part of the wide connecting veranda which looks out over the garden. Watch flocks of sparrows taking a dust bath in the dirt path that wends its way down to the the jetty, where the Fort House's boat 'Nova' bobs about. With great views over the harbour and a much-loved café serving some of the best food in Fort Kochi, this is a simple, unusual, charming base and great value. *Try island hopping on Fort House's new boat.*

rooms	9: 4 bamboo huts for 2, 5 brick huts for 2.
price	Rs950. Peak season: September–February.
meals	Lunch & dinner from Rs200.
closed	Rarely.
directions	In Fort Cochin between the coast guard & the boat jetty.

Mrs Nova Thomas

tel	+91 484 2217 066
fax	+91 484 2217 103
e-mail	forthouse@hclinfinet.com
web	www.forthousecochin.com

Guesthouse

 map 9   entry 137

Malabar House

1/268 & 1/269 Parade Road, Fort Kochi, Kochi, 682 001, Kerala

With his Spanish wife Txuku, Joerg Drechsel, an ethnographic exhibition creator with enviable taste and style, has created a slice of heaven: old temple carvings cast shadows across lively ochra, turquoise or white walls and every piece of furniture has been perfectly chosen. The central courtyard is as Eden might have been; Joerg built the hotel around a vast, drooping, vine-and-frangipani-clad rain tree. Creeping green vanilla climbs up white-washed walls, and the petal-sprinkled plunge pool sits beneath a hanging red-tiled roof. Tables from the verandaed restaurant spill out under the trees and bamboo overhangs the open-sided courtyard brushed by sea breezes. Txuku concocts the food (delicious), a delicate harmony of east and west. Colonial four-poster teak beds stand opposite vast Keralan masks, subtlety lighted works of contemporary art are mixed with ancient ones; this is no hotel 'tat'. Though most of the building is new, every inch reflects Joerg's architectural vision and commitment to the Keralan vernacular. Old and new seamlessly combine; the luxury is perfectly simple. Joerg and Txuku deserve those many awards.

rooms	17: 13 doubles, 4 suites.
price	$150. Suites $170-$250. Plus 15% tax. Prices increase by around $45-$75 20 December-10 January. Peak season: 1 October-31 May.
meals	Lunch & dinner from $15.
closed	Rarely.
directions	From seaside Kochi you'll see signboards. Do not get taken to Taj Malabar!

Mr K P Francis

tel	+91 484 2216 666
fax	+91 484 2217 777
e-mail	info@malabarhouse.com
web	www.malabarhouse.com

Boutique Hotel

avail 30/12 – 2/1
4/1 – 5/1 £57

KER

Old Courtyard Hotel

371 Princess Street, Fort Kochi, Kochi, 682 001, Kerala

A whitewashed courtyard with an old well-head, whitewashed steps snaking up the outside wall to the next floor, the balcony winding round two sides of the yard. The Portuguese builders built a retreat from the worst of the sun for a large family, with communal spaces tucked into an inner courtyard. There is an unexpected wooden staircase, too, creakingly ancient and massively dignified. The corridors are also wooden, a delight to anyone who despairs of modern hotels. One room has a vast four-poster bed under white bedcover and sheets – magnificent. The floors are wooden, the walls are white and there is a vast bathroom attached. Here there is less protection from the heat but it is big and easy – and with plenty of hot water. Other rooms are more or less handsome. Breakfast can be in the courtyard, or nearby in an excellent café; the hotel provides a very good dinner. There are often music recitals in the courtyard – a nice touch. The staff are kind yet unobtrusive, and create a gentle, modest mood in this delightful hotel.

rooms	8: 6 doubles, 2 suites. Some a/c.
price	Rs1,000-Rs2,000. Suites Rs2,500-Rs3,500. Plus 10% tax. Peak season November-March.
meals	Lunch $7. Dinner $10.
closed	Rarely.
directions	On Princess Street in heart of Fort Kochi. Walk from Chinese Fishing nets to St Francis Church. Ask anyone.

	Mrs Rose Kuruvinakunnel
tel	+91 484 2216 302
e-mail	reservations@oldcourtyard.com
web	www.oldcourtyard.com

Heritage Hotel

Plantation Homestay

Mundackal Estate, Pindimana PO, via Thrikkariyur, Kothamangalam, 686 698, Kerala

You approach the house along a bumpy farm track that winds through a rubber plantation on the edge of the Salim Ali Bird Sanctuary. Seeing no official boundaries, birds of every description come to sing over breakfast, their seranade the only disturbance in this calm oasis. Daisy and Jose, whose father was a leading Keralan politician, are a warm and generous couple, perhaps a little too eager to make you leave feeling more circular than when you arrived. This is a real Indian homestay – you sleep in quite bare but adequate rooms, and feast on mountains of food (Daisy can teach you a few culinary tricks). It is fascinating to see, on Jose's plantation walk, how rubber is tapped and turned into sheets, and to spot the many eastern spices growing wild. Though it is not the most remarkable of houses, and has small splashes of kitsch, the setting makes it. Secluded, green and with birds to excite twitchers, it offers a chance to dip one's toes into the lives of a working plantation family. An engagingly real Indian experience, particularly for anyone with ornithological or gastronomic leanings. *Kodanad elephant training camp nearby.*

rooms	3 doubles. 1 a/c.
price	Full-board only, $100. $125 for a/c room.
meals	Included. Full-board.
closed	Rarely.
directions	Kothamangalam 57km from Kochi on way to Munnar. Plantation House is 7km from Kothamangalam. Don't try to find it on your own.

	Jose & Daisy Mundackal
tel	+91 485 2570 717
e-mail	nestholidays@hotmail.com

Homestay

Windermere Estate

Pothamedu, , Munnar, 685 612, Kerala

What cool, green relief from the heat and stickiness of the coast, here in Munnar. Sprays of bougainvillea and morning glory cover the garden walls of this stunning spot which is perched above miles of steep-sided tea estates and wooded slopes. It is green beyond imagination and as colourful as a Devonshire spring garden. Almost alpine in feel, the modern chalet-like building is simple but extremely comfortable. There is a long shaded terrace with wicker chairs in which to read, and gardens in which to stroll. Though the building is modern and you might find an embroidered alpine milkmaid watching you from the dining room wall, the setting is stunning and the tranquillity total. The early morning or evening walk through the cardamom forest takes you into another world of birdsong and arboreal paradise. The trees are vast, buttressed giants that play host to hundreds of species of birds and wild bee colonies, beneath which sprout the jungle-like cardamom plants. Windermere is intimate if not entirely Indian – one of those rare finds which you are reluctant to share. Do watch the sunrise from the hilltop look out.

rooms	5 + 1: 5 doubles. 1 cottage for 4.
price	Half-board only. $110. Cottage $145. Peak season: October–March.
meals	Included. Half-board. Lunch $8. Dinner $9.
closed	Rarely.
directions	Fom Kochi, right on a narrow bridge 2km before Munnar. Follow signs to Windermere Estate for 2km along road. Estate is on right.

Dr Simon John

tel	+91 4865 230 512
fax	+91 484 2427 575
e-mail	info@windermeremunnar.com
web	www.windermeremunnar.com
res. no.	+91 484 2425 237

Guesthouse

map 9   entry 141

avail 1-5 Jan £151

Shalimar Spice Garden

Murikkady P.O., Kumily, Idukki District, 685 535, Kerala

Maria Angela has created her own sylvan paradise hidden in this exquisite miniature valley. An architect by training, but an interior designer too, she has created what most people could only dream of. Thatched huts are dotted about among the trees – the interiors smack of those tiny hill top Greek temples, all whitewash, low doorways, candles in arched niches and thin cotton curtains blowing about the paneless windows; bathrooms are reached through stooping doorways. There is something zen about the place: beams of sunlight illuminate the oldspice tree in the lobby which lies across a wooden bridge, swing chairs hang in cushioned balconies, all pink flowing cotton and dark wood. Breakfast of fresh mango juice and scrambled eggs is served on rough granite-topped dining tables; a low-slung, thatched ochre Ayurveda and yoga centre beckons. The place is run with a gentle hand, the staff are as serene as Maria herself. There are precious few places in Kerala, let alone anywhere else, which are quite so tranquil – "a balm for the tired psyche" reads the guest book and we agree. Perfection. *5km from Periyar Tiger Reserve.*

rooms	15: 8 doubles, 6 cottages for 2, 1 cottage for 4.
price	$110. Cottages $140. Plus 7.5% tax. Peak season: November–March.
meals	Lunch & dinner from $15. Full-board available.
closed	Rarely.
directions	5km from Kumily bus stand. 4–5 hours from Kochi & Trivandrum airports.

Mr Aditya Garg

tel	+91 4869 222 132
fax	+91 4869 223 022
e-mail	shalimar_resort@vsnl.com
web	www.shalimarkerala.com

Boutique Hotel

entry 142   map 9   C

Kanjirapally Estate

Vandiperiyar P.O., Vandiperiyar, 685 533, Kerala

An unusual homestay, and an untypical farmhouse. Built 30 years ago on a cardamom and coffee plantation bordering the Periyar Tiger Reserve, this modern, angular building is cool and colourful, with reds and yellows, bright terrazzo floors and modern art. It's funky yet restrained, smart yet informal. Gita and Mathew are young, sophisticated, interested and involved. Both are passionate conservationists and twitchers and can take you for long bird-spotting walks around the plantation that spreads its green, forested tentacles across kilometres of steep hillside. (It also plays occasional host to the wandering furry, hooved or feathered residents from the next-door reserve.) Having cut their teeth in the hotel world, Gita and Mathew are perfectionists – yet the house has an easy style that belies the huge amount of thought that goes into every corner. And they can cook up a storm in the kitchen! Come here for the quiet, the birds, the conversation and to savour a more cosmopolitan India with a refreshing absence of kitsch. Lovely. *Guided trekking, rafting, plantation walks & visits to a local cardamom auction.*

rooms	3: 2 doubles, 1 single.
price	On request.
meals	Included. Full-board.
closed	April–June.
directions	Directions given on booking. The estate borders the Periyar Tiger Reserve, 200km from Cochin.

	Gita & Mathew Eapen
tel	+91 4869 252 278
e-mail	kanjirapallyestate@hotmail.com

Green Mansions

Kerala Forest Development Corporation, Gavi, Vandiperiyar, Idukki District, 685 533, Kerala

Rarely does a government-run spot feel so cared for and dynamic, or a place leave you as revived as Green Mansions. Getting there is half the fun; the three-and-a-half-hour jeep ride rattles even the most well-travelled bones but sets souls soaring. Fly through tropical forest, neat plantations and stark grassland hilltops, through some of the most awe-inspiring scenery in the country. On its own little hillock overlooking Gavi Lake, the building is snug and unassuming, and rooms are simple though far from uncomfortable – perfect for those with fond memories of youth-hostelling days. Vegetarian meals are served in the open: breakfasts in the lakeside straw gazebo after a sunrise trek, camp fire dinners under the stars. It's wonderfully calming to feel miles from nowhere; blankets of pristine forest roll out in all directions, and the knowledge that a man as passionate about the region as Bashir is caring for it will makes you sleep well. His vision has made Green Mansions a centre for local employment and organic small holdings. An unbeatable spot and inspiring people. *Incredible trekking and opportunities for wildlife sightings.*

rooms	3 doubles.
price	Full-board only, $70.
meals	Included. Full-board.
closed	Rarely.
directions	30km from Vandiperiyar. 120km incredibly scenic drive from Kottayam. Prior permission from the Forest Department is required.

	C A Ardul Bashir
tel	+91 486 9252 560
fax	+91 481 2581 205
e-mail	kfdcgavi@rediffmail.com
web	www.kfdcgavi.com
res. no.	+91 481 2581 205

Ecolodge

E

Serenity at Kanam Estate

c/o P.V. George, Payikad, Kanam P.O., Vazhoor, 686 515, Kerala

Yet again the Malabar House team have come up with something new, and employed their perfect taste and style – using modern minimalism to reveal the simple grandeur of the Keralan architectural heritage. This two-storey 1920s plantation house is enclosed by trees, a grand white edifice with open sides that allow natural ventilation to take the edge off humid summer heat. The windows are wooden-shuttered, not glass, and the main living room has latticed screens instead of walls. The whole building is designed to let the outside in: dark inside and with slate-tiled floors, the communal rooms are open to the breeze, and the high ceilings create a fine sense of space. The bedroom interiors are classily restrained, the coir matting, cotton curtains and the gentle oranges and greens of the walls softening the typically austere use of dark wooden interiors. This is not a hotel, but a house, albeit luxurious, over which you can briefly reign. You have your own space on one of the wide wooden verandas, yet your meals can be shared with other guests. Grand yet homely – the perfect stop-off between Periyar and the backwaters. *Good trekking.*

rooms	5: 3 doubles, 2 twins.
price	$160. Breakfast included. Plus 10% tax. Peak season: October–April.
meals	Lunch & dinner $30.
closed	Rarely.
directions	On Kanam Estate between Kottayam & Kumily. Don't try to get here on your own.

	Mr K P Francis
tel	+91 481 456 353
fax	+91 484 2217 777
e-mail	escapes@malabarhouse.com
web	www.malabarhouse.com
res. no.	+91 484 2216 666

Catered cottage

map 9   entry 145

Kumarakom Lake Resort

Kumarakom North, Kottayam, Kottayam District, 686 566, Kerala

Despite being a new resort and using many of the usual 'heritage' techniques of the backwaters, this one finds a place in this book for its bold luxuriousness. There are some parts where you can sense that the architect has been given room to entertain his fancies. Sitting by the horizon swimming pool feels like being in a stylish photo shoot – expensive cloth umbrellas cast shade over heavy wooden sun loungers, coconut trees waft in the breeze and hushed pool attendants ready themselves with towels. The heritage cottages are beautiful, luxurious, and more ornate than most. Painted temple drawings cover the wall above the wide bed, and double doors open to the plant-filled garden into which is sunk a vast mosaic bathtub. The restaurant is a 300-year-old Keralan royal house, through which one of the canals passes, and the 'women's balcony', from which regal ladies would watch courtly happenings, still remains. The feeling is of polished history – there are no cracks in this place. The meandering pool villas are more modern and resort-like, but good for families. Watch the sunset from the tea garden – a treat.

rooms	50: 22 heritage cottages, 26 pool cottages, 2 suites with private pool.
price	Heritage villa $195-$250. Pool villa $250-$300. Suites $500. Plus 15% tax. Peak season: October-March.
meals	Breakfast $10. Lunch & dinner $15.
closed	Rarely.
directions	90 minutes from Kochi airport via Chertala. 3km from Kumarakom on backwaters. Free transfers from Kottayam train station or Muhamma Jetty.

Mr Shelly Thayil

tel	+91 481 2524 900
fax	+91 481 2524 987
e-mail	klresort@vsnl.com
web	www.klresort.com

Resort

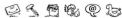

Coconut Lagoon

Kumakarom, Kottayam, Kottayam District, 686 563, Kerala

Tourism has a stormy relationship with environmentalists, yet here is an example of eco-ingenuity that doesn't cut corners on comfort. All the tricks – *biogas* (dung fuel), water recycling, organic rice paddies – are used here, yet nothing you'd want from a backwater resort is missing. Endangered rare-breed Vechur cows graze tethered between the cottages and a butterfly garden juts out on a small spit into the paddies. The quaint heritage bungalows are made from parts of old Keralan houses – simple dark wooden furniture, plain cotton bedthrows and cool, red-tiled floors are discovered through a tiny, heavy wooden door. You may experience a frisson of grandeur as you arrive by boat through a small channel crossed by bridges and step into the low-slung, wooden, verandaed reception to be greeted graciously with a coconut and jasmine garland. The days can be full of activities, yet there's ample space to swing in a hammock. It is, undeniably, a resort, yet one that strives to make a difference. It is at once calm, easy-going and fun, and ideal if you have children with you.

rooms	50: 42 doubles, 8 suites with pools.
price	$149-$171. Suite $319. Plus 25% tax. Peak season: 21 December-20 January.
meals	Breakfast $5. Lunch & dinner from $10.
closed	Rarely.
directions	Only accessible by boat from Kumakarom. Contact hotel to arrange pick-up.

Mr P Subrahmanian

tel	+91 481 2524 491
fax	+91 481 2524 495
e-mail	contactus@casinogroup.com
web	www.casinogroup.com

Resort

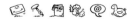

 B map 9 entry 147

Philip Kutty's Farm

Pallivathukal, Ambika Market P.O., Vechoor, Kottayam District, 686 144, Kerala

Come to be marooned, happily, on an island. Vinod has brought to his 'homestay' an unusual professionalism. Each of the three cottages is new and solidly built along old architectural lines using tiled, wooden overhanging roofs and heavy shuttered windows. They have huge, luxurious showers, small living area and are spotlessly clean, and all lie along the waterfront of this 750-acre island created from land reclaimed by this Syrian Christian family in the 1950s. The homestay atmosphere is dominated by Vinod, a principled, strong but interested man who clearly enjoys intellectual jousting with guests, yet knows exactly when to let them have privacy. His delightful mother is a fine chef (and runs cookery courses here), and meals are communal, conversational occasions under the outdoor pavilion – with Vinod as the patriarch. It's a working plantation, criss-crossed by hundreds of water channels that create narrow strips of land for the coconuts, nutmeg and coffee plants. You can be alone or involved, take out punts or just read in one of the most comfortable of Keralan homestays. *Cooking or painting holidays.*

rooms	3 cottages for 2.
price	Full-board only, $135. Peak season: October-March.
meals	Included. Full-board.
closed	Rarely.
directions	From Ambika Market, Church road for 1km. Boat will collect you from jetty. 1 hour from Kochi.

Mr Vinod Kumar & Anu Mathew

tel	+91 4829 276 529
e-mail	mail@philipkuttysfarm.com
web	www.philipkuttysfarm.com

Homestay

Privacy at Sanctuary Bay

TP111/185 Kannamkara P.O., Muhamm, Thaneermukkom, Kerala

Huge sliding screens give onto the veranda with its bamboo blinds and views right across the lake. This must be one of the most heavenly spots in Kerala – and it is almost entirely yours while you're there: there are only two rooms in this small thatched bungalow. There can be few places more idyllic to eat an evening meal – candlelit, outdoors and close enough to the shimmering lake to be able to dip one's toes. The interiors are colourfully minimalist, true to the Malabar House design genius that uses old Keralan buildings to house its bold simplicity. Nothing is here that isn't beautiful, and balance and symmetry underpin the subtle placing of the few ethno-graphic collectables. 'Your' waiter/cook is present but not overbearing, the focus being on total privacy. The food is delicious – delicate curries and fresh juices, served as and when you want. You'll see no-one but passing fishermen, and be disturbed by nothing but the cawing of crows. Stay here for a memorable experience and a place to call your own, for the duration, in one of the most exquisite settings on the Vembanad Lake.

rooms	2 doubles.
price	$160-$180. Plus 10% tax. Peak season: October-May.
meals	Breakfast included. Lunch & dinner $30.
closed	Rarely.
directions	10-minute drive from Chertala.

Mr K P Francis

tel	+91 478 582 794
fax	+91 478 582 794
e-mail	escapes@malabarhouse.com
web	www.malabarhouse.com
res. no.	+91 484 221 6666

catered cottage

map 9   entry 149

Motty's Homestay

Murickanadiyil, , Kidangamparambu Road, Thathampally, Alappuzha, 688 013, Kerala

The first things you'll notice are Motty's deep infectious chuckle and his eye for beautiful things. Motty and Lali's home is crammed with objects d'art from all over India and beyond, but his interior designer instinct has made the most of the space — nothing looks too busy. There is as much communal space ouside as in: the beautiful plant-strewn verandas are at front and back, smooth teak pillars hold the front veranda, and the rear one has carved jackwood tressle and arches. The bedrooms are big, stylish and private; each has its own entrance and one has a splendid four-poster bed and a surprisingly beautiful collection of walking sticks that splay out at the foot of the bed. Lali's Keralan cooking is great, and she'll be delighted to chat about it. Central Alleppey is five minutes' rickshaw away, but you wouldn't know it. It's great value too, and Motty has fingers in many tourism pies. He'll make sure you make the most of your time. *He can easily organise rice barge cruises on the Keralan backwaters. Please arrange in advance during the peak season.*

rooms	2 doubles.
price	Full-board only, $50.
meals	Breakfast $5. Lunch & dinner $15.
closed	Rarely.
directions	5 minutes from cental Alappuzha.

	Motty & Lali Mathew
tel	+91 477 2260 573
e-mail	motty1@satyam.net.in

Tharavad Heritage Home

West of North Police Station, Sea View Ward, Alappuzha, 688 012, Kerala

A stroll round the house feels like a tour of a lived-in museum; there's an abundance of curios and everything is properly ordered. An antique rosewood gramophone and a brass and wooden *para* (for measuring rice) are two of the living room discoveries, and the vast rotund brass pot used by Madhu's great-grandfather for mixing Ayurvedic oils squats on the glistening veranda. Each of the bedrooms has its own antique *objet*: a huge metal safe in one room, an ornate set of trinket boxes in another. Madhu is calm and smiling, perhaps more hands-off than other homestay hosts, but as involved as you want him to be. This is his grandfather's house, now shared with his brother and mother. They sometimes take meals with guests in the stone-floored dining room that opens on to a garden dappled in shade cast by the impressive 100-year-old mango tree. Alleppey town isn't far — Madhu will help to organise boating from there — but far enough away to escape the urban hum. Excellent value.

rooms	5: 4 doubles, 1 single.
price	Rs600–Rs800. Single Rs375. Peak season: August–March.
meals	Breakfast Rs75. Lunch & dinner from Rs150.
closed	Rarely.
directions	1km from train station near North Police Station Road. Rickshaws will know the way from Alappuzha town. If you arrive at Kochi or Trivandrum airport, Madhu will arrange pick up.

Mr Madhu A Mohan
tel +91 477 2244 599
e-mail alleppeytharavad@sify.com

Keraleeyam Ayurvedic Resort

Thathampally, Alappuzha, 688 006, Kerala

The owning group, SD Pharmacy, has 60 years of experience in Ayurvedic health, which is one reason to include Keraleeyam. This resort offers the real thing, and isn't just clinging to the coat tails of the current Keralan cash cow. The air-conditioned 'heritage' cottages have dark ornate wooden doors giving on to pristine bathrooms – you can almost see yourself in the gleaming white tiles. Non-air-conditioned cottages are great fun; they are made entirely of coconut thatching – locals re-thatch every month; one sits on top of another and there are views over the gentle backwaters from the top cottage veranda. Tradition meets modernity in the wonderful open-air bathrooms; the view to the stars above may have you singing an extra verse in the shower. Cottages are worth the extra, but the double rooms are good too; all have fresh simple furnishings and there's not an ounce of 'tat'. The L-shape dining room is dark and simple, with chunky wooden furniture – come for the great Indian tradition of 'tea and snacks', or just to retreat from the heat. An idyllic spot, and Ayurveda to trust in. Wonderfully good value.

rooms	14: 5 doubles, 9 cottages. Some a/c.
price	$25-$40.
	Peak dates: September-January.
meals	Breakfast Rs90.
	Lunch & dinner Rs240.
closed	Rarely.
directions	On the backwaters 3km from Alappuzha train station.

Mr R S Nair

tel	+91 477 2231 468
fax	+91 477 2251 068
e-mail	mail@keraleeyam.com
web	www.keraleeyam.com

Resort

Kayaloram Lake Resort

Avalookunnu PO, Punnamada, Alappuzha, 688 006, Kerala

The gardens are right on the water that stretches for silvery kilometers. Kayaloram is in one of the most stunning spots on the western side of the Vembanad lake. The resort is low-key but has an easy feel that can only exist in such a small place. This is the original backwater resort, the first to use parts of old Keralan houses, and each low-slung 'house' containing several rooms stands in well-tended, open gardens that centre around a small pool. Postcard-perfect sights are easily found all over the Keralan backwaters, but the views from the lake-facing rooms at Kayaloram, through the coconut trees and out across the mirror-like lake, are breathtakingly lovely. This is not luxurious and the service is informal, but it's perfect for those who want something a little more intimate and less resort-like than most other backwater haunts. They have rice barges for backwater cruises, a ping-pong table and a small, attractive, open-sided restaurant for which you have to place your orders at least an hour in advance. Slightly eccentric, but worth the wait. *Air-conditioning at night only.*

rooms	12 cottages.
price	$70. Plus 15% tax. Peak seaon: October–March.
meals	Breakfast $3. Lunch & dinner $6.
closed	Rarely.
directions	Access by pre-arranged boat from Alappuzha.

	Mr M K Mathew
tel	+91 477 2232 040
fax	+91 477 2252 918
e-mail	kayaloram@satyam.net.in
web	www.kayaloram.com

Resort

Emerald Isle

Kanjooparambil-Manimalathara, Chathurthiakary, Alappuzha, 688 511, Kerala

You are cloaked in romance from the word go - a dug-out canoe glides you across the Pamba river to the ancient, low-slung wooden bungalow tucked away on a little island on the backwaters. A sprawling veranda dotted with inviting wicker chairs hugs the contours of what one guest described as the "mother of all bungalows". Settle in with a book or some *chai*, this is a soporifically relaxing place just to 'be'. The furniture is dark and satisfyingly heavy; much of it is original, including the carved teak bedroom doors giving on to the veranda — even their hinges are wooden. Vinod's great-grandfather renovated the place years ago; family property deeds etched into 250-year-old palm leaves are hung in the cool dark living room. Vinod is genuine and friendly, keen to share the history of this dreamy place, but never intrusive. He will organise any backwater adventure you desire, or just point you to a gentle amble through the maze of canals to the paddy and coconut fields of the 10-acre estate — hammocks have been strategically placed en route. A delightfully peaceful way to spend your time in India.

rooms	5 doubles. Some a/c.
price	Full-board only, Rs2,800-3,500. Peak season: May-September.
meals	Included. Full-board.
closed	Rarely.
directions	10km from Alappuzha. No road access, you'll be collected from boat pick-up point near Nazareth Junction. Call for detailed instructions.

	Mr Vinod Job
tel	+91 477 2703 899
e-mail	info@emeraldislekerala.com
web	www.emeraldislekerala.com

Guesthouse

E-F

Marari Beach Homes
Marari Beach, Alappuzha, Kerala

In a country that prides itself on hospitality, somewhere you can look after yourself and live at your own pace is a real find. Disused fishermen's shacks have been cleverly converted to classily simple self-catering beach cottages; a terracotta and pale yellow combination washes the walls, there's coir matting underfoot, and a bright pink or yellow bedspread beckons for siestas from the sun. Each cottage has its own shady veranda – they are dotted with lazy chairs and have uninterrupted views to the sea, which rolls rhythmically just yards away. An archway draws you through to the second bedroom of the family house; there's plenty of space, and a big horse-shoe veranda winds round to a private bar. There are well-equipped kitchens of course, but you are not bound to them; you can give a shopping list to the staff if you don't want to explore the markets yourself, and chefs can be arranged if you are staying for more than a week. The Marari Beach restaurant is a few sandy paces along the coast. An engagingly different way to do a beach holiday.

rooms	5: 4 cottages for 2, 1 cottage for 4. Some a/c.
price	$50-$80. Plus 15% tax. Peak season: November-April.
meals	Breakfast $5. Lunch & dinner $10. Self-catering available.
closed	Rarely.
directions	On the Kochi-Alappuzha National Highway turn west at Marari Junction. On Marari Beach itself, 15km from Alappuzha.

	Mr M K Mathew
tel	+91 477 2243 535
e-mail	motty1@satyam.net.in

Self catering cottage

Arakal Heritage

Chethy P.O., Alappuzha, 688 530, Kerala

Carved elephants squat on the sand-scattered steps of the heritage cottage – a Keralan sign of welcome. Duck through the intricate antique door to a four-poster bed, a cosy dressing room hung with Abi's great-grandmother's tapestry work, and an outdoor bathroom decked out in funky leaf-print tiles. Inside, things are snug but there is a veranda to lounge on too; you can take your meals there, or eat off banana leaves in the family dining room. There are also two extremely basic double rooms… family miscellany may have to be shifted to give you space, so it's a good idea to pay the extra for your own cottage, and if you're in a group the space could be useful. Abi and Mini are warm and engaging hosts; come here to share in rural family life, and get a feel for real village India. Wander to the sea through sandy coconut plantations past fishermen's huts and locals making coir or tapping toddy. You're in the thick of it here, worlds away from cosseted hotel living. No frills, just a very real Indian experience with genuinely delightful company.

rooms	3: 1 double, 2 cottages for 2.
price	Full-board only, $25. Cottages $40-$50.
meals	Included. Full-board.
closed	Rarely.
directions	18km from Alappuzha, 11km from Cherthala. Just a couple of km down the beach from the Marari Beach Resort.

	Abi & Mini Arakal
tel	+91 478 2865 545
e-mail	abiarakal@sify.com

Homestay

F

Mankotta House
Alappuzha, 690 514, Kerala

The story behind Mankotta is unusual enough, the woman-made island having been the life's work of Jai's formidable grandmother. She carved out this 450-acre rice island from backwater swamp, bringing with her the seven men whose descendants are the isle's only dwellers. The house is simple, a real working farmhouse, yet the company is sophisticated. Music reigns, and the legendary jazz jammin' sessions with Jai on the clarinet into which musical guests are roped, must be the only interruptions to the serenity of this place. The bedrooms are in the old seedling storage rooms, sharing a narrow porch that looks out onto the shaded garden and over the river Pamba to the paddy fields beyond. They are spartan yet comfortable, with plain, big bathrooms. Watch the duckherds steer their quacking flocks past the garden in the evening. Jai's tales from his days as a commander in the Indian Navy provide a raucous backdrop to any evening, and Laila's easy, dignified presence make them a remarkable couple. This must be the only Indian farmhouse with a makeshift squash court in an old granary!

rooms	3 doubles.
price	On request.
meals	Included.
closed	April-May.
directions	Given on booking. The island of Mankotta is midway between Kochi and Trivandrum airports (135km).

	Laila & Jai Chacko
tel	+91 477 2212 245
e-mail	mankotta@vsnl.com

Homestay

map 9   entry 157

Graceful Homestay

PHRS No. 20 Philip's Hill, Pothujanam Road, Kumarapuram, Trivandrum, 695 011, Kerala

Sylvia is high energy and hugely smiley, a self-confessed workaholic and cat freak. Through her UN work as an administrator for CARE, she has travelled all over the place, gathering tales and knick-knacks along the way. Stories are told over relaxed meals on the generous balcony, and the eclectic collection of handicrafts — from Botswanan wooden carvings to weavings and metal work from Kosovo — adorn the walls of this modern home, lent a colonial air by the white-washed mass of arches and verandas. Tajikistani art will soon be the next addition; our inspector visited just hours before Sylvie rushed off for a six-month stint there. In Sylvia's absence her brother Giles is in charge, and lives in the original family home just across the lush garden. Take up the invitation to eat at his place, or wander in to the attached kitchen and invite them over to yours. Things are very relaxed here, and you can be as independent as you like. The bustling centre of Trivandrum may be just minutes away, but gazing out across a carpet of palms to the thin blue line of the Arabian Sea, you'd never know it. *A/c on request.*

rooms	4: 2 doubles, 2 singles.
price	$40–$45. Singles $35.
meals	Lunch & dinner $5.
closed	Rarely.
directions	Half-way between Trivandrum airport & the Medical College. In Kumarapuram turn up Pothujanam Road & continue until you reach the house.

	Ms Sylvia Francis
tel	+91 471 2444 358
e-mail	southernsafaris@yahoo.co.in

Homestay

Wild Palms Guesthouse

Mathrubhoomi Road, Vanchiyoor, Trivandrum, 695 035, Kerala

Hilda and Justin spent the last 30 years in the London rat race, though they always knew they'd return to their Keralan roots. Wild Palms is their retirement dream – a large, somewhat grand townhouse in central Trivandrum, 10 minutes from the sea. More formal than a homestay (you all have keys to your rooms), the house is an eclectic mix of 'designer' and 'ethnic' – the elegant dining room chair design was poached from a Charles Rennie Mackintosh catalogue, and the beds are heavy traditional Keralan. The house is modern, indulging a miscellany of architectural fancies – it sort of works. Inside, the central atrium has an almost church-like resonance, wide marble spaces, a sweeping wooden staircase and leaded windows. Downstairs, an ornamental fountain tinkles in the hallway; upstairs, the rooms have more space than you need and private balconies that sit out over the garden. The atmosphere is easy, you come and go as you please and eat with the family around the wooden expanse of the dining table, though the restaurants of Trivandrum are a 10-minute amble away. A peaceful suburban retreat.

rooms	6: 5 doubles, 1 suite. Some a/c.
price	Rs845-Rs1,295. Suite Rs1,595. Plus 7.5 % (non-a/c)-15% (a/c) tax. Peak season: August-January.
meals	Lunch & dinner from Rs125.
closed	Rarely.
directions	6km from Trivandrum airport. Next door to Mathrubhoomi newspaper office & very close to Holy Angels Convent; 20-minute walk from MG Road.

	Hilda & Justin Pereira
tel	+91 471 2471 175
fax	+91 471 2461 971
e-mail	wildpalm@md3.vsnl.net.in
web	www.wildpalmsguesthouse.com

Guesthouse

Lagoona Davina
Pachalloor Village, Trivandrum, 695 027, Kerala

Davina has played out all her fantasies here. A cultured, attractive English lady in her fifties, she was evidently seduced by the raucous colours and textiles of India. This is not so much a resort as a sophisticated traveller's den. Yogic-looking European ladies sit cross-legged in conversation on palm-shaded, low, cushioned platforms overlooking the lagoon, wearing flowing cotton dresses and mirror-embroidered bags bought from the lean-to boutique, while their personal flunkies make sure that their every need is tended to. The rooms are fantastical, like a clairvoyant's tent, all billowing ceiling drapes, gold stencilled borders, rich, ochre walls, old inlaid wooden trinket boxes and four-poster beds – all under thatch. The whole place feels handmade. Some rooms open onto the sandy waterfront garden where books are read in hammocks and food is served at cloth-covered tables. Others are tucked around the back, with small sandy alleys running between them to create a village feel; some are very small. People come to practise yoga, experiment with Ayurveda, or just lounge in this feminine retreat.

rooms	13 doubles.
price	$75–$132. Plus 7.5% tax. Peak season: November–May.
meals	Breakfast $6. Lunch $9. Dinner $15.
closed	Rarely.
directions	4km before Kovalam on the road south of Trivandrum.

	Ms Davina Taylor
tel	+91 471 2380 049
fax	+91 471 2462 935
e-mail	lagoonadavina@hotmail.com
web	www.lagoonadavina.com

Resort

Bethsaida Hermitage

Pulinkudi, Mulloor P.O., Trivandrum, 695 521, Kerala

The set-up is unusual but endearing – for several reasons: you choose your room according to its (rather brave) colour; and there's a surviving affection for moulded concrete. But stranger still is the fact that every cent earned by the resort helps to support the orphanage next door. The huts have been built over time, each new batch in a different style – there are quaint rondavels with brightly coloured outdoor bathrooms, arched terraced cottages that you'd imagine would house Willy Wonka's oompa-loompas, and a traditional Keralan *tharavad*. There is not an ounce of stuffiness here: the staff are not uniformed and meal times are not observed. Yet everyone is unfailingly helpful and the food is better than you might find in many more formal kitchens. Breakfast on the grassy lawns overlooking the sandy cove is memorable: carved melon bowls, endless coffee and spectacular views. What this resort lacks in groomed hospitality management and facilities it more than makes up for with its setting, informality and admirable purpose. Green, cosy and for those who like their tourist dollars to make a difference.

rooms	33: 19 cottages for 2, 14 cottages for 1. Some a/c.
price	Cottages for 1, $60; for 2, $80-$95. Plus 10% tax.
meals	Lunch & dinner from Rs350.
closed	Rarely.
directions	9km on road south of Kovalam. Follow signs to Surya Samudra. 21km from Trivandrum.

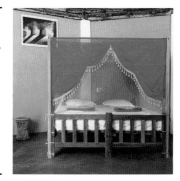

Mr Frederick Thomas

tel	+91 471 2267 554
fax	+91 471 2268 131
e-mail	bethsaida@satyam.net.in

Resort

Karikkathi Beach House

Mulloor, Thottam, Pulinkudi, Trivandrum, Kerala

Foreign diplomats bring their families here as an antidote to the social whirl. It is secluded and comfortable yet wonderfully simple. Mr Sajjad's is an unusual concept in the Indian travel scene, on this stunning spot of terraced shoreline, looking out over the Arabian Sea with a small private beach, and shaded by swaying coconut trees. Perfection! Yet this is only one small house, with only two simple bedrooms – the whole idea fuelled by Sajjad's disgust at the burgeoning concrete desecration of Kerala's coastal beauty. The house, designed by Swiss architect Karl Damschen, uses local materials and natural colours. The roof is palm thatch on lashed wooden poles, the floors are country-red tiles, and the shuttered wooden windows can be flung open to reveal a view of the blue horizon. The beds are cane and comfortable, with linen sheets and cotton throws, and the bathrooms are big and white-tiled. A chef comes to cook when and what you want, and there's a 'boy' on call. Pure escapism – so idyllic that we tell you about it with some reluctance. *Hire a snorkle & wooden canoe from the beach next door.*

rooms	2 doubles.
price	$90. Cottage $190. Peak season: December–January.
meals	Personal chef, all meals for $15 per day.
closed	Rarely.
directions	Just before Surya Samudra Beach Garden on main road south of Kovalam. Arrive at Nagar Bhagavathy Temple at Mulloor Thottam, then a 5-minute walk to the south among the palm grove.

Mr Shaina Sajjad
tel	+91 471 2400 956
e-mail	karikkathi@yahoo.co.in
web	www.pulinkudi.com

Catered cottage

Surya Samudra Beach Garden

Pulinkudi, Mullur P.O., Trivandrum, 695 521, Kerala

One of the first 'heritage' retreats in Kerala, Surya Samudra was started by a German professor from Madras University as his personal beach retreat from city life. His 'octagon' house, now the best room, with glass double doors that open on four sides, gives you a bird's-eye view of the rocky promontory and the sea. Wide stone steps lead grandly down through the sandy garden from the reception, flanked by 15 ancient carved lions from Tamil temples. The mood is hushed and exclusive, the guests are mature and there is total calm. The rooms are all old Keralan houses, dark wooden affairs with verandas and lazy chairs; the sea-facing (more expensive) ones have stunning views through the wide shuttered windows to the blue horizon beyond and you don't even have to stir from your bed to get them. The natural quarry swimming pool built into the rocks overlooking the cliffs is spectacular, and the restaurant is a granite-pillared verandaed semi-circle that has panoramic views over the sunset horizon – one of the most charming places to eat on this stretch of coast. The food's heavenly, too.

rooms	14+ 7: 14 doubles. 7 cottages for 2. Some a/c.
price	$200-$240. Cottages $120-$180. Plus 15% tax. Price increase by between $100 & $200 over Christmas & New Year. Peak season: November-March.
meals	Lunch & dinner fixed menu $17.
closed	Rarely.
directions	8km south of Kovalam; signed.

Mr Vikrant Pathak

tel	+91 471 2267 333
fax	+91 471 2267 124
e-mail	info@suryasamudra.com
web	www.suryasamudra.com

Resort

Somatheeram & Manaltheeram Ayurvedic Resorts

Chowara P.O., South of Kovalam, Trivandrum, 695 501, Kerala

A favourite, with rambling green gardens that tumble down to the clifftop, and cottages that feel more genuine than most. This is the original Ayurvedic resort, and has won the state prize for its treatments for the last five years. Every room dotted up the steep slope has its own little grassy terrace with hammock or table and chairs; the sea-facing ones have views along the gently curving crescent beach that stretches for miles. The steep, stepped gardens have lush, palm-shaded mini-lawns, colourful climbers and hundreds of flower pots bursting with colour through which the paths wind. The buildings feel effortlessly 'heritage', the resort appears to belong here. Thatch, wooden poles, old tiles and brick blend into the surroundings and there is little that doesn't feel natural. The restaurant is at the top of the resort, a buzzing candlelit nest whence you can see the procession of fishermen's lights snaking for miles along the coast. The beach is alive with activity at sunrise, as the early haul is accompanied by Keralan chants. A wonderful resort with a well-deserved reputation.

rooms	94: 93 doubles, 1 suite.
price	$53–$169. Suite $209. Plus 17.5% tax. Peak season: 15 December–15 January.
meals	Breakfast $6. Lunch & dinner from $11.
closed	Rarely.
directions	On main road south of Kovalam towards Balarampuram. 21km from Trivandrum.

Mr Baby Mathew

tel	+91 471 2268 101
fax	+91 471 2267 600
e-mail	somatheeram@vsnl.com
web	www.somatheeram.com/

Duke's Forest Lodge
Anappara, Trivandrum, Kerala

Being here feels massively indulgent, but that's the idea. Claustrophobic hotel rooms are up there at the top of Bailey's pet hate list so he designed this place to give you all the space you could possibly want, plus a wee bit more. The five villas sit at the edge of his organically farmed family estate, overlooking the river at the foot of the forest. The ground floor of each villa houses a small pool-cum-jacuzzi, but if being private isn't your style, the curvaceous communal pool sprawls out enticingly beneath the rooftop restaurant. The bed and bathrooms are on the top level of each villa; unique carved antique beds (king-size, naturally) dominate, yet the feel is one of luxury rather than overstated extravagance. Big verandas are great spots for catching a glimpse of the visiting birds from the nearby reserve. There's good trekking round here and if you need some spicy material for your postcards you could take a day trip to the only natural bonsai forest in the world – really. If you deserve a treat, prefer your own space, and want to see some of Kerala's least-visited natural wonders, you'll be more than happy here.

rooms	5 villas for 2.
price	Full-board only, $150.
meals	Included. Full-board.
closed	Rarely.
directions	48km from Trivandrum airport on the Ponmudi Road. Follow the signs.

	Mr Jacob Bailey
tel	+91 471 2268 822
fax	+91 471 2267 822
e-mail	nest@sancharnet.in
web	www.dukesforest.com

Resort

Photography by Victor Dey, Tranquil Plantation Hideaway

karnataka

Four Winds Estate

Mysore Road, Madikeri, Kodagu, 571 201, Karnataka

The Colonel's enthusiasm for India and Kodagu (Coorg) is infectious and enchanting. He is a remarkable, kind and interesting man, well-read and educated, easy company – and the main reason for including his modern house in this book. The house is basic but comfortable, cosy, without frills or luxury, with pleasant views to the distant hills and with no rules. You have a large double bed, a window onto the garden, brightly coloured curtains, good lighting, interesting books to read. You share the sitting room with Pradeep, as Colonel Uthaya is called; it is cosy and traditional, with wooden sofas and lightly checked covers, a dark red floor and traditional rug, and a miscellany of objects. If you want lunch or dinner the Colonel will take you into town; it is all very new and he hasn't quite 'got going' yet, but there is stacks to do in the area and Pradeep can organise anything – even himself (with car) if you are lucky – and will collect you if you come by bus. This is no smooth-running tourist machine – just a delightful and very human encounter with the best of modern India. *Trekking, golf, angling, birdwatching.*

rooms	2: 1 double, 1 single.
price	Rs600. Single Rs500. Peak season: November–May.
meals	Lunch Rs250. Dinner Rs250.
closed	Rarely.
directions	2km from Madikeri centre on road to Mysore. The Colonel will pick up, or direct you in more detail.

	Lt Col K G Uthaya
tel	+91 8272 225 720
e-mail	speedy8@rediffmail.com
web	www.gurudongma.com

Homestay

Sandbanks

Polaycad Estate, Ammathi P.O. 30, South Kodagu, 571 211, Karnataka

A feast for the eyes, mind, body and spirit – in the bend of the Cauvery river and with hills just to the west. It is often the people who make a place special and Micky, his wife, mother and children, wonderfully kind and generous, are rooted in this place and treat you as friends. Upon arrival you might sit in the thatched gazebo for a chat, the peace of the place washing over you. Their modern bungalow on the gentle green slopes of the garden is elegant and beautiful. You sleep in a purpose-designed gazebo with a bedroom, bathroom and veranda and a place for casual eating. The furnishings are warm without being opulent. It is simple, beautifully decorated, with high ceilings, plenty of light and all mod cons. The 'vestibules' have terracotta tiles, cream walls and orangey bedspreads. There is also a very large tent pitched under a thatched gazebo, with a double bed and its own bathroom block close by – fun for anyone but especially so for children. Prakesh, the serving-man, is always available but you never feel suffocated by service – as can often happen in India. A special place indeed, in gorgeous countryside. *Good trekking.*

rooms	3: 2 doubles, 1 thatch-covered tent for 2.
price	Rs1,500. Tent Rs750. Peak season: October–May.
meals	Lunch & dinner from Rs110.
closed	Rarely.
directions	110km from Mysore & 185km from Mangalore.

Mr Micky Kalappa
tel   +91 8274 452 130
e-mail kalaps@sancharnet.in

Homestay

 F–G   **map 9   entry 167**

The Green Hotel

Chittaranjan Palace, 2270 Vinoba Road, Jayalakshmipuram, Mysore, 570 012, Karnataka

Once a film set, this palace, just outside Mysore, was built in the 1920s by the Maharaja for his three unmarried sisters, and very nice it is too – not too big, with plenty of air, space and original character. Rooms in the main house are the best: the Maharani suite with its four-poster bed and antiques, the two Bollywood rooms with dark wood furniture and bright, but pleasing, framed photos of stars of the Indian screen. The annexe rooms are more modern, pleasantly, simply furnished and overlook the lawns – mind the monkeys don't get your bananas. Blooming with marigolds and bougainvillea, the garden is fragrant and lovely at breakfast time and after dark; eat in the shaded restaurant area, candlelit at night – Indian, Chinese or continental. This is a fine place to relax, on a cane chair on the veranda, or on a window seat – there are plenty of books and games. There's also a travel desk and helpful staff; Srirangapatnam and the Ranganathittu Bird Sanctuary are beautiful and peaceful. The hotel is 'green' because it aims to be a model of sustainable tourism and its profits go to Indian charities and environmental projects.

rooms	31: 24 doubles, 5 suites.
price	Rs1,500–Rs3,750. Suites Rs2,250–Rs4,750. Plus 12.5% tax. Peak season: October–8 March.
meals	Lunch & dinner from Rs110.
closed	Rarely.
directions	Leaving Mysore on road to Madikeri, hotel signed to right, 50–100m after Basappa Memorial Hospital. Your landmark is old Premier Film Studios.

Mr J Hilel Manohar

tel	+91 821 2512 536
fax	+91 821 2516 139
e-mail	grenhotl@sancharnet.in
web	www.greenhotelindia.com

Heritage Hotel

Alath Cad Estate

Ammathi P.B. No. 7, South Kodagu, 571 211, Karnataka

There are 65 acres of lush green coffee plantation all around the bungalow and distant mountain views through a million shades of green. You are in splendid isolation from the world, though neither from the bird life nor the butterflies – both ubiquitous and beautiful. The family has been here for generations and has done lovely things with the building and gardens. There is a delightful red-tiled courtyard area, the bedrooms are charming, with – perhaps – blue and white chiffon curtains, white walls and views onto the garden. There is a cottage with suites, in similar style but with big, beamed ceilings. All is simple, in good and imaginative taste and the family are delightful company... strong-willed, amusing, energetic, kind and friendly. They live separately but are always on hand – able to organise treks, bike rides (bikes are there for your use), fishing, golf, birdwatching and picnics by the river. It is a fine place to which to retreat, perhaps with a group of friends, and centre yourself, and you are only 70 miles from Mysore, one of the most 'amenable' of Indian cities. *Cycling, birdwatching, fishing.*

rooms	10 doubles.
price	Half-board only, Rs2,000.
meals	Included. Half-board. Lunch Rs240.
closed	Rarely.
directions	2km from Ammathi. Well signed, or if in doubt, ask. Mysore 110km. Virajpet bus station 12km.

Mrs Kannu Muddaiah

tel	+91 8274 452 190
e-mail	mudhus@rediffmail.com
web	www.alathcadcoorg.com
res. no.	+91 80 3683 2747

Homestay

  map 9   entry 169

Orange County

Karadigodu Post, Siddapur, Kodagu, 571 253, Karnataka

Comfortable and elegant - Orange County manages to avoid the 'pack 'em in' ethos that dominates other resorts. The place exudes calm; it is has captured something special, an edge over others. The atmosphere is mature, the service impeccable and the comfort total. The architecture is an intriguing, thatched, mock-Tudor whose white walls and red tiled floors create breezy, open spaces within to counter the close, dense forest without. Wooden beams span thatched ceilings and dark wooden furniture sits invitingly on balconied living areas, guarded by rosewood and brass doors. However, what earns Orange County the 'resort' title, aside from the buffet meals, are the many activities and facilities, from Ayurvedic Spa to gym, all tucked into low-slung, unobtrusive buildings. Venturing beyond the resort is made easy – *mahseer* (Canadian salmon with fight) fishing, birdwatching, golf and jungle safaris are effortlessly arranged, and all nearby. A peaceful, luxurious retreat for those wanting to relinquish responsibility for their holiday. *Good trekking.*

rooms	50: 48 cottages for 2; 2 private pool villas.
price	$120-$140. Villa $270.
meals	Breakfast $6. Lunch & dinner $9.
closed	Rarely.
directions	5km from Siddapur on road to Mysore. Well-signed. 245km (5 hours) from Bangalore, 200km (5 hours) from Mangalore.

Mr Sanjay Sinha

tel	+91 8274 458 481
e-mail	coorg@trailsindia.com
web	www.trailsindia.com

AYURVEDA

The word *ayur* means life, and *veda*, the science or the knowledge. Ayurveda is a holistic philosophy that prescribes certain practices for achieving a healthy, happy, comfortable and advantageous life – physically, mentally and socially. It focuses on prevention rather than cure and is widely practised by southern Indians, for whom it is part of their everyday existence.

Many hotels and resorts that cater for Western tourists have realised the commercial benefit of offering Ayurvedic treatment, and do so with varying levels of professionalism. Ayurveda treatment is not 'a quick fix', but should be received over a long period – and preferably during the monsoon when the conditions are thought to be perfect. There is wide debate as to whether the short treatment usually taken by holidaying Westerners outside the monsoon period might not, in fact, be harmful.

There have been some reports about charlatan masseurs not only practising dangerous versions of Ayurveda, but of being indecent when 'treating' female patients. The resorts listed in this book that offer treatment should introduce you to a safe environment in which to experience Ayurveda. However, it must be said that short-term treatment should be seen as rejuvenation and not as a cure-all.

Photography by Michael Busselle

tamil nadu

Jungle Retreat

Bokkapuram, Nilgiri District, Masinagudi, 643 223, Tamil Nadu

The 35-acre estate goes right to the feet of the Nilgiri hills – lushly beautiful countryside, especially in the rainy season. To sit up in one of the gorgeous bamboo treehouses and take in the view must be one of India's most seductive holiday experiences. It is wild, remote and irresistible, for Hermie and her son Rohan are remarkable, too, and seem to love having people around. They have created some interesting spaces in their bamboo-and-thatch cottages which are simple and small but charming and full of character. All is made from natural materials and each room is like a cottage, with its own semi-open-air bathroom with shower in an airy brick 'outhouse'. The family rooms are done out with rosewood and teak, including the beds, with batik on the walls and their own tiled bathrooms. There are deluxe rooms too, of stone, wood and impeccable taste. (Note that there is a tented children's camp here in the summer holidays, so check the dates if you want to join in or avoid.) The communal bar/dining room, with snooker table, has a relaxed mood. A wonderful place. *Camping, trekking & Toda tribal village visits.*

rooms	5 + 7: 5 family rooms. 7 cottages. Some a/c. Tented accommodation as required.
price	Rs1,000-Rs2,000. Peak season: mid-April-mid-June.
meals	Breakfast Rs150. Lunch Rs200. Dinner Rs250.
closed	Rarely.
directions	6km from Masinagudi on the Bokkapuram Road. Right at the temple & follow signs.

Rohan & Hermie Mathias

tel	+91 423 2526 469
e-mail	bookings@jungleretreat.com
web	www.jungleretreat.com

Homestay

Glyngarth Villa Resorts

Golf Club Road, Finger Post, The Nilgiris, Udhagamandalam (Ooty), 643 006, Tamil Nadu

Famous for its serene eminence, Ooty is one of India's best known colonial hill-stations. And here, touching the 'heavenly clouds' at about 7,600 feet is the splendid old Glyngarth, built in 1850 by Sir Walter Moude in the colonial style. It's all very nostalgic for British visitors. It is also rather homely, with a big reception area and a wooden staircase to the light and airy rooms. The mood is casual and 'family', in spite of the fact that this is a hotel. There's lots of wood, comfort, and atmosphere – though a lick of paint would be welcome. There's a big sitting room with wooden floor, cream walls, window seats, floor-seating and sofas. The dining table seats 10 and is a snug focal point, especially in winter, when log fires may be lit. All around are the terraced fields where their vegetables are grown, tall pine trees (and others) rolling down the hills to the fine views. The garden is well looked after and has shaded seating areas. A thoroughly decent place with charming staff and a lovely setting, though you can just hear the traffic in the distance. *Take a drive in the Hillman 1951 classic. River rafting, hang gliding, horse riding, trekking and golf.*

rooms	5 doubles.
price	$35-$45. Plus 12.5% tax. Peak season: 14 April-15 June; 15 October-15 January.
meals	Lunch & dinner Rs200.
closed	Rarely.
directions	4-5km outside Ooty on the road to Mysore, 500m before the Golf Club. Entrance on the right.

Mr Sahid

tel	+91 423 2445 754
fax	+91 423 2445 440
e-mail	glyngarth@sify.com
web	www.glyngarthvilla.com

Resort

  map 9 entry 172

The Tryst

Carolina Tea Estate, P.O. Box 6, Coonoor, Nilgiris, 643 102, Tamil Nadu

An Aladdin's cave of 'things', either antique, interesting, odd or baffling. What to make of the old telephones and toy cars, the half-dozen gramophones and the biscuit tins? There are Ann's tapestries and embroideries, not to mention framed jigsaw puzzles, lace table covers and home-made fire-screens. It is a wild and energetic clutter, in a house that is stuffed with personality. Not for the steel-and-teak minimalist but there is something engaging about the sheer unexpectedness of it all. You could spend many happy rainy days in the library, games room, music room (two pianos), billiard room – even the exercise room. It's is in the loveliest possible place among the tea plantations, with rolling views and great walks and Coonoor out of sight behind a hill. Sathya worked for 17 years as a doctor in Liverpool where he met Ann and then brought her back here. They are fun, mildly eccentric, enthusiastic, imaginative and generous (they have a bedroom with hot water and TV, for drivers). And they will organise your whole holiday if you give them half a chance. *They run the Salutary Trust for sustainable development.*

rooms	6: 5 doubles, 1 cottage for up to 10.
price	Half-board only, Rs3,500. Family cottage Rs6,000. Peak season: September–March.
meals	Included. Half-board. Lunch Rs150–Rs175.
closed	June–1 August.
directions	2km from Coonor bus stand. Take road going up opposite the Coonor railway crossing. After 1km follow signs down the left fork. The Tryst is 1.5km away.

	Dr Sathya & Ann Rao
tel	+91 423 2207 057
fax	+91 423 2207057
e-mail	drrao@trystindia.com
web	www.trystindia.com

Homestay

Bison Wells

'Camp George', Oberservatory P.O., Kodaikanal, 624 103, Tamil Nadu

One well provides water for washing and another for the kitchen; the third well is for the bison that come out of the forest to drink. The forest teems with life and at night the noises are exhilarating. Your view is across a shallow and wooded valley to thickly forested hills, for you are on the edge of a natural reserve – the reason why George built this remote lodge made of clay and wood. He is a serious ecologist and you learn much from him. He lives in Kodaikanal but comes to be with guests and sleeps down the hill in a little hut. Your space is basic and unremarkable, in natural earthy shades of yellow and green and without frills. The little bathroom is equally rustic and simple, with buckets to empty down the loo – but it all works perfectly. The helper, Williams, prepares your meals in the little kitchen and you eat out on the veranda – you'll while away many hours here. Walk a few yards from the house and you are in deep nature – and there are many lovely walks to do, perhaps with a guide from the lodge. An unusual and rich experience. *Trekking, birdwatching and jungle trails.*

rooms	1 cottage for 2-3.
price	Full-board only $30.
meals	Included. Full-board.
closed	Rarely.
directions	90-minute drive from Kodaikanal. Contact George in Kodaikanal for provisions & transport.

	Mr George Roshan
tel	+91 4542 240 566
e-mail	bisonwells@rediffmail.com
web	www.wilderness-explorer.com

Ecolodge

Mayuram Lodge

Kallarackal Farm, Govindaperri Village, Ambassamudram Taluk, Tirunelveli District

Paddy fields dotted with palms meet the Western Ghats - this is a beautiful place. Rajesh is a bubbling source of ideas on environmental issues such as rainwater harvesting and he is re-establishing an indigenous forest on his estate. Close at hand are walks in the wooded hills and among lakes, with the relief of swimming in mountain streams. The great variety of habitat makes it superb for bird watchers. Rajesh, educated in America, used his skills as an architect cleverly to design the guesthouse around a court with an ornamental pool – in keeping with the architectural vernacular. The bedrooms open onto a generous balcony overlooking the estate. The farm is some distance from a main road so you need to make certain that you know where you are going. If Rajesh is not going to be there you can ring him anyway to get him to pass any special requests to the servants; they don't speak much English but will look after you very well. They will also serve you excellent Indian food, which you can digest in the small library.

rooms	3 doubles.
price	Full-board only Rs3,150. Peak season: November-15 March.
meals	Included. Full-board.
closed	Rarely.
directions	135km from Trivandrum. 235km from Kochi. See web site for directions.

	Mr Rajesh George
tel	+91 4634 240 715
e-mail	prakrti@vsnl.com
web	www.mayuramfarm.com
res. no.	+91 484 2307 955

Ecolodge

Cardamom House

Athoor Village, Dindigul, 624 701, Tamil Nadu

Few places in Karnataka, let alone India, dish up such a fine lamb hotpot with mashed spud. Chris is a foodie, a traveller, a gentleman and a comic. A retired British doctor, he has poured energy and passion into creating his Utopia. His humour and zest infuse the place, the staff wear the broadest smiles in Dindigul and the place sweeps you into its warm embrace, leaving stuffiness banished. The house stands alone at the foot of a steep hill, huddled in a horseshoe of scrub hills with views across the lake to the Western Ghats beyond. In three separate buildings, the rooms are a picture of taste and restraint – tiled red floors, crisp white linen and a single fresh flower on the bed. Verandas crouch beneath bougainvillea cascades of every colour, creating hidden spots in which to escape into a book; rooftop terraces sit beneath a nocturnal frenzy of Indian stars. Ultimately, the feeling is of conviviality, of sharing the treat of having discovered a moment of true happiness in the remote heart of rural India. *Chris loves introducing interested guests to 'real' India, and will arrange trips into the local village.*

rooms	7: 6 doubles, 1 suite.
price	Rs3,350. Suite Rs4,000. Peak season: December-March.
meals	Breakfast Rs150. Lunch Rs200. Dinner Rs300.
closed	Rarely.
directions	27km from Dindigul, 65km from Madurai. Off the beaten track so contact Chris for his set of detailed directions, he will arrange a motorcycle escort for the last 5km from Athoor.

	Dr Chris Lucas
tel	+91 451 2556 765
fax	+91 451 2556 795
e-mail	cardamomhouse@yahoo.com
web	www.cardamomhouse.com

Homestay

The Bangala

Devakottai Road, Senjai, Karaikudi, 630 001, Tamil Nadu

After bumping across many miles of scarred road to get here you may have begun to wonder why. The beautiful manners of Mr Gopalakrishnan soon banish memories of the dust and heat of the journey. Karaikudi has its other secrets, too. This is the centre of the Chettiars, a small coterie of families who wielded immense commercial influence under the Raj. Their 'palaces' are thick on the ground in a scattering of small villages in this area, and in Karaikudi itself. Imagine turning the corner in a bamboo-and-dust village to be confronted by a long avenue lined on both sides with a tatterdemalion collection of villas, mansions, manors and mini-palaces from every conceivable era and European country. You shake your head to throw off the dizzy moment – but they are still there. The Chettiars poured their riches – some made from Burmese teak – into these monuments and into their local temples. The results are astonishing. The Bangala, more like a villa, serves superb food and is run with kindness and discretion – all is elegant, comfortable and understated. It is like a country house whose owner is absent but there in spirit.

rooms	8 doubles.
price	Full-board only, Rs6,000. Plus 5% tax.
meals	Included. Full-board.
closed	During Diwali Festival.
directions	At the beginning of Devakottai Road, in the Senjai area of Karaikudi. Trichy & Madurai train stations are within easy reach.

	Mr A K Gopalakrishnan
tel	+91 4565 220 221
fax	+91 44 2493 4543
e-mail	bangala@vsnl.com
web	www.thebangala.com
res. no.	+91 44 2493 4912

Guesthouse

Sterling Swamimalai

6/30B Thimmakkudy Agraharam., Swamimalai, Kumbakonam, Tanjore District, 612 302

Ayurveda is hard to avoid in southern India, and here it is the very essence of the place. Few hotels are so devoted to the practice and you can genuinely learn a great deal and be magnificently treated, perhaps in the unusual copper sauna bath. (Many hotels offer Ayurvedic treatment but much of it is dubious.) The hotel is in an old villa, in six acres of land amid coconut groves. The buildings are enchanting, done with an eye on authenticity, and the bedrooms are plain, simple and gently attractive – with, perhaps, soft beige walls and wooden beds. The facilities and activities are impressive: herbal oil massage, classical and folk theatre, pottery, swimming pool and health centre. You are on the banks of the river Cauvery, in a "confluence of leisure, heritage, health, nature, aesthetics, spirituality, fine arts and fun that creates harmony for the body, mind and soul" to quote the splendid brochure. The staff are unusually delightful and the food is delicious. Note that this is very much a resort hotel – although with a strong difference – and you will encounter groups here. But they are likely to be good company.

rooms	25: 22 doubles, 3 suites.
price	$94. Peak season: October-March.
meals	Breakfast $4. Lunch & dinner $8.
closed	Rarely.
directions	91km from Trichy; 211km from Madurai; 300km from Chennai. All these cities have airports.

	Mr Senthilnathan
tel	+91 435 2480 044
fax	+91 438 2481 705
e-mail	swamimal@md4.vsnl.net.in
web	www.sterlingswamimalai.net
res. no.	+91 44 4984 114

Resort

 D

 map 10   entry 178

Hotel de L'Orient

17 Rue Romain Rolland, Pondicherry, 605 001, Tamil Nadu

In the pretty, pastel charm of colonial Pondicherry, you could be forgiven for forgetting this is India. The hotel, formerly the French Department of Education, is an elegant pink-and-white 18th-century mansion in which the 14 rooms are decorated with antiques, terracotta statuettes, rhinestone-studded oleographs and Savonnerie-style dhurries made on the looms of Jaipur. For your own private terrace, complete with pillared recess and terracotta-tiled floor, choose the Karikal Suite. From the vast and superior Chandernagore Suite to the tiny crow's nest of Gingy, reached via treacherous, ladder-like steps, each room is rich in individual character, with the boring essentials of life secreted in teak cupboards and dowry chests. Some of the high, beam-ceilinged, wood-shuttered rooms overlook the internal courtyard, where Creole food – a blend of French and Tamil – is served. Breakfasts are delicious, with fresh tropical juices and delicious Neemrana jams, which can be bought in the hotel. Listen hard, and you might just hear the ripples of the Bay of Bengal lapping against the shore a short, two-street hop away.

rooms	14: 10 doubles, 1 single, 3 suites.
price	Rs2,250-Rs2,750. Single Rs1,750. Suite Rs3,500. Peak season: September-March.
meals	Breakfast Rs100. Lunch Rs250. Dinner Rs350.
closed	Rarely.
directions	In central Pondicherry. 175km from Chennai railway station and 160km from Chennai airport.

	Mr Anthony Gabriel Thomas
tel	+91 413 343 067
fax	+91 11 2435 1112
e-mail	orient1804@satyam.net.in
web	www.neemranahotels.com
res. no.	+91 11 2435 6145

Heritage Hotel

WHAT'S IN THE BACK OF THE BOOK?

TRAVEL AGENTS & TOUR OPERATORS

Not all of the following tour operators are bonded (see introduction). If they are, we say so. We have indicated where this is the case.

UK Western & Oriental Travel Ltd (www.westernoriental.com) have a thorough knowledge of India and real expertise in running tailor-made tours throughout the subcontinent. Their advice has been invaluable in the compiling of this guide. Tel: 020 7313 6611. E-mail: info@westernoriental.com Contact: Georgie North. *Bonded.*

Kerala Connections (www.keralaconnections.com) – a small outfit run by a husband and wife team that arranges trips to the southern coastal state. Their website has useful information about travel in Kerala. Tel: 01892 722 440. E-mail: info@keralaconnect.co.uk. *Bonded.*

India Some of our owners run their own travel companies, which we mention in the italics section of our write-ups. Here are others that you might contact:

Banyan Tours & Travels Private Ltd, Delhi plus regional offices – can organise all manner of travel within India. Will organise cars, trains, hotel bookings, flights and the fiddly aspects of getting around India. Tel: (00 91) 11 2435 0435. E-mail: banyan.delhi@vsnl.com *(Banyan work in association with Western & Oriental.)*

Choomti Travellers, Delhi – Simon Blazely, a true gentleman, organises individual travel throughout India, and has particular sympathies for the less mainstream tourist of any budget level. However, he can organise travel for any pocket. Tel: (00 91) 11 2331 1194. E-mail: choomti@vsnl.com

Sundale Tours, Kochi, Kerala (www.sundale.com) – a charming, small outfit that organises homestays, cookery holidays and backwater cruises and can help with any travel arrangements in southern India. Tel: (00 91) 484 2380 127. E-mail: tropical@vsnl.com

Explore Culture & Tours, Delhi (www.exploreculturetours.com) – specialists in North Indian travel, trekking and mountaineering with a strong focus on low-impact travel. Tel: (00 91) 11 2335 8711. E-mail: ect@bol.net.in

TRAVEL AGENTS & TOUR OPERATORS & GLOSSARY

Timeless Tours and Excursions, Delhi (www.timelessexcursions.com)
– specialist advice for both gay and disabled travellers to India,
as well as tours focused on pottery, museums, fishing and tea
gardens.
Tel: (00 91) 11 2626 1198. E-mail: timeless@vsnl.com

*Though we are happy to recommend the above companies, we are not
responsible for any dealings you have with them.*

Explanation of Indian words that appear in our descriptions

chai	Hindi for tea
chhatri	small ornamental pavilion beneath a cupola
cupola	small, delicate dome resting in pillars
dhurrie	flat-woven cotton rug
durbar	large hall used for holding court or audience
haveli	a large town mansion with courtyards, built by royal families for their courtly visits to main towns
jharokha	a decorative protruding balcony, usually filled with bolsters and cushions
jali	ornamental pierced or latticed stone screen. Designed to keep the hot desert air out and let the light in, and to allow women to see but not be seen
mahal	palace
tharavad	Keralan ancestral home
ghat	steps down a river bank, often used for washing

GENERAL ADVICE

Water scarcity and responsible tourism

India is suffering – the monsoons are failing to arrive more often than ever before, water tables are dropping dramatically, people and livestock are dying. It is a serious problem and the Indian government realises it can no longer be brushed aside. Though lack of monsoon rains is part of the problem, deforestation, extravagant use of water, poor conservation and bad management play their part. Indian communities have coped with poor rains and semi-arid climes for generations – they have been frugal and innovative, adapting with each successive year of meagre rains.

Yet the Indian population is ballooning beyond sustainable levels, and the advent of Western technologies and tastes, and furious consumerism, has stretched resources to breaking point. The growth of tourism in India has made a bad problem worse. Huge demands are made by foreign visitors whose love of deep, wallowing baths and power-showers takes no account of the scarcity of water. Hotels in the desert regions with huge water gardens and miles of infinity pools are drilling further and further down into the ground each year to slake their thirst, while nearby villages find their communal taps running dry and their animals dying from starvation.

It is the great paradox – India's tourism brings the foreign exchange desperately needed to fuel its growth, yet many of her people are suffering as a direct result. A more considered, careful approach to tourism is needed, and visitors to India must understsand that their behaviour can send damaging ripples beyond the hotel walls. So be aware of where you are – do not run baths in the desert.

Culture clashes

India's beaches are undeniably beautiful and, for many, the main lure of the country. Yet for coastal fishing communities the beach is something entirely different – their work place and often their home. The sight of scantily clad tourists causes huge offence to more traditional Indians of all religions, and topless sunbathing in public is utterly intolerable.

For tourism to sit happily alongside local communities, foreigners must be aware of their behaviour and its effects on the local communities around them. Indian women in particular will rarely bare much flesh and would certainly be grateful if you followed suit – especially around religious sites.

GENERAL ADVICE

Communities visited by tourists often complain that their
children are abandoning school to hound tourists for money.
Though it may go against your instincts, you should not give
money, sweets and pens to school kids. Leave donations with
established Indian charities instead.

Getting involved   There are hundreds of charitable organisations needing help
in the shape of both money and time. Below are a few that are
running interesting projects, and who would happily welcome
donations. Though help is always needed, it is often difficult to
organise the sort of short-term work that holiday-makers would
be able to offer.

• CRY (Child Relief and You) www.cry.org – based in Delhi
(with offices in Mumbai, Bangalore, Chennai and Kolkatta)
this organisation concentrates on rescuing children from slums,
educating and supporting them. You can sponsor individual
children.
Tel: (00 91) 11 2649 3137. Address: DDA Slum Wing, (Barat
Ghar), Bapu Park, Kotla Mubarakpur, New Delhi 110 003.
E-mail: cryinfo.del@crymail.org

• DCWA (Delhi Commonwealth Women's Association) – runs a
community support centre that offers cheap medication, family
planning and ante-natal support, cancer and tuberculosis
detection programmes, and pre-school education facilities.
Tel: (00 91) 11 2642 7878. Address: DCWA Medical Centre,
Zamrudpur, Kailash Colony Extension, New Delhi 100 048

• Rotary International www.rotary.org – runs many localised
projects across India (and elsewhere). Their major polio
eradication programme, among others, needs continual funding.
Tel: (00 91) 11 2374 8108. Address: Rotary International,
Thapar House, 124 Janpath Lane, New Delhi 110 001.
E-mail: bholav@rotaryintl.org

• Father Tony Fleming Memorial Trust – a leprosy rehabilitation
and eradication project working in Jharsaguda, Bilaspur in the
eastern state of Orissa. Donations can be made to Tony's niece,
Angela Devonport.
Tel: 01626 832 500. Address: Wildbank, Chapple Road,
Bovey Tracey, Devon, TQ13 9JZ.

GENERAL ADVICE

Planning your trip

Getting your jabs

Plan your course of injections well in advance, as there are fears that having a quick succession of vaccinations might lead to health problems. Most GP practices will have information about travel clinics or you can consult these websites:

The Scottish NHS provides a brief overview (www.fitfortravel.scot.nhs.uk) of the risks and precautions when travelling anywhere.

The Travel Doctor (www.traveldoctor.co.uk) is a comprehensive site which also lists official travel clinics.

When to travel

Within this vast country is every geographic extreme, from the parched Thar desert of Rajasthan to the unending tropical greenery of Kerala and the jagged glacier-carved peaks of the Himalayas. There is no 'perfect' time to visit India – when Gujarat is creaking and baking in the searing summer heat, Ladakh is emerging into blissful spring sunshine, the flowers bursting through the melting snow. But there are times when certain areas will be impossible to enjoy and others when they will be in full splendour. Below are the months during which you're likely to have the easiest time:

Southern India October to March

Rajasthan, Gujarat and central-Northern India October to March

The Himalayan foothills March to September

The Himalayas May to September

Where there are no fans or no air-conditioning, this is generally for a good reason. You do not need a fan in Sikkim, just as you do not need an open fire in coastal Kerala. All the hotels in the book will be geared towards the local climate, so fear not if you don't see the symbol for a fan in the Himalayan foothills. However, not everywhere in India's hotter parts has air-conditioning. Sticky nights can be the price you pay for glorious, unbroken sunshine. Be prepared for a little discomfort. Where air-con has been laid on for the passing tourists, be prepared to pay more for the privilege of being cooled – electricity is expensive in India.

GENERAL ADVICE

Festivals and Public Holidays

There are hundreds of religious and cultural festivals in India, some peculiar to tiny regions and others that bring the country to a standstill. They are colourful, sometimes loud and occasionally of epic proportions.

National Holidays:

Republic Day (26 January) – a spectucular, jingoistic parade of India's military might down Rajpath in Delhi. Tickets from Delhi Tourism Office.

Independence Day (15 August) – the country's biggest secular celebration, marking independence from Britain.

Public Holidays

Id-ul-Zuha (February) – the Muslim feast of sacrifice.

Holi (7 March 2004; 26 March 2005) – a key Hindu festival to mark the end of the winter, where effigies are burnt and coloured powder thrown liberally in riotous crowds.

Dussehra (20-22 October 2004; 20-22 October 2005) – nine days of celebrations depict the victorious battles of Rama with Ravana, ending in the burning of vast effigies.

Diwali (12 November 2004; 1 November 2005) – Rama's return to Ayodhya is celebrated in almost every Hindu village, with the burning of oil lamps in every home.

Popular festival dates

Bikaner Camel Fair (Bikaner, Rajasthan)
6-7 January 2004; 24-25 January 2005

Nagaur Fair (Nagaur, Rajasthan)
28-31 January 2004; 15-18 February 2005

Desert Festival (Jaisalmer, Rajasthan)
4-6 February 2004; 21-31 February 2005

Elephant Festival (Jaipur, Rajasthan)
6 March 2004; 25 March 2005

Hemis Festival (Leh, Ladakh)
2004: June/July – like the Kumbh Mela, this year's festival is an extra special one that comes around only once every 12 years.

GENERAL ADVICE

Teej Fair (Jaipur, Rajasthan)
19-20 August 2004; 8-9 August 2005

Marwar Festival (Jodhpur, Rajasthan)
22-23 September 2004; 12-13 September 2005

Pushkar Fair (Pushkar, Rajasthan)
18-26 November 2004; 8-15 November 2005

Puram Festival (Kerala) 30 April 2004

Onam Festival (Kerala) Culminating in the spectacular Nehru
Trophy Boat Tace in Alappuzha: 28 August 2004

Travel in India

Arriving in Delhi

Most people coming to India arrive in the capital city. Here's
how to cope:

Stepping through airport security into the main throngs of
Indira Ghandi International Airport can be a bewildering
experience and getting a taxi organised before you enter the
main crowds outside the gates is the best idea. In the arrivals
area, just before you get to the first crowd of waiting family
members and hotel drivers, go to the official 'Pre-Paid Taxi'
counter but make sure it's the government counter (yellow).
There are several other companies that could charge you triple
the standard rate of Rs300 into central Delhi. You will be issued
with a chit that you take outside to any green and black taxi.
You do not need to pay anything further to the driver.

If you feel uncomfortable letting a porter disappear with
your luggage firmly refuse any help and insist on pushing
your trolley yourself.

Where possible, book a hotel before arriving, and go straight
there. A common scam used by taxi drivers is to tell you that
your booked hotel is now closed because of some drama (fire
or building problems, for example) and then take you to an
expensive hotel of their choice.

Moving on

The Indian public transport system is truly remarkable – it is
possible to get anywhere you want for a song, and in hugely
varying degrees of comfort. You can travel the length of the
country by first class train, spending the nights snuggled under
fresh white sheets in air-conditioned cabins, or you might bounce
along rutted dirt roads in prehistoric buses, squeezed in among
whole families and their clucking, bleating livestock.

GENERAL ADVICE

Train Travel

One legacy of British colonial rule that Indians will admit to
being grateful for is the train system. The second biggest in
the world, it is absolutely vast (the largest employer in the
world with over 1.6 million workers on the pay roll) and it
stretches from the coastal ports right up into the foothills of the
Himalayas. It can be a romantic way to travel and is something
of an institution among travellers, though it remains a vital
artery for 12 million Indians each day. At first glance it looks
like complete chaos, yet it seems to work with remarkable
efficiency. Reservations made on chits of scrappy paper in
dishevelled offices appear as lists of printed names on the side
of each carriage, your name, sex and age there for all to see.

Not all Indian trains are as infuriatingly slow as you're led to
believe. The main metropolitan areas (Kolkatta, Delhi, Mumbai
and Chennai) are connected by the Rajdhani Express, while
other localised express routes have, in places, halved old journey
times. The Shatabdi Express has also been introduced as a
commuter and tourist train between certain cities and tourist
honey pots. It is fast, air-conditioned and generally on time,
and included in the ticket price are drinks and meals (and fresh
linen if you are on a sleeper).

Classes

The trains have several classes (sometimes as many as seven)
that offer quite different experiences. However, listed below are
the ones that all but the hardiest of travellers use.

1st Class a/c Apart from the joy of going to sleep in Rajasthan
and waking up in Mumbai, the appeal of using trains is the
amount you save compared to using India's domestic airlines.
This is not the case with 1st a/c, which is barely any cheaper
than flying, though unarguably very comfortable.

2nd Class Sleeper Most travellers use these carriages. They are
pretty safe, comfortable and cheaper than flying. You will share
the cabin with three or five other people so you might want to
attach yourself to a group of other travellers. You can pay more
for air-conditioning in 2nd Class, though many prefer not to be
sealed behind an opaque double-glazed window.

GENERAL ADVICE

(2nd Class Unreserved is half the price, though rough wooden benches and serious overcrowding make it little better than hitching a lift in a cattle truck.)

Special Trains Apart from the quaint 'toy trains' that wind their way between numerous hill stations, India's luxury 'Royal' trains are overpriced, naff and outdated – a failed attempt to resurrect the once-splendid manner in which maharajas and viceregal entourages used to travel. Unless you are a railway fanatic, you could be disappointed.

Indrail Passes Those wanting to travel all over India should consider buying this pass. Issued for anything between one day ($43, 2nd class) and 90 days ($530), it is good value if used heavily. They are available at major hub railway stations in the foreigner's travel bureau and from travel agents; you can only buy the pass in foreign currency.

Booking A certain number of seats on every long-distance train are saved for senior government employees, though most are never used. Those not used are released for sale the day before departure, so there is nearly always a chance to get a seat. However, it is best to book well in advance, especially on popular routes during the high season. A cunning trick is to buy your ticket when you can, knowing that cancelling right up to the day before will incur only a Rs50 cancellation fee.

For timetables and availability you can sign up for a government train site (www.indianrail.gov.in). Tel: 00 91 011 2340 5156

Travelling alone as a woman

Women do occasionally get hassled in train carriages, especially at night. Though it tends not to be serious, it is at least infuriating. There are women and children's carriages that provide sanctuary for those not wanting to be ogled. Make sure you demand to be placed in this carriage when making a booking.

Security on trains

It is not uncommon for bags to go missing while you are asleep. Be sensible – keep your vital belongings with you, tied around your waist. If you haven't already got one, you may be able to buy a chain and padlock on the station platform to lock your larger bags to the seats. Befriend your fellow cabin passengers; this might encourage them to keep an eye on your belongings.

GENERAL ADVICE

Road Travel

Using the roads in India is an experience, and not always an
enjoyable one. The traffic in built-up areas is hectic, loud and
undisciplined, and a smooth stretch of tarmac without potholes
is rare. European driving conventions are not followed; the
horn is used more than the brake and the vehicular pecking
order goes according to size.

Buses

Buses reach all those parts that trains do not. They are dirt-cheap,
generally quite uncomfortable, but are undoubtedly part of the
India experience. However, certain main routes, between Delhi
and Jaipur for example, are served by air-conditioned coaches
that can be of European standards.

Car and Driver

Hiring a driver and car takes much of the toil out of travelling
in India – something that many people find the hardest side of
holidaying there. The average cost is between £12-£20 per day,
and many drivers double up as guides (you pay more for modern
cars and a premium to have the luxury of air-conditioning).

You can arrange for a car and driver through most Indian tour
agents. Some are listed earlier in this section.

Air travel

The time taken to travel the huge distances in India has meant
that air travel has become hugely popular among those who can
afford it. A four-day journey can be reduced to a four-hour flight,
but expect to pay European prices.

Though there are several domestic Indian airlines, they vary in
coverage and reliability.

Indian Airlines (00 91 011 2462 0566), a government venture,
covers most routes though some passengers tell stories of being
left for hours on the tarmac while waiting for a government
minister to finish his dinner in the airport lounge.

Jet Airways (00 91 011 5164 1414) has a good reputation
worldwide and is one of India's true success stories. It operates
on most popular routes and offers Visit India passes starting at
$250 www.jetairways.com.

GENERAL ADVICE

Other airlines such as Sahara (011 2335 9801) operate, on limited routes www.saharaairlines.com.

Phones

The phone system reaches even further than the rail system and can be equally erratic. Some lines are clear, while others crackle and fizz at the first drop of monsoon rains. Domestic (STD) and international (ISD) call booths have yellow signs countrywide.

Mobile phones

The cost of using mobile phones abroad can be as much as £2 per minute (check with your service provider before leaving). And don't forget to activate your phone before you leave.

Given hefty costs, it is often more attractive to buy an Indian SIM card, available on almost every street corner for approximately Rs300 (£4), which allows you to make cheaper calls to Indian numbers. The rates are somewhat higher than using the landline system and you need a photocopy of your passport to buy one.

Each provider has regions of good and bad coverage, while some will not work at all outside their area. If you are travelling through several states it may not be worth buying a card. But, if you do not plan to travel widely, find out which local provider is most popular and then buy their SIM card when you reach your destination.

E-mail

Connection speeds can be a little temperamental, but e-mailing in India has become easy and very cheap. Most urban areas have plenty of internet cafés, and hotels are often hooked up to the net, though they may charge above average rates.

Those without online accounts such as Hotmail or Yahoo can access the mail on their computers at home by logging onto the website www.mail2web.com. Using the password and log-in name for your home account allows you to send and receive e-mails.

A POTTED HISTORY OF INDIA

India's history is too deep and complex to tackle between the pages of this guidebook. Prehistoric sites dating back 250,000 years have been unearthed, and by 2500 BC a sophisticated urban civilisation had emerged in the Indus Valley. The arrival of the Aryans and the subsequent laying of the foundation stones for the Hindu faith, the birth of Buddhism, the rise and fall of the Mauryan Empire, the emergence of the Deccan dynasties in the south, the arrival of Islam in the 13th century, the coming of the Mughals, and colonisation by the Europeans – to over-simplify things – have created a richly-layered and fascinating history that mesmerises scholars, travellers and religious pilgrims from every corner of the earth.

What strikes most travellers when passing through India, and what forms the focus for the tourist gaze, are the architectural landmarks left as the legacy of various empires and civilisations. Though the arrival of the Aryans and the beginning of the evolution of the Hindu faith is central to the character of modern India (85% of India's population are Hindus), the era's architectural legacy is not so apparent. (However, later Hindu culture created some truly astouding temples to their Gods, such as Konarak in Orissa.) The period during and since the Mughal reign holds most intrigue for the majority of travellers. It is an era of great change, of wealth, violence, cultural greatness and of spectacular rises and demises – and of superb craftsmanship that still stands proud among the encroaching mess of modern India. It is on these last 500 years, which have seen India pass from the hands of despotic, wild leaders to an entangled relationship with their European rulers, that I shall concentrate.

arrival of Islam

Islam arrived in India with the Turkic invasions from Central Asia (908 AD onwards). Spurred by tales of the outlandish wealth of India's Rajputs (royal dynasties), the Muslim invaders made incursions across the border, battling ferociously with the royals, plundering temples and returning time and time again to take home the spoils of war. Many eventually stayed, settling alongside fellow scholars, merchants, preachers and artists, to establish their own dynasties that would leave an indelible imprint on the religious, cultural and artistic landscape of the Indian subcontinent. The Delhi Sultanate, the first of many Muslim dynasties and one of the most powerful, ran for more than 300 years, finally ending with the internecine battles of the

A POTTED HISTORY OF INDIA

Lodis (responsible for the Lodi Gardens of Delhi). Though they began by controlling small chunks of India, by the reign of the Tughluqs (1320-1414) their grip had extended towards the Deccan and the South as they gobbled up swathes of land previously under the control of Rajput kings. Yet, as with all powerful kingdoms, bloody battles, great wealth, revolt and rivalry led to eventual decline, spawning independent kingdoms such as Gujarat and Bengal.

During this era huge changes took place in India. Great wealth was being generated, thanks partly to the new agricultural and administrative methods introduced by the Muslim rulers. Novel ideas about irrigation made India's fields more productive and trade with Arabia, Southeast Asia and Europe created a fury of activity. In this climate new arts and crafts flourished, and lavish architectural fancies were entertained, still visible in the tombs and forts left standing among the creeping modernity of Delhi's urban sprawl.

The Mughals

The arrival

The Mughals arrived in 1526 in the shape of Babur, a great tactician, poet and leader, and descendant of Timur (a notorious Central Asian conquerer) and Genghis Khan (the Mongolian ruler). Having defeated the Lodis, last of the Delhi Sultanates, he fought off challenges from confederacies of Rajputs, and held back Afghan attempts on his position, creating an empire that stretched from Kabul in Afghanistan to the borders of Bengal – a vast area to conquer in just four years.

Yet his son, Humayan, was less successful. A volatile, difficult, feckless and enthusiastic character, he was prone to long periods of hedonism during which he would abandon his duties as ruler. It was during an indulgent sojourn in Agra that he was outwitted by Sher Khan Sur in 1539, losing great chunks of land to the Afghan raiders and being forced to retreat to Persia while the victors overran Delhi.

However, in 1545 Sher Khan was killed in battle and Humayan took full advantage of this vacuum of power to re-establish himself as ruler of the empire his father had fought to create. His death a year later left his 13-year-old son, Akbar, to consolidate the empire and to succeed where he had failed. Though helped greatly in his early years by trusted aides of

A POTTED HISTORY OF INDIA

his father, Akbar grew to become one of the most important Mughal rulers – a magnetic character and a brilliant general. He clinched great stretches of India and, using his administrative genius, secured revenue from the conquered states through consultation with peasants and landowners – a tactical manoeuvre that guaranteed that no parties felt exploited. He employed local community leaders and landowners *(zamindars)* to collect the revenue and, in accordance with his admirable policy of religious tolerance, made sure that Hindu *zamindars* were as involved in political and economic life as their Muslim counterparts. Critical to his popularity and success was this policy of religious harmony – he held famous consultations with Jains, Hindus, Goan Catholics and Parsis – which eventually led him to dream up the idea of 'divine kingship' central to which is the toleration of all religions. His marriage to the Hindu daughter of Raja Man Singh I of Amber was just one of the alliances he forged to bring peace and resulting prosperity to his empire. This great statesmanship and liberal ideology helped to create a solid foundation for the Mughal rulers that followed the end of his reign in 1605.

The glorious years

The period that followed Akbar is seen as the great age of the Mughals, when wealth and excess reached new heights and during which artistic fancies and whims were lavishly indulged. Both Jahangir (1605-27) and Shah Jahan (1628-57) were great patrons of the arts. Jahangir loved the art of miniature painting, a craft seen in its adopted and evolved state in many Hindu Rajput palaces. Though he also commissioned great buildings, it was Shah Jahan whose artistic vision and inspiration is most remembered, still embodied in the astoundingly beautiful Taj Mahal, and both the Red Fort and Jama Masjid in Delhi.

A slightly darker period follows in Shah Jahan's life. Not only, some argue, had his wild spending on projects such as the Taj Mahal put strain on the empire's coffers, but his two most powerful sons, Dara Shikoh and Aurangzeb, corrupted by aspirations of power and supremacy, connived to thwart each other's attempts at succession. While Shah Jahan was convalescing after a serious illness in 1657, the two sons clashed spectacularly. Aurangzeb was victorious, wiping out Dara Sikoh's army and slaughtering his son and nephew.

A POTTED HISTORY OF INDIA

He then incarcerated his father, Shah Jahan, in Delhi's Red Fort where he lived out his last years in an opium-induced delirium.

Aurangzeb was a great warmonger, unleashing his fury and his armies against anyone who threatened his supremacy. His brutal suppression of Sikh separatism after the refusal of Guru Tegh Bahadur to embrace Islam, and his violent confrontations with Rajput partners left many around him disenchanted. In a move against the non-sectarian diplomacy perfected by Akbar, Aurangzeb began to mete out hefty taxes on non-Muslims, creating an atmosphere of intense disaffection, while his successful pushes for more territory left his empire overstretched and rendered him incapable of managing his increasingly divided nobles.

The fall

Aurangzeb had created such chaos that by the end of the reign of his son, Bahadur Shah (1707-12), disintegration was in full swing. Hindu landholders were in revolt, and several major Muslim states had broken off into independent states (Hyderabad and Bengal, for example), leaving the empire on its knees and open to attack from the Nadir Shah of Persia who sacked Delhi in 1739 after defeating the tired Mughal army.

Though the Maratha kingdom, a congomlerate of Rajput leaders and their fiefdoms helped the Mughals drive back yet another raid by on Delhi in 1757, this time by Afghans, they were eventually overwhelmed by the Afghan Ahmad Shah in 1761. However, the victor never made it to the throne, thwarted by his own soldiers who mutinied over lack of pay. Though the Mughals still hung on to the last of their power in various pockets, their grip had essentially slipped. Thus, a vacuum of power was created in which the Europeans began to flourish.

The British in India

The early years

The British had long had a presence in India by the time the Mughal empire fell. By 1665 trading posts had been well established by the East India Company in Fort George (Madras), Fort William (Calcutta) and Bombay. Victorious defeats over rival French trading companies in southern India, and the defeat of the nawab (Muslim prince) of Bengal in 1757 marked the beginning of true British power in India, and

A POTTED HISTORY OF INDIA

prompted the weakened Mughal emperor to reluctantly
hand over the collection of revenue in certain key provinces.

The status quo didn't last for long – the British parliament
decided to appoint its own governor-general after the East India
Company skated perilously close to the edge of bankruptcy.
Warren Hastings, the first appointee, managed to reform
the revenue collection system, gradually introducing a more
European administration. As the British machine in India
became smoother and better-run, so its power grew. Under
Lord Wellesley the most feared rivals of the British were
conquered and the more powerful independent kingdoms
subjugated, leading to the annexing of great tracts of India
from Tamil Nadu to Gujarat. Much of the success of the British
was in roping in 'loyal allies' in the shape of easily manipulated,
greedy independent rulers who wanted to hang onto their
lavish, courtly lifestyles in exchange for playing the British
game. (In fact, the British rather enjoyed having regal friends
with whom they could indulge in high culture and excess.)

In such a way, the great British machine steamed forth with
huge momentum, finally gobbling up the last of the Maratha
opposition and the few remaining independent kingdoms.
By 1852, the British reigned supreme.

All was not sweet, however. After centuries of back-to-back
battles the subcontinent was suffering. Gangs of outlaws were
spreading terror throughout the hinterland, the re-organisation
of agriculture by the British (for export) had led to rioting by
the peasants, and Britain's cultural imperialism was hitting a
raw nerve among the more traditional Hindu communities.
The concerted push for the Anglicisation of India, and
especially its education system, was creating a climate of
growing infuriation, while the less slavish members of the
Indian ruling class were beginning to become worried that
they would be entirely usurped.

The Mutiny 1857

The mastery of the British over the Indian provinces was partly
thanks to their ability to draft in Indian soldiers. Yet this was to
be the root of one of the first major threats to their rule. Not
only was the imperialism of the British increasingly resented
among the Indian people, but Indian soldiers in the British army

A POTTED HISTORY OF INDIA

were also growing disenchanted with their masters. The straw that broke the camel's back was the order to clean the new Enfield rifles with cow and pig grease, offensive to both Muslim and Hindu conscripts. With such an apparent affront to their religious beliefs, the soldiers decided to revolt. On 10 May 1857, the uprising began. Thousands of soldiers, soon joined by civilian masses, marched into Delhi to take the British by surprise. The taste of victory lasted just over a year, the remaining strongholds of the Mutiny laying down their guns in June of 1858, but the ripples were felt all over the country. It was as a result of this uprising that the ruling powers of the East India Company were handed to the British crown which realised the unpopularity of the Company's behaviour, and turned India from a trading entity to an independent kingdom.

The Raj 1857-1947

Astonishingly, the British governed an Indian population of 300 million, at one stage, with only 2,000 members of the elite Indian Civil Service (ICS), who braved the extreme climates to extend British values and administrative systems throughout the subcontinent. Their relationships with the communities in which they lived were not always fraught – ICS officers and their families had close ties with the higher echelons of Indian society – though many of the postings were in difficult and troubled regions. Churches, schools and hospitals were established, still much in evidence today, and ports and railways were built with staggering speed.

The British success in laying down thousands of kilometres of railways oiled trade within India. Local Indian businessmen began to invest heavily, and primary industries flourished. Yet Britain was not being entirely selfless, her economy benefiting hugely from the cheap raw materials from India and the growing demand for her manufactured goods.

The proliferation of Western knowledge and British educational ideas was also creating a middle class, which gradually became discontent with the way in which British values and systems were being imposed and Indian interests subjugated. It was then that an idea of the Indian national consciousness began to take form, and the first rumblings of the Independence movement were uttered. The British allowed the founding of the Indian

A POTTED HISTORY OF INDIA

National Congress as a token gesture to placate the educated classes. Yet it quickly became a forum for serious protest at continued British rule as more hard-line protagonists of independence fought for the reigns.

The British realised, after their protracted European battles during World War I and the hugely controversial attempted partition of Bengal in 1905, that their imperial drives were no longer sustainable and that they would have to relinquish their grip over India.

Strangely, the British did not abandon their elaborate plans to move the capital from Calcutta to Delhi, a project that involved huge construction projects and vast expense. As home-grown political movements, both Hindu and Muslim, were joining forces to present a united front, the British produced the Royal Proclamation in 1917 which promised self-government.

Gandhi

Yet all was not harmonious. British rule was still in place and heavy-handed measures were still being used to quash minor uprisings. It was in response to this that Mohandas Karamchand Gandhi began his peaceful protests. Educated as a lawyer in England, he was deeply influenced by liberal ideas, especially the tenets of Christianity, Jainism and humanitarianism, from which he created the doctrine of non-violence (*ahimsa*) and the pursuit of truth (*satya*). These beliefs became the foundation upon which Gandhi built his efforts to achieve an independent India. Among his greatest fights was one for the 'untouchables', whom he renamed 'children of God' (*Harijans*). Adopting the dhoti and shawl to identify himself with the masses, Gandhi headed protests against the maltreatment of Harijans, and inspired many with his nonviolent civil disobedience (satyagraha). His epic fasts to encourage peace between Hindu and Muslim communities, and his incessant self-sacrifice for the 'average Indian' were, for many, the inspiration to continue the drive for complete independence.

Having been frequently incarcerated for his disobedience Gandhi was becoming an icon of the independence movement and of Congress, which by 1924 was being led by the radical Jawaharlal Nehru. The great Salt March of 1930 was, many think, the beginning of the end for the British in India.

A POTTED HISTORY OF INDIA

It began as a protest against the salt tax imposed by the British – a march led by Gandhi from his ashram to the illegal salt pans of Gujarat. On the 241-mile march, the Mahatma's village speeches whipped up great crowds and the march grew into a vast procession. Upon reaching the pans, Gandhi ceremoniously picked up a rock of salt, an illegal act which his fellow marchers copied and which prompted the British authorities to sling thousands of protesters into jail. By the end of the year almost 100,000 of Gandhi's followers had been incarcerated as they held strikes and protests across the country. A truce was finally drawn between Lord Irwin, the Viceroy, and Gandhi, after which Mahatma was invited to London as the only Indian representative to discuss the future of Indian independence.

While Gandhi was instigating his 'Quit India' campaign, Mohammed Ali Jinnah, a Muslim lawyer from Bombay, was advocating the formation of a separate Muslim state. As head of the Muslim League he preached his case for 'two nations', finding mass Muslim support against the Indian National Congress that was so dominated by Hindu members. As Indian terrorism surrounding this issue grew, Britain realised that a workable solution for preserving Indian unity in independence was impossible. Enfeebled by WWII, and prompted by the growing new socialism and liberal ideology at home, Britain's last Viceroy, Lord Mountbatten, announced the creation of Pakistan and Indian independence on 15 August 1947.

The move that Gandhi had fought so hard to avoid was a humanitarian disaster. With a casual stroke of the Imperial pen, the new borders were drawn through Bengal, turning families that were once neighbours into enemies, and forcing millions of Pakistani Hindus and Sikhs to flee to India, and millions more Indian Muslims to take sanctuary in the new Pakistan. Great numbers died. The assassination of Gandhi in 1948 by Hindu extremists was the final tragedy of the partition saga.

Independence

Independent India made rapid advances under Jawaharlal Nehru, who proved himself a charismatic, popular and imaginative leader. In spite of the problems with getting certain princely states to join the union of India, Nehru managed to progress towards a united India that was, suddenly, the world's largest democracy. Women and 'untouchables' were granted new rights to lift them out of their morass; economic and social reforms were pushed through to eradicate poverty, increase agricultural production and encourage industry, and foreign aid and assistance was secured to speed up the process.

Indira Gandhi 1966-1984 – The 'Iron Lady'

Nehru's death in 1964 brought great sadness to the Indian people. He had been an inspirational leader and the 'father' of independence. His daughter, Indira, took the reigns of Congress with great zeal, pushing forward radical socialist reforms that saw the nationalisation of banks and the removal of maharajas' privy purses.

Hugely driven and immensely powerful, Indira was both feared and loved. Her success in the liberation of East Pakistan (Bangladesh) in 1971 was becoming overshadowed by growing unrest as inflation rates rose and corruption spread. In 1974, as murmurings of discontent grew to serious rumblings and a threat from the opposition to overthrow Indira, she declared a State of Emergency during which hundreds of opposition members were thrown into prison, the press was heavily censored and civil liberties were suspended.

Though she had managed to stem inflation and tackle corruption, when she finally called an end to the emergency in 1977 and released all political prisoners, Indira's rule was doomed. Forced sterilisation of men and vicious slum clearances in Delhi had been deeply unpopular, leaving the 'Iron Lady' a clear loser in the 1977 elections. After a brief term out of office, she returned in 1980 only to have her political candle snuffed out for good in 1984, the result of a fatal policy error.

Sikh terrorists, calling for a separate Sikh state of Khalistan, were using the Golden Temple at Amritsar as their base from which to plan acts of violence not only against Hindus but Sikh moderates too. Responding to a national call for an end to the terror, Indira sent in the troops for a battle which left the Sikh's holiest religious site desecrated. Later that year, her Sikh bodyguard took revenge, ending her rule with a single bullet.

Modern tumult The years since Indira's death have not seen the end of the corruption that is so rife in India. It has been a time of great political upheaval, much of which has followed religious wranglings between the Hindu and Muslim right-wing establishments.

A POTTED HISTORY OF INDIA

One of the greatest thorns in the side of India has been the battle over Ayodhya, a 16th-century Muslim *masjid* (mosque) built on the supposed third site of the birthplace of Ram. The right-wing Bharatiya Janata Party (BJP) has periodically carried the torch for hard-line Hindus wanting to rebuild a Hindu temple where the *masjid* now stands. Many attempts were made to tear down the *masjid*, often instigated by the BJP leader LK Advani. Finally, in December 1992, a throng of extremists and fanatics, too large to be stopped, demolished it brick by brick. Terrible rioting followed as religious intolerance bubbled to the surface. India's self-image as a democratic, secular state was rocked by the ensuing terrorism and extremism.

Though the Congress Party had been in power almost continually since independence, the BJP was profiting greatly from the uncertainty and religious antipathy brought about by Ayodhya. To top it all, the devastating earthquake in Gujarat of 1993 sowed the seeds for an epidemic of cholera and typhoid, a situation which left the Indian people desperate for guidance and support. It was during these difficult, strained times that the Hindu right wing found itself becoming increasingly popular.

Though the BJP took several attempts and a few years to develop its majority, by 1998 it won the election as part of a conservative coalition under the leadership of Atal Behari Vajpayee who, as we go to print, is still in power as prime minister. His time in office has seen the Indo-Pak relationship reach new lows. Jousting sessions of missile tests followed by dangerous posturing and frigid diplomatic relations have been the subject of intense international diplomacy and worry.

So, corruption is still endemic, poverty is still rife and frightening numbers of politicians remain hounded by allegations of murder, extortion and illegality. Cronyism and power struggles dominate the political realm, superseded occasionally by cross-border posturing and occasional battles with Pakistan. Holding together a country the size of India, with as many cultural, linguistic and social differences as you'd find within Europe, is a Herculean task. Perhaps it is thus beyond mere mortals.

With grateful thanks to The Rough Guide to India

A POTTED HISTORY OF INDIA

Post-independence place name changes

Many of the better-known Indian towns and cities have had their British names replaced with more Indian variations. Listed below are a few in case you have troubles with modern Indian maps:

- Allepey is now **Allappuzha**
- Bombay is now **Mumbai**
- Calcutta is now **Kolkata**
- Calicut is now **Kozhikode**
- Cannanore is now **Kannur**
- Cochin is now **Kochi**
- Coorg is now **Kodagu**
- Madras is now **Chennai**
- Ooty is now **Udhagamandalam**
- Palghat is now **Palakkad**
- Quilon is now **Kollam**
- Simla is now **Shimla**
- Trivandrum is now **Thiruvananthapuram**

WHAT IS ALASTAIR SAWDAY PUBLISHING?

Twenty or so of us work in converted barns on a farm near Bristol, close enough to the city for a bicycle ride and far enough for a silence broken only by horses and the occasional passage of a tractor. Some editors work in the countries they write about, e.g. France; others work from the UK but are based outside the office. We enjoy each other's company, celebrate every event possible, and work in an easy-going but committed environment.

These books owe their style and mood to Alastair's miscellaneous career and his interest in the community and the environment. He has taught overseas, worked with refugees, run development projects abroad, founded a travel company and several environmental organisations. There has been a slightly unconventional streak throughout, not least in his driving of a waste-paper-collection lorry, the manning of stalls at jumble sales and the pursuit of causes long before they were considered sane.

Back to the travel company: trying to take his clients to eat and sleep in places that were not owned by corporations and assorted bandits he found dozens of very special places in France – farms, châteaux etc – a list that grew into the first book, *French Bed and Breakfast*. It was a celebration of 'real' places to stay and the remarkable people who run them.

The publishing company grew from that first and rather whimsical French book. It started as a mild crusade, and there it stays – full of 'attitude', and the more appealing for it. For we still celebrate the unusual, the beautiful, the individual. We are passionate about rejecting the banal, the ugly, the pompous and the indifferent and we are passionate, too, about 'real' food. Alastair is a trustee of the Soil Association and keen to promote organic growing and consuming by owners and visitors.

It is a source of deep pleasure to us to know that there are many thousands of people who share our views. We are by no means alone in trumpeting the virtues of resisting the destruction and uniformity of so much of our culture – and the cultures of other nations, too.

We run a company in which people and values matter. We love to hear of new friendships between those in the book and those using it, and to know that there are many people – among them farmers – who have been enabled to pursue their decent lives thanks to the extra income our books bring them.

WWW.SPECIALPLACESTOSTAY.COM

Britain

France

Ireland

Italy

Portugal

Spain

Morocco

India...

all in one place!

On the unfathomable and often unnavigable sea of online accommodation pages, those who have discovered **www.specialplacestostay.com** have found it to be an island of reliability. Not only will you find a database full of trustworthy, up-to-date information about all the Special Places to Stay across Europe, but also:

· Links to the web sites of all of the places in the series

· Colourful, clickable, interactive maps to help you find the right place

· The opportunity to make most bookings by e-mail – even if you don't have e-mail yourself

· Online purchasing of our books, securely and cheaply

· Regular, exclusive special offers on books

· The latest news about future editions and future titles

The site is constantly evolving and is frequently updated with news and special features that won't appear anywhere else but in our window on the worldwide web.

Russell Wilkinson, Web Producer
website@specialplacestostay.com

If you'd like to receive news and updates about our books by e-mail, send a message to newsletter@specialplacestostay.com

FRAGILE EARTH SERIES

The Little Earth Book
Now in its third edition
this book as engrossing
and provactive as ever
and continues to
highlight the perilously
fragile state of our
planet.
£6.99

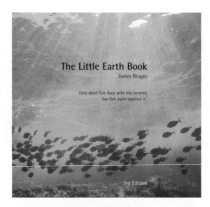

The Little Food Book
Makes for a wonderfully
stimulating read – one
that changes your
attitude to
the food choices
you make daily.
£6.99

The Little Money Book
This Little Book could
make you look at
everything from
your bank statements
to the coins in
your pocket in a
whole new way.
Available November 2003
£6.99

This fascinating series has been praised by politicians,
academics, environmentalists, civil servants – and 'general'
readers. It has come as a blast of fresh air, blowing away
confusion and incomprehension.

SIX DAYS

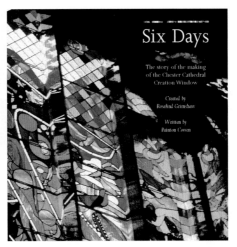

Celebrating the triumph of creativity over adversity

An inspiring and moving story of the making of the stained glass 'Creation' window at Chester Cathedral by a woman battling with debilitating Parkinson's disease.

"Within a few seconds, the tears were running down my cheeks. The window was one of the most beautiful things I had ever seen. It is a tour-de force, playing with light like no other window ..."

Anthropologist Hugh Brody

In 1983, Ros Grimshaw, a distinguished designer, artist and creator of stained glass windows, was diagnosed with Parkinson's disease. Refusing to allow her illness to prevent her from working, Ros became even more adept at her craft, and in 2000 won the commission to design and make the 'Creation' Stained Glass Window for Chester Cathedral.

Six Days traces the evolution of the window from the first sketches to its final, glorious completion as a rare and wonderful tribute to Life itself: for each of the six 'days' of Creation recounted in Genesis, there is a scene below that is relevant to the world of today and tomorrow.

Heart-rending extracts from Ros's diary capture the personal struggle involved. Superb photography captures the luminescence of the stunning stained glass, while the story weaves together essays, poems and moving contributions from Ros's partner, Patrick Costeloe.

Available from Alastair Sawday Publishing £12.99

ORDER FORM UK

All these books are available in major bookshops or you may order them direct. **Post and packaging are FREE within the UK.**

		Price	No. copies
French Bed & Breakfast	Edition 8	£15.99	
French Hotels, Châteaux & Inns (Nov 03)	Edition 3	£13.99	
French Holiday Homes (Jan 04)	Edition 2	£11.99	
Paris Hotels	Edition 4	£9.99	
British Bed & Breakfast	Edition 8	£14.99	
British Hotels, Inns & Other Places (Nov 03)	Edition 5	£13.99	
Bed & Breakfast for Garden Lovers	Edition 2	£14.99	
British Holiday Homes	Edition 1	£9.99	
London	Edition 1	£9.99	
Ireland	Edition 4	£12.99	
Spain	Edition 5	£13.99	
Portugal	Edition 2	£8.99	
Italy	Edition 3	£12.99	
Europe with courses & activities	Edition 1	£12.99	
India	Edition 1	£10.99	
Morocco (Dec 03)	Edition 1	£10.99	
The Little Earth Book	Edition 3	£6.99	
The Little Food Book	Edition 1	£6.99	
The Little Money Book (Nov 03)	Edition 1	£6.99	
Six Days		£12.99	

Please make cheques payable to   Total £ ———— ————
Alastair Sawday Publishing

Please send cheques to: Alastair Sawday Publishing, The Home Farm Stables, Barrow Gurney, Bristol BS48 3RW. For credit card orders call 01275 464891 or order directly from our web site **www.specialplacestostay.com**

Title   First name   Surname

Address

Postcode   Tel

If you do not wish to receive mail from other like-minded companies, please tick here ☐

If you would prefer not to receive information about special offers on our books, please tick here ☐

IND1

REPORT FORM

Comments on existing entries and new discoveries

If you have any comments on entries in this guide, please let us have them. If you have a favourite house, hotel, inn or other new discovery, please let us know about it.

Book title: _____

Entry no: _____ Edition no: _____

New recommendation:

Country: _____

Name of property: _____

Address: _____

_____

_____

Postcode: _____

Tel: _____

Comments: **Report:**

_____

_____

_____

_____

_____

_____

_____

Your name: _____

Address: _____

_____

_____

Postcode: _____

Tel: _____

QUICK REFERENCE INDICES

QUICK REFERENCE INDICES

QUICK REFERENCE INDICES

INDEX BY PROPERTY NAME

INDEX BY PROPERTY NAME

INDEX BY PROPERTY NAME

HOW TO USE THIS BOOK

explanations

❶ rooms

All rooms, in this example, are 'en suite'.

❷ room price

The price shown is for one night for two people sharing a room. A price range incorporates room differences. We say when price is per week.

❸ meals

Prices are per person for a set two-course meal. If breakfast isn't included we give the price.

❹ closed

When given in months, this means for the whole of the named months and the time in between.

❺ directions

Use as a guide; the owner can give more details, as can their web sites.

❻ map & entry numbers

Map page number; entry number.

❼ type of place

❽ price band

Price ranges, see last page of the book.

❾ reservation number

❿ symbols

See the last page of the book for fuller explanation:

- smoking restrictions exist
- credit cards accepted
- premises are licensed
- food served
- working farm
- air-conditioning
- @ internet connection available
- swimming pool

sample entry

RAJASTHAN

Neemrana Fort-Palace
Neemrana, 301 705, Rajasthan

If the marauding hordes descending on this maze of a palace got as lost I did, the inhabitants might never have been defeated. The warren spreads over 10 layers, the ramparts and colonnaded walkways leading to open courtyards and as confusing as an Escher sketch. A sensitive, modest, yet beautiful restoration of near ruins, this 'non-hotel' is a powerful example of the triumph of good taste and moderation over the evils of standardised luxury. Built over ten years, the rooms have slowly taken shape, reflecting the mindfulness of history that runs throughout this special place. Some have their own jarokha balconies facing out onto plains peppered with plots of bright mustard, while others have bathrooms open to the skies. You can sleep in the old royal court, or in a tent atop the highest turret. All are simply furnished with colonial and Indian antiques in the eclectic style so well executed here. This place embodies holiday calm – there are no TVs or phones in the rooms, just endless corners, courtyards and lush gardens to sit and read – one of the few hotels where one can always have a turret or courtyard to oneself. *The smaller rooms are very cosy. Yoga, meditation.*

rooms	43: 21 doubles, 1 single, 18 suites, 1 family room for 4. Some A/C.
price	Doubles Rs2,200-Rs3,300. Singles Rs1,100. Suites Rs4,400-Rs6,600. Family room Rs12,000. Plus 10% tax. Peak season: September-March.
meals	Breakfast Rs200. Lunch, & dinner Rs400.
closed	Rarely.
directions	2 hours southwest of Delhi along NH8 to Jaipur. Turn right at the signs in Neemrana Village.

	Mr Ramesh Dhabhai
tel	+91 1494 246 006
fax	+91 11 2435 1112
e-mail	sales@neemranahotels.com
web	www.neemranahotels.com
res. no.	+91 11 2435 6145

❼ Heritage Hotel ❾
❻ entry 37   map 5   E-F ❽
❿